Take Me Home

Take Me Home

Parkinson's, My Father, Myself

JONATHAN TAYLOR

Granta Books
London

Granta Publications, 2/3 Hanover Yard, Noel Road, London N1 8BE

First published in Great Britain by Granta Books 2007

The author would like thank the following for permission to quote:
The Society of Authors as the literary representative of the Estate of
Katherine Mansfield, Faber and Faber Ltd for 'The Love Song of J. Alfred
Prufrock' from *Collected Poems 1909–1962* by T. S. Eliot, John Murray
Publishers Ltd for *Parkinson's Law, or the Pursuit of Progress* by
C. Northcote Parkinson and Gustav Mahler *Memories and Letters*,
translated by Alma Mahler, ed. Donald Mitchell and Knud Martiner,
Rev. Awdry for the quote from *Small Railway Engines*, Blake Morrison
for the quote from *And When Did You Last See Your Father?* published
by Granta Books, 'Delight' by J. B. Priestley (copyright © Estate of
J. B. Priestley 1951) used by permission of PFD (www.pfd.co.uk)
on behalf of the Estate of J. B. Priestley.

Some of the proceeds from this book are donated to the
Parkinson's Disease Society of the United Kingdom
(Registered Charity no. 258197).

A CIP catalogue record for this book
is available from the British Library.

1 3 5 7 9 10 8 6 4 2

ISBN-13: 978-1-86207-955-7

Typeset by M Rules

Printed and bound in Great Britain by
William Clowes Ltd, Beccles, Suffolk

There is no such thing as *forgetting* possible to the mind.

(Thomas De Quincey, *Confessions of an English Opium-Eater*)

This book is dedicated to my father, John Taylor (1928?–2001), who would probably have hated it.

CONTENTS

PART ONE

PART TWO

PART THREE

PART FOUR

PART ONE

Preface

'Who are you?' my father would ask me on opening the front door.

Or: 'Where are you taking me?'

Or, worst of all: 'What have you done with my son?'

These questions made me feel like a stranger in a strange land.

It's that strange land which I want to map in this book.

A Diagnosis

There is a moment – some time in distant 1981 – when, standing near the desk of a Saturday morning group called 'The Explorers' for talented, chess-playing children like my elder brother and their tag-along siblings like myself – there is a moment – a moment which now makes my hair stand on the back of my neck, but which, for years afterwards, was just a Sunday-dinner anecdote – a moment when my dad – at this point still working, still raven-haired, still capable of smiling – forgot my baby sister's name – like a paper shred gusted away – and with a laugh, and somewhere deep inside a vertiginous panic, had to grab my sleeve and ask what it was. As ever, I didn't understand quickly enough, didn't help.

The memory may mean nothing except in retrospect, but I still feel the tug on my shirt as he lunged towards me. 'My mind just went blankety blank,' he'd say. Was this the first inkling, my family wonders now – was this the first one-way street his mind mistakenly turned up?

But there are many other possible first inklings, some of them lost in the dead ends of *my* memory. A disease like his is so gradual, so much a continuum of greynesses, one can

properly remember only the most recent state – which now is
death. All I can provide are fragments of memories – a list of
vanishing points and partial origins:

May 1983: I was nearly ten years old. Apart from some nasty
bullying which persisted through my school years like the
weather, I *personally* don't remember anything particularly start-
ling about that spring – even though my father was in the
process of quitting his headmastership, having a nervous breakdown and contemplating serious self-harm. My mother had to
ask my elder brother Robin to 'keep a careful eye on Dad' whenever she went to the shops, in case razors, pills or kitchen knives
were put to alternative use. My father had been prescribed
Amitriptyline (an anti-depressant), on which he was dependent
till 1989. He was also sent to regular sessions with a psychiatrist.

I don't recall noticing any of these things. Perhaps it seemed
that my mother put her hair in curlers more often at this time –
a sure indication that she was in a fraught mood – but, otherwise, nothing. It seems incredible to me now: how blind was I
that a father's breakdown could pass me by?

Except that . . . well, except that there was one thing, there
was one afternoon, clambering up the stairs, my parents' bedroom door ajar in front, overhearing as I reached the top step
my dad on the phone, saying that, 'Yes, I've decided to change
my mind and accept the early retirement offer you made,' – and
then scampering back down the stairs, knowing that I've heard
something I shouldn't have, feeling that what I've done is
wrong, but not able to tell a soul. A few weeks later, the second
sign of his retirement visited my imagination: an electric
Teasmade (one of those 80s quiz-show prizes which made tea in
bed for you when the alarm went off) appeared in the dining
room. What a lavish leaving present for thirteen years' service

as headmaster of the toughest school in Stoke-on-Trent. Thirty-two years' work as a teacher = a Teasmade, which also = ten minutes on a second-rate quiz show. This was a simple, simultaneous mathematics equation like the ones my dad used to help me with. To my frustration, the Teasmade stayed in the box – despite my insensitive, childish fascination – and eventually merged with the attic dust.

August 1987: I'm fourteen. Friends of my computer come round to play. My dad wanders in to ask us if we want a cup of tea or anything (non-alcoholic, of course) to drink. Then he shuffles off. Sometimes, he comes back an hour later to ask if we want a cup of tea or anything to drink. Sometimes, he doesn't come back at all. Sometimes, he comes with the wrong things balanced precariously on an Isle of Man tea tray, biscuits swimming in what's been spilt. The first time my friends laugh and say to me, 'You ask your dad for a cup of tea one day and you get an orange squash next week – the only thing slower than his tea making is his driving,' I laugh too. The second time my friends laugh and say to me, 'You ask for a cup of tea at your house and you get it next month,' I laugh with them, swearing to myself that I won't laugh next time – that I'll put up a fight. The third time my friends laugh and say to me, 'You ask for a cup of tea and a jammy dodger at your house and your dad goes off and milks the fucking cow,' I smile and stay quiet, as he comes into the room, slightly lopsided, like a faulty Teasmade.

Spring 1988: My father's shakiness, stooped gait, spidery handwriting, slow driving, depression, nightmares, poor tea-making skills are all lumped together and diagnosed by a young neurologist looking for medals: '*I know what you've got!*' he exclaims. No one else knows. No one else found it out. Just him. My father's condition is at the extreme end of the Parkinsonian spectrum, partly because it is 'early onset' Parkinson's; he's only sixty years old and Parkinson's is 'usually an old person's disease', as if that makes it better.

No one told me about the diagnosis, of course. I thought 'Parkinson's' was a law which stated that toast always falls buttered-side down. (In some ways, I still do – even though I realize I was mixing up Parkinson's and Murphy's Law.) Family illness was never discussed in anything but the vaguest terms: I had an operation when I was seven, but only found out what it was for at seventeen. I'd been out of anaesthetic for a long time.

April 1988: A crisis. One evening, my mother says to me that I should stay upstairs, because a police officer with the picturesque, if rather paradoxical, name of Sergeant Flowers is calling. As normal, I am given the barest of details, but it seems that a van had been parked at the top of my parents' drive, and that my father, reversing out, hadn't seen it, and had hit it. Quite how he managed to do any damage I can't think, given the speed he and the old green Avenger generally agreed on. 'The man in the white van', who'd been visiting our neighbours, was furious to the point of wanting my 'imbecilic' father 'off the road, bollocked, thrown in jail, crucified and generally fucking dead'. So Sergeant Flowers had had to intervene – to berate my terrified dad further and threaten him with prosecution. My father never drove again. In this sense, Parkinson's was a disease of gradually giving things up: the Avenger was given up to my brother, driving to my mum. Only the terror of Flowers did he retain for himself.

February 1991: A long-haired, unwashed teenager (known as myself) is sitting on one of the chairs in the living room, grasping hold of the arms, believing that, if he holds on tightly enough and stares at *Cagney & Lacey*, his mother won't notice that he's drunk three-and-a-half pints of cider at the local pub (illegally).

Mum is knitting in her green, comfy chair as ever, Dad is asleep in his green, comfy chair as ever. The teenager wonders why murders and scenes with incidental music happen to Sharon Gless on *Cagney & Lacey* and never in his life, never in Stoke-on-bloody-Trent. He wonders why he's condemned to live in a family where there is nothing but the straightforward, the mundane, the non-murderous, the a-musical. No Sharon Gless needed here, thank you – there are no hidden skeletons, pasts, heroics or even different chairs in this living room. There's only the gradual cardiganization of parental ageing.

Mum asks a question and son answers, detaching each word from its neighbours in order to avoid telltale signs of slurring. Dad suddenly snores, alerting everyone that he'll wake up if anyone interferes with the channel. Son turns his head and fails to focus on drooling father, seeing instead a magazine on the coffee table next to him. He stares at it for a moment, reading each separate word in the same way he's just spoken: *The Parkinson: The Magazine of the Parkinson's Disease Society.*

That was the first time my dad's twitches, shufflingness and peculiar tempers were given a collective diagnosis. Instead of being sat down and told about it, instead of hearing what the name meant, what it would mean in the future, I stumbled across it like some drunken idiot. But then, that's not dissimilar to how my parents found out about it. Parkinson's disease: a label which sounded important, serious – something inevitably suggesting a piece of toast fallen buttered-side down.

Help Help Help

As time and the disease proceed, difficulties increase ...
the patient seldom experiences a suspension of the agita-
tion of his limbs ... The propensity to lean forward
becomes inevitable ... The sleep becomes much disturbed ... The bowels ... demand stimulating medicines of
very considerable power.

(James Parkinson, 'An Essay on the Shaking Palsy')

'Help' – the word my mother heard more than any other.
With his eyes shut, his head hunched forwards and his
left arm outstretched, my father would shake his chair, shouting
'Help' and hitting the wall behind him in a kind of syncopated
drum-and-bass rhythm ('Help' bang 'Help' bang 'Help help'
bang). He'd do this even if we were in the room and there was
nothing *visibly* wrong. The call for help wasn't necessarily a
demand for any particular object – my father just wanted some
unspecified and, in the end, unrealizable help of some or all
kinds. It was one of the only ways he had left to communicate
with the world. For that reason, we shouldn't have begrudged
him the word so much.

'Help' – there were countless ways in which he could cry out the word: desperate wail, psychopathic whisper, Wagnerian fortissimo, Puccinian heart-wrench, Gilbert-and-Sullivanian patter ('Help helphelpmehelpmehelphelphelpmehelp'), Beatlesian urgency ('Help, I need somebody'), Banaramanian farce . . .

'Help. Help.' Bang bang bang bang bang.

'What do you want?' I ask, looking over my shoulder at him from the piano, where I'm banging away myself without much more musicality.

It's May 1995, and I'm cross. In a test conducted this morning on my father, he has failed to distinguish between a photo of me and a photo of Humphrey Bogart. This might have been flattering, had he not gone on to mistake Bogart for a giraffe and ultimately everything for everything else. A doctoral student from Birmingham University has been visiting for months now, collecting data about my father's condition for a research paper. 'He didn't want to play today,' says my mother, nonchalantly shoving a handful of pills into his mouth and pinning his head back with a glass of water. The student has left, but Mum is worried that my father's unwillingness 'to play' will mess up the poor girl's research results. 'Last week, he managed to identify the photos till he switched off, but today, he wasn't in the mood.'

I reassure her – the student probably wants 'bad' results anyway. They'll make the research more interesting. And I'm right. Years later, after his death, I happen across the research paper the student published about my relationship with my father. It's called 'Delusional Misidentification: A Neuropsychological Case Study in Dementia Associated with Parkinson's Disease'. In it, my father is 'Case 1' (there's no Case 2 – uniqueness is built into Parkinsonism), and I'm 'Junior'. Retrospectively, I find out Case 1 suffered from a form of dementia called Lewy body disease, and a variant of 'Capgras syndrome', whereby he misidentified Jr and believed he was being impersonated or even taken over by a villainous double. Case 1's Capgras, I discover, also involved elements of 'Fregoli' and 'Intermetamorphosis' syndromes, both of which involve the misrecognition of a stranger as a 'significant other'. My father's form of misrecognition, the writer suggests, is a peculiar one which blurs the boundaries between Capgras, Fregoli and Intermetamorphosis syndromes, demanding a rethink of these terms. 'Typical Dad,' comments my mother on seeing the article. 'Even his delusions had to be different from other people's.'

I find it hard to grasp, but there are sections of the brain – in the right hemisphere – which are devoted to processing and recognizing faces. Thus, damage of the right hemisphere might mean damage of this processing system, as it did with my father. Imagine that (if it's possible to *imagine* it): your ability or inability to differentiate faces and to know to whom they belong is a biological function, built into the material of your brain. What does that mean for supposedly spiritual or mental concepts like 'love' or 'hate'? Does it mean that the kind of serial monogamist we all know, who transfers his or her love all too easily from one partner to another, has a weak facial-recognition processor, so that lovers become interchangeable? Does it mean that racism might be a neurological syndrome? When an unregenerate member of the BNP says 'they all look the same', is this because his or her right hemisphere is damaged? In the ultimate irony, is it *racism*, not race, which is biologically based? Questions, questions.

For my father, one of the routes to the facial processor had become impaired by disease. And the result was that I was no longer me. Instead, the double – the bodysnatcher – who had villainously invaded my body was a deputy at his old school, whom he hadn't got on with (to put it lightly). Let's call him Gil-Martin for the sake of this book, after the famous doppel-gänger in James Hogg's *Private Memoirs and Confessions of a Justified Sinner*.

I had no conception of these things at the time, no knowl-edge of the theories or syndromes. I didn't even know who had so discourteously snatched my body, wasn't really aware my body *had* been snatched (but then, nor do people in science-fic-tion films). I was merely aware that certain symptoms were happening, and I didn't recognize the person he recognized as me. He was furious at me, shrank from me, shrieked for help when I was already trying to help, and I didn't know why. I just thought he was confused and took me for some generalized baddie, or (worse) that he *did* recognize me and no longer liked what he saw. And I couldn't always blame him for that – some-times I didn't like the violent dictator his incessant 'Helps' teased out of me.

Years later, over a croissant, I asked my mother why I was the one, in particular, who he misidentified. And she told me it was because both the deputy and I had long, straggly hair. What a let down, I think. What a paltry cause for something so bizarre, so science-fictionish. I had known that my father never liked my hippy hair, but not that it was a major cause of his delusions. Why didn't anyone tell me at the time? I could easily have had it cut to cure him, for God's sake.

Meanwhile, back in May 1995, he pushes the glass violently away from his mouth with a grunt.

'What was that for?' my mother demands. My father keeps pushing at her, bouncing up and down in the chair to get up.

'It was *him*!' he says, pointing at me. '*He* did it!'

'Don't be ridiculous, and stop pushing me,' says my mother

back. 'I've got to finish making tea. You need to stay sitting for a while. Watch the television or you'll fall.'

'No – not while *he's* around!' I can still remember the stress on any pronouns referring to me when he was in this frame of mind. Almost by definition, pronouns invite misidentification. They can so easily slip from one person to another, allowing the mind to slip with them. My father never used real nouns when he was angry or paranoiac.

Now, though, his anger has started trailing off into tiredness: 'He's out to get me . . . I tell you what he was doing. He . . . he was . . .' A loud advert on the television for conservatories supervenes, and he finishes his sentence with the peculiar accusation that I was '. . . building an Edwardian-style porch with double . . . double . . . double-gla . . . zing . . .' He yawns, we laugh and, within a few minutes, he's sitting down on the chair again, drooling and snoring, whilst I crash away at the piano. He only wakes once to point and laugh at the pink goats he sees sitting next to my elbow, who are accompanying me with complex Wagnerian harmonies.

Then there's a loud chariot race on the television, and he comes to, muttering something over and over about a teacher collecting the schoolchildren from the playground. Eventually, there's a crescendo to: 'Help help help help help' – and it's more desperate, insistent this time.

'Help with what?' I ask, suspending my piano playing.

'Help.'

'You want help with help?' = facetious winding.

'Go away – I don't want you . . . It's not *you*.'

'What *do* you want?' = aggressive impatience.

'I want your mum.' Bang bang bang bang bang.

'Stop doing that.' I saunter over to him and move his hand back on to his lap. 'Don't disturb her. She's busy' = authoritative self-righteousness.

'Help.'

'She's cooking tea. She can't come at your beck and call' =
more self-righteousness.

'Help help help help. Help help help. Erm,' – he seems to
lose his thread, and then recovers it: 'help.'

'Come on, Dad, be reasonable' = pretend imploration.

'No. Help help help help. Get *him* away from me.' Bang bang
bang bang. 'Get the pupils in from break.'

'You're at home, Dad. You've been retired years. You don't
have to worry about school any more' = patronizing reassurance.

'Help! Get *that person* away from me.' Bang bang bang.

I take hold of his hand to stop its mechanical thumping of
the door. He wraps his fingers round mine in a grip which
would crack walnuts. So weak and clumsy and fragile, yet he
has what the doctors call a 'prehensile grip' – as if his out-of-
control body is somehow flashing back to the strength of
nut-cracking, tree-swinging gibbons. I can feel that grip now;
somehow, somewhere, the bruises remain.

'I want to go home.'

'You're *at* home – in your own sitting room.'

'I want to go home. Help help.'

'Oh, for God's sake . . . Come on, Dad.' As normal, I'm starting to laugh, and I don't know why. It's a kind of reflex action,
no different to crying.

I lose attention for a moment, glancing at the television
behind, letting my hand be crushed. Someone who was once
well known as an ex-police chief is now less well known as a
seller of remortgages for happy elderlies.

'What's going on here then? What are you up to, darling?'
asks my mother as she comes in through the door, wiping her
hands on an Isle of Man tea towel.

'It's always *me*. You always take *his* side. It's not me. It's him –
that person,' – he jabs an accusing finger at me with his spare
hand.

'That's Jonathan, your son,' says my mother.

'No it's not. Can't you see? It's *that* fraud, playing tricks on
me.'

Not knowing what reaction I should have, I laugh again.

My father pushes at me, as if trying to expel whoever I am
from his past. But he's unable to release his own grip, unable to
let go of something he himself is grasping. 'It's this . . . *sod* –
that's what he is.'

I'm still laughing, and my laughter sends his fury spiralling
upwards. His grip tightens.

'Sod.'

'I don't hear language like that,' my mother says.

'Help.'

'Come on now, darling.'

'Help.'

'What do you want anyway?'

'He doesn't want anything.' I say this to wind my father up
further, knowing it's not true.

'I want to go home. It's him – he's kidnapped me. I tell
you – he's . . .' His fury's too much to allow him to finish the
sentence. Instead, he shouts: 'It's him . . . ever since he came
to the school, ever since he . . .' – and finishes the sentence
by flailing at me again. He stares at me with white-eyed
paranoia.

'Gosh, look at that face,' comments my mother, and we both
smile down at a face paralysed into a scowl. There's a silent
horror movie from the 1920s where a clown is mutilated when
young; afterwards, all he can do is grin, even when he is
murderously unhappy. Parkinsonism does the opposite, gradu-

ally petrifying your face muscles into those of a miserable, wrin-
kled, growling clown. It's what's known as 'masking'. Day in,
day out, my father had to watch us smiling and laughing, whilst
he couldn't join in. *Vesti la giubba.*

'It's him . . . I told you – it's him – one of your fancy men.
You're both out to get me. He's kidnapped me. Bundled me
away. Your fancy boy. Kidnapped me.'

'You're starting to hurt my hand,' I say, out of embarrassment
trying to ignore what he's saying. 'Let go, Dad.'

'Let go of his hand now.'

'Tell him to go away. I don't want him.'

'I can't bloody well go away till you let go,' I say, bending his
fingers back off my wrist. His unsnipped fingernails dig in to my
palm.

'Let go, darling.'

'Come on, Dad, let go.'

'Let go, darling.' My mother starts working on his fingers as
well.

Suddenly, they snap away, and my hand is free. Immediately,
he snatches back at the air, trying to grab the hand again.

Instead of mine, he grabs my mother's wrist this time.

'Ow, that hurts. Let go.'

'Help.'

'Let go, darling, that hurts me.'

'Help.'

'Let go of Mum, Dad.'

We're both peeling at his fingers now, trying to release the
monkey grip.

'Tell her to let go then.'

Laughter. 'But you're the one who's doing it.'

My sister Helen comes in and starts peeling too. Everyone's
joining in. 'Let go.'

'Let go.'

'Let go, Dad.'

'Come on, I've got to do tea. Let go.'

Even he's echoing the catchphrase now – 'Letgoletgoletgo-letgo' – though that doesn't mean he is actually releasing his grip.

'Okay, do it then.'

'Yes, let go.'

'Let go.'

'Let go.'

Every word, every phrase, every everything had to be repeated over and over again to my father, just as my father himself repeated actions over and over again. I can't put down here the amount of repetition involved; it would be a waste of trees. But for the carers as for the sufferer, Parkinson's and dementia seem to me to be all about repetition, and the repetition of repetition. For the patient, repetition is built into the diseases. As regards dementia, there's going to be a hell of a lot of repetition since you've forgotten what you've said, or what you've been told from one minute to the next. A million different moments might be cited as examples: 'Where did you say my jumper with reindeers on was?' 'In the top drawer.' Pause. 'Where did you say my jumper with the reindeers on was?' 'In the top drawer.' Pause. 'Have you found it yet?' 'What?' 'The jumper with the reindeers on.' 'No, where is it?' 'In the top drawer.' 'What's in the top drawer?' 'The jumper with the reindeers on.' 'Why do I want a jumper with reindeers on?' 'Because it's Christmas.' 'When's Christmas?'

Similarly, in terms of Parkinson's, many of the neurological symptoms are based on automatic repetition. They have beautiful sounding names: 'palilalia' is the repetition of words;

'palipraxia' is the repetition of actions; 'echopraxia' is the repetition of other people's actions; and the most magical sounding
of all, 'echolalia', is my father automatically repeating 'Let go
let go let go' after we've said it to him a dozen times. It was only
recently, by reading Oliver Sacks's book *Awakenings*, that I
myself found out that these are recognized, neurological symptoms. Back in 1995, I just thought my father was suffering from
a well-known symptom called 'paininthearse-alia'. Since finding out the official names of his symptoms, though, I've started
seeing palilalia, palipraxia, echopraxia and echolalia everywhere, in infirmaries, on phones, in parks, symphonies,
novels . . .

Looking back to 1995, these compulsive repetitions certainly
echoed from patient to carers (and back again): lift him up, sit
him down, lift him up, sit him down, untwist his emaciated
legs, relax his shaking arms, untwist his legs, relax his arms,
make him drink some pop, make him eat some food, make him
drink some pop, teeth in, teeth out, teeth in, sit him down, lift
him up . . . and so on and on, as if the carers reflect the patient
in a hall of echolalias and echopraxias. A simple 'let go' or
'stand up' becomes 'let go let go let go let go' or 'stand up stand
up for fuck's sake stand up you're breaking my back stand up'.
It's not just the sufferer whose syntax breaks down: you the
carer have to repeat everything without punctuation, without
let up, in the same tone 4,562 times.

And the point of all this repetition? It wasn't necessarily – or
wasn't just – to cajole my father into doing something, in the
hope that, if said enough times, the message would get through.
Oh no. Just because you repeat an order twice or thrice to a
waiter who doesn't speak English doesn't mean they'll understand you better. All that repetition was there to fill time, to
feel we were doing something whilst we were really waiting for

the symptoms to change, for one of the pill cycles to kick in or kick out, for the muscles to relax or get going, for him to open his eyes or fall asleep – for him to capitulate to our wishes without input from his own volition. Care is a kind of siege, a war of attrition in that sense.

Time-filling was made easier to an extent by the routines to which we clung. Every so often, I'd take over from my mother for a few days and look after Dad on my own – whilst she had a break by driving 240 miles to visit and help my sick grandparents. Whilst my mother was with them in Torquay, I'd hold on to the schedule set by my father's pills, toilet visits and home helps with a desperate, prehensile grip. With many variations, by 1997 the schedule went a bit like this:

7.25 am: Lying in bed, waiting for the five minutes till the alarm went off, sometimes hearing 'helps' or a rhythmic banging noise coming from the next room, wondering if he'll mine a knuckle hole in the wall between us. In the early 90s, when I first took over from my mother, I was so anxious about his waking up or falling or wrecking the bedroom, I'd get up before six, and drink five cups of tea whilst watching reruns of *Joe 90*. I'd go up and down the stairs every four minutes to peek in at him, push his legs back into bed and tell him to be quiet till the 'nurse' came.

8.05 am: Still waiting for the Social Services home help (the 'nurse') to arrive and get him up. He's shaking and shouting and trying to pull off the 'pad' – a euphemism for a huge nappy that he wears round his nether regions, to keep the wet in at nights.

8.25 am: The irrepressible, indomitable Doreen from Social Services bustles in and upstairs, smelling of cigarettes and coffee. I make her another coffee, setting out pills according to colours. In the early days, the pills were my great panic – there was a baroque, colour-coded, size-coded, shape-coded system of them which I invariably got wrong. At different times, the system included Sinemet (for the Parkinson's), Benzhexol, Madopar, Oxybutynin (to control his bladder problems), Thioridazine (which shut him down), Risperidone (an anti-psychotic which worked him up), Paroxetine, Sulpiride, Selegeline, Flucloxacillin . . . The list sounds like a pantheon of Wagnerian nymphs. In fact, some of them sounded so alluring, I considered trying them myself. Dennis the Cat put me off that idea. One day, after lining up my father's narcotic nymphs, the cat jumped on to the sideboard and swallowed one of them whole. For the remainder of the morning he proceeded to twitch around the kitchen like a robot-cat with rusty cogs.

8.30 am: I start making breakfast, lighting the fire, putting the rubbish out, feeding Dennis the Cat (food, not pills), digging a grave for the dead pigeon Dennis has left for me on the doorstep, etc, etc. I take Doreen's coffee, my father's pills and a cup of tea upstairs. I continue making the breakfast, lighting the fire, putting the rubbish out, feeding Dennis, shovelling the dead pigeon into its shallow grave. I return to my father and Doreen. She announces that he has achieved a successful bowel movement after drinking his tea. 'A good cup of tea,' she remarks every morning, 'gets the bowels open and sets us up for the day.' This is the Doreenian Universal Theory of Everything: cup of tea + digestive biscuit = bowel movement = human happiness. And perhaps she's not far wrong, though I do wonder why she herself drinks coffee. I help her troop my father downstairs and into the sitting

room. She leaves, after chattering about her own illnesses
and injuries.

9.10 am: I take at least ten minutes putting my dad's teeth in –
a peculiar operation involving some pink glue, the possible loss
of fingers on my part, a gallery of grimaces from my father, and
panic in case he manages to swallow the dentures lengthways.

9.20 am: The next ten or so more minutes are spent reopening
my father's eyes. Parkinson's often makes eyes light-sensitive –
though this was yet another symptom where the dividing line
between what he couldn't and wouldn't do was frustratingly
ambiguous.

Finally, his eyes are open, and I convey him the five yards
into the kitchen for breakfast, conducting his legs 'one two one
two', trying to drill them to move in anything but the tiniest of
slides. I'm told now that this symptom of Parkinsonism is
known as 'micro-ambulation', though at the time it was just
'fucking annoying'. Worst case scenario for the 'fucking annoying' micro-ambulation towards breakfast: he stops dead and
collapses on the floor.

9.30 am: By the time I've got Dad sitting at the table having
breakfast it feels like the day's half over. My father's teeth
(which I have positioned wrongly) come out in his croissant –
as if he's trying to eat by proxy – and have to be cleaned off and
put in again.

10.40 am: Father is in his armchair. I've washed up, tried to
force-feed him some Fybogel (a drink which promotes
Doreenian happiness) through a straw, and now we're sitting
down, listening to a scratchy Beethoven LP. I give my father

the record sleeve to look at, he holds it for a minute, and then starts using it as the foundation stone for what we call his 'sculptures'.

He'd frequently sit forwards in his chair, and (for hours if we let him) arrange the record sleeve, foot stool, fake stuffed badger, magazines, teacups and any cushions which were to hand into an improvised piece of installation artwork, balancing everything on top of everything else. If he lacked enough materials for the structure he had in mind, he'd call out and point at one of the cushions on the sofa, asking us to hand him a 'square'. For some reason, he could never find the word 'cushion' after he got ill and had to substitute 'square' for it instead. Cold geometry replaced comfort.

Not remembering the word for cushion is a symptom I've never seen mentioned in any books on Parkinson's. There is, though, a separate condition called 'anomic aphasia', often caused by damage to the brain's temporal lobe – the part responsible for recognizing objects. Anomic aphasics mislay nouns for objects and call things squares or another portmanteau word, in place of specific nouns, like cushion, or stuffed badger. Let's claim every illness we can think of for my father, and say he had anomic aphasia too; let's become a posthumous hypochondriac-by-proxy . . .

After we'd handed him numerous squares, the pyramidical structure he was building would become increasingly intricate, precarious – until I lost my temper with the painstaking laboriousness of it all and cruelly toppled his artwork, putting its constituent parts out of reach.

11.40 am: After my father has listened to the music for ten minutes and not listened to it for a further fifty, I get him some limeade. A limeade duel ensues: I try to force-feed him the limeade through a straw and he, in turn, tries to force it on to the floor. He's meant to drink five pints of liquid a day to avoid infections. He normally manages one.

12.10 pm: In later years, Doreen would call again, just to put him on the commode. From the word go, toilet manoeuvres were always a major and structuring part of the regimen.

1.05 pm: We have lunch, consisting of marmite toast, under-cooked eggs, force-fed limeade, and the reappearance of the star of the show, the false teeth. We retire to the sitting room where, if I'm feeling lazy or it's near Christmas, I watch an afternoon film starring James Stewart. A lull, until . . .

3.00 pm: . . . and probably the most common time at which crises occurred – although the Protean disasters of Parkinson's could take such varying shapes that any time of day or night was worry-time. Disasters I faced (or ran away from) included: finding my father and the claustrophobic downstairs toilet covered in claustrophobic shit while workers were painting the porch next door (perhaps he was echopraxically mirroring their job?) . . . discovering unconsumed pills swimming in the toilet upstairs where he'd spat them out when no one was watching . . . watching my father somersault backwards down the stairs, making horrid noises as he hit each step in turn, like the piano in the Laurel and Hardy film . . . conveying him a thousand and one times to the toilet to relieve an infected bladder . . . being sworn at, shouted at, shoved, ineffectually punched (and, with less excuse, returning the favours) . . . losing him and finding him wandering and confused near the park . . . having to wrench him up over and again from a floor on which he insisted on falling over and again (or so I reckoned at the time) . . . and – what was worse – the constant, *unreal-*ized threat of disaster in his repeatedly shuffling to the edge of the chair, ready to precipitate himself forwards . . . so I'd lift him back on to the chair and then he'd shuffle to the edge again and I'd lift him back on to the chair and he'd shuffle to the edge again . . . and, in this way, he'd be threatening a fall on a loop for hours until I'd lose my temper and shout abuse and he'd tell me I'm a devil and he'd always had his eye on me ever since I started at the school and I'd release my frustration and headaches in a torrent of bullying blasphemy . . . help help help help help help help bang bang bang bang bang bang help help help bang bang – until I'm not sure who is doing this, him or me, any more.

This kind of incessant fidgeting is one of the things peculiar to Parkinson's. The 'Shaking Palsy' (as Parkinson's is also known) merges movement and paralysis, activity and stillness, so that Parkinsonians are least at rest when they're most at rest – fidgeting and shaking and aching when they're suppos-edly sitting still. When you can get them to move, the fidgeting, the trembling generally stops. Sometimes, I just had to move my father's arm for the tremoring to stop. Gradually, though, movement becomes more agonizingly difficult, and it too becomes infused with shufflingness and paralysis – until all that's left is an unstill stillness and an unmoving motion.

4.35 pm: Never underestimate the value of tea breaks and the biscuit tin, at least to mark time.

6.25 pm: Another toilet visit and round of pulling down trousers, waiting till he's done, wiping his bottom, pulling up trousers, and walking or wheeling him to tea – which I've been hygienically preparing simultaneously.

During these pre-tea time toilet visits, whilst saucepans are boiling, and the meat is blackening, I'd find myself having arguments of a Monty Pythonesque circularity with my father: 'Go to the toilet, and then come to the table and we can have tea.' 'It's tea?' 'Yes, but go to the toilet first, and then we can have tea.' 'When's tea?' 'After you've been to the toilet.' 'Isn't it bed time?' 'No, it's toilet time.' 'Yes it is,' he agrees, shuffling away from the toilet door. 'Where are you going then?' 'To tea.' 'No, you're meant to be going to the toilet first. Look, the tea's burning.' 'If the tea's burning, let's go.' 'Okay, then, so you don't need the toilet.' 'Yes I do, and you won't stop me.' 'Go then.' 'I don't want to.' He sits down for tea, and I start serving up. 'I need the toilet,' he says, jumping up. And so on and on.

Sit down to tea. Get up from tea because I've forgotten his pills. Sit down to tea. Get up from tea because his teeth are missing. Teeth found hiding down the corner of the sofa. Begin to think teeth have malevolent life of their own and chatter about me when I'm not around.

11.15 pm: Sometimes, a district nurse comes round to help put him to bed, and maybe sit with him overnight. She usually finds me on the sofa with a bottle of sherry. Putting my father to bed was a ritual which changed a lot in the last year, when he could no longer get upstairs. Before then, I'd always proudly pulled him up the stairs – it was one thing I was able to do that no one else could. By his last year, though, the upstairs had become a forbidden garden. Putting him to bed was now a step-by-step process of ointments, pads, bowls, flannels, hot water, catheters and teeth – which, out of contrariness, would now not come out without a fight. If I left them in, I used to worry all night that they'd get dislodged, and I wouldn't hear him choking to death.

When I looked after him that last year, all I could do was bide time, pray that my father didn't shatter before my mother returned, pray that the colostomy bags didn't need emptying. No doubt lots of people have to deal with these every day; but I'm ashamed to admit that my queasiness got in the way, and I was relieved when my mother stopped giving Dad his usual dose of laxatives before she went away. It made putting my father to bed easier for me, if not more comfortable for him.

11.45 pm: Finding no sex on Channel 5 to watch now my father is in bed, I down some more sherry to a programme called *When Good Kids Go Bad*. Looking in on him once more, I go to bed too.

3.40 am: Lying in bed, dreaming of my cartoon head being hit with a cartoon girder, gradually realizing I'm awake and that it's the sound of my father banging the wall between us. I go into his bedroom, and the sheets are wet, the 'pad' shredded across the room. I spend the next half hour swearing, rearranging the bed, clearing up the mess, putting a new 'pad' on him. I go to bed again. Worst case scenario: more cartoon girders, more shredded pads, more wet sheets, less sleep . . . And then again, trying not to cry because I've lost my temper – and might not ever be able to recover it. I'm horribly rough with him as I pull his bony, bent legs back into bed. 'There's such a thing as sleep, you know, Dad.'

Sleep was, of course, a precious quality for my mother. I sometimes think that the years passing for her simply meant that she looked more and more tired. Since I was young, I can't remember seeing her fully rested. Even after my father's death, she still seems to be catching up. In the early 90s, my father would get up during the night seven or eight times for the toilet, stumbling and falling and lost in the dark. From my sleep, I'd hear my mother pleading with him to hold on, to control his bladder, pleading that inevitably led to shouts full of crying. Other times, he'd shake uncontrollably in his sleep, making my mum feel like she was on a building site. And sometimes I'd start awake in my room, hearing a scream which pierced my dreams – and no doubt my mother's – wide open: 'I was being chased by a giant bee,' cried my dad.

At least that was better than the waking nightmares about miners. These were sleepless worryings, drawn out for long post-midnight hours, most of which only my mum heard. One of the largest mines in Europe, one of the only pits still open in Stoke after Thatcher, ran hundreds of feet under our house. My parents had received a letter, saying that they were excavating under their street – and generously offering a council address where you could get a form if you thought your home was subsiding.

The pit was called Hem Heath, and my father had once been taken down into its darkness in a rickety elevator. After just one visit, his mind seemed to confound its darkness with his own. He'd listen awake for hours at night, his eyes white open, convinced he could hear the distant sounds of the miners working, scrabbling, tapping, picking far beneath the house. What bothered me so much about this particular anxiety was that I sometimes lay awake too, waiting for silence enough to hear them – wondering if it were just possibly possible. Of course it's ridiculous, I'd laugh to my mother, telling my father to be quiet, but then I'd wonder.

7.25 am: And . . . back to the beginning again.

Of course, my mother repeated the 'and again' part every day, every month, every year, repeating the routines over and over like we repeated orders to him and he repeated his cries for help. Whole months, years repeated themselves in an ever-decreasing spiral.

For me, the 'and agains' would only happen three or so times in a row, and I'd go back to university, far away from these repetitions. Too far, perhaps: whilst studying for my PhD, I had too few routines. I had nothing pressing to do, nowhere I was supposed to be at any particular time. So I wandered and frittered away days and weeks, time flaking away like my father's dry skin. I could have spent more time looking after him, helping my mother or even writing the useless piece of fire-paper that was the PhD itself – but instead, I let the days flake away and got drunk at night.

Travelling back to university after looking after my father, I'd decide to get off the train in random, unknown places, for no reason at all. I'd wander round the centre of Derby or Sheffield or Nuneaton because I didn't know anyone there, wasn't likely to be (mis)recognized by anyone for anyone . . . And I'd do this for hours, looking in shop windows, toying with CDs and videos I couldn't afford, buying dozens of second-hand books I wouldn't read. And everything seemed tinged with Parkinsonism, and everyone round me would have a shuffling gait, shaking hand, twitch or quirk I couldn't quite define.

Until once, about two-and-a-half years into my PhD, an old man in ill-fitting trousers shuffled up to me whilst I was hovering round the top shelf in a rundown Sheffield newsagents. He was shouting 'Cedric!' and people were staring as he grabbed my hand and shook it, tears in his wrinkles. It had been decades since he'd last seen Cedric, his half-brother, who'd gone to Korea. I tried to tell him he wasn't seeing him now, but he was still shaking my hand and crying. Perhaps he was happy that he'd found someone who might pass for Cedric for a moment – a moment he had to keep repeating every day with new, fake half-brothers.

I haven't been to Sheffield since.

Salvation Army, King's Cross

In December 1998 I went back to Stoke for a weekend. I was wandering round the house chatting to my mother, whilst she force-fed my father some Dandelion and Burdock . . . when she stopped, turned and said to me, 'Sit down at the kitchen table. There's something, erm, I want you to see. It may be a bit of a surprise.' So I sat, knowing already this was something important, because she'd shut the kitchen door between us and my father, and had even switched off the television. My father could be heard murmuring to himself in the sitting room.

My mother reached up to one of the shelves in the corner, where important documents were kept out of reach when we were children. 'Only your brother's seen this so far. And he was really good about it.' She smoothed down three letters in front of me. I don't remember reading the letters end to end, but certain things stuck out and I supplied the rest from old fantasies I'd had as a child: first, I noticed the slightly bent paperclip my mother's trembling hand removed from the papers, then . . . Salvation Army . . . Colin . . . ref. 497/3339 . . . John Taylor . . . First marriage . . . Children . . . Barbara . . . Divorce . . . Search.

My mother's commentary seemed just as fragmentary:

'Robin was really good about it. I haven't told Dad yet. I
don't know how to. I asked the solicitor, and he was sceptical.
He thought some kind of money motives, you know the sort
of thing . . . But I don't see what this Colin would have to
gain. Dad made his will a long time ago. He wouldn't be
capable, now, of changing it . . . Robin was really good about
it.'

'Did you know about this before?' I ask.

'Yes. We never told you because it never seemed, well, relevant to anything. It wasn't a secret – it just never came up. I
don't suppose these things do "come up" as a general rule. As
you got older, we lost sight of everything else, and he lost touch
with the other children.'

The top letter was from the 'Contributions Agency' of Social
Security, and was a list of bullet points, bold type and instructions about what not to do:

Why we are sending you this form:
- We have been asked to forward the enclosed, **and**
- It seems you **may** be the person the sender is trying to find
Please note:
- The letter has **not** been issued by this office and we are **not**
  responsible for its contents
What to do now:
If the letter is for you:
If you are the person mentioned in the letter, and you have
any further queries, please:
- Contact the sender
- **Do not contact us**

In the washing-of-hands way of Social Security, the letter
seemed most concerned with *not* eliciting a reply – rather

peculiar for a letter, it seemed to me. The second letter was a little less minimalist:

The Salvation Army
King's Cross
London
21 August 1998

Please quote reference 497/3339

Dear Mr Taylor

Re: John TAYLOR   Born: 05.08.1928
Last known address: Enville Street, Stourbridge

You may be aware of the excellent work of the Salvation Army in endeavouring to bring together members of families who have lost touch with one another. In connection with a family enquiry we are anxious to contact the above-named person.

We would be grateful if you could let us know whether or not you are the person we are seeking so that we may acquaint you with the nature of our enquiry. If you cannot be of assistance, please inform us accordingly in order that we need not trouble you again. Please quote the reference above in all correspondence.

Yours sincerely
Christopher Fairclough, Lieut-Colonel
Director – Family Tracing Service

All I could think at the time was that this letter read like a strange fusion of advertising and militaristic imagery – adver-

tising for the Salvation Army's 'excellent work', and misplaced
army imagery in its application of 'Lieut-Colonel' for someone
who tries to find, not shoot family members. I already knew
that my father and 'ref. 497/3339' were one and the same.

The next document, a letter from my mother's solicitors, was
more understandable, though at first I misread it as a missive
from the nineteenth century:

Bishops Solicitors
Est. 1808

Dear Mrs Taylor

Re: SALVATION ARMY ENQUIRY

As instructed, I requested from the Salvation Army further
details to be disclosed in connection with the enquirer,
namely their full name, possible relationship to Mr Taylor
and their last point of contact. The Salvation Army have
now responded in supplying the following details:

1. The enquirer's name is Colin Michael John Matthews.
    The enquirer's name was formerly Taylor, but he reverted
    to his mother's maiden name following the divorce of his
    parents.
2. The enquirer is believed to be the son of J. Taylor and
    was born May 1952, in Stourbridge. His minor years were
    spent living in Worcester and the surrounding area.
3. Contact between the enquirer and J. Taylor ceased some
    years ago following the separation of his parents. His
    mother's full name was Barbara Muriel Jane Matthews
    (Barbara Muriel Jane Taylor when married) who is now

deceased. It is believed the enquirer's parents were
married in 1950 in Wolverhampton. The Salvation
Army state that the enquirer is seeking his father due to
his belief that he unfairly blamed him following the
break up of his parents' marriage.

I hope the information provided supplies some further
details which may explain the situation.
I. R. Wilson

'There was also a daughter,' added my mother after I'd read the
letter. A throwaway remark and you gain another family
member. 'Turn over other stones and we might find more siblings hiding underneath,' my sister Karen used to say afterwards.

'Dad and his first wife got divorced. I don't know what happened to her – it seems she's dead now. They were married
when he was young, but it went horribly wrong and the divorce
lasted years. He had a huge breakdown and went into a mental
hospital. He was still getting the divorce when I first knew him.
I never met the children, but he kept in touch with them for a
while after we were married. I wonder why they broke off contact. Dad never wanted to talk about it, and I know it seems
funny now, but I never thought of asking. It's too late to know
anything now.'

'One has to wonder,' she says after my father's death, 'if Dad
would ever have told you, if he'd been well. If he'd got that
letter, I guess his initial reaction would have been to throw it
in the bin. He might have regretted it afterwards, but by then
it'd have been too late. After all, when I eventually showed
him the Salvation Army letter and asked if it was about him,
he just said "No" sharply: "No, it's not me. Not me." He was
so definite about it.'

The day after finding myself in a rather larger family than I'd thought, with a strange, angst-ridden history opening behind us, I pull up a chair next to my dad, whilst my mum's out at the Co-op. I heave my father up so he's sitting straight, and then give him a record sleeve to look at: 'It's what I've put on – Bach.' This time, he doesn't use the sleeve to make a sculpture with. Instead, we sit together whilst Bach's Orchestral Suites are playing, and I look at him now and then, wondering about his life. And I cry a little at the music and the non-memories to which neither my father nor I now have recourse.

PART TWO

Under the Clock, King's Cross Station

When I asked my mother how she met my father, she wrote me a letter:

Dear Jonathan

Of course I remember the first day your dad and I met. I was nervous – this might turn out to be a 'wild-goose chase'! We arranged to meet under the clock on King's Cross Station, mid-morning on 26 August 1965. Dad was there, wearing a brown sports jacket, smart, and carrying a mac over his arm. That was how I was to recognize Dad – by the mac over his arm.

Reading this again, I find it strange that – in recounting a time before any of us were born, before they were engaged, before the divorce from his first wife – my mother already uses 'Dad' to describe my father. It's as if, for her, he had always been husband-and-dad-in-waiting – waiting, that is, under the clock on King's Cross for the moment when his true nature would be discovered. The letter continues:

We went first for a cup of coffee, and then we walked and walked and walked. I remember him taking me round Westminster Cathedral, I hadn't been there before, and Westminster Abbey, through the parks, along the river; we looked around some ship (Captain Scott's?), and St Paul's. We had tea in a Lyon's Corner House, and sat down in a News Theatre in Trafalgar Square. We walked everywhere, hardly stopping. By the end of the day my feet ached and ached. I've relived that day in my imagination many times afterwards.

I left about seven in the evening on the suburban train for Hertford, where my grandmother lived. He kissed me goodbye. I think we fell in love at first sight, give or take a couple of hours – as Dad used to say.

From that point on, my mother would travel up every weekend from Kingston, Devon, on the Plymouth to Paddington line, to see my father and his mac. After they'd spent the day together, she'd take the local train to Stapleford in Hertfordshire, to stay with her grandmother – or she'd stay in Maida Vale with Reni, an 'auntie' of mine.

'Reni was sympathetic to me and your dad,' my mother says. 'If it hadn't been for her, the wedding might never have happened, and none of you would have happened. Your Auntie Reni let me stay at her flat – it was from there that I went to the wedding.'

Reni wasn't really an 'auntie': the term was used liberally when we were younger to include relatives, friends, any woman who was older than us. That's one of the reasons why working out a family tree has proved difficult. Reni, for example, is both family and not-family at the same time. She was born in 1930s Berlin to German-Jewish parents. She came to England with her sister in 1939, as part of the Kindertransport scheme which rescued thousands of Jewish children from the Nazis. Eventually, Reni and her sister ended up in rural Hertfordshire, where they were looked after by my maternal grandparents. Reni's father – who had Parkinson's – died after they left; Reni's grandmother committed suicide when the deportation order came through; Reni's mother sent letters to her daughters in England, letters which got shorter and shorter. She died in Auschwitz in 1943.

In this way, my parents' King's Cross is distantly linked to the end of the line that is Auschwitz. My parents' micro-history is touched, even determined, by terrible, international events. When my mother says that 'if it hadn't been for Reni, none of it might have happened' whole vistas open up behind us.

Today, in 2003, we're in Shropshire, a long way from the end of the line. We're driving through the rain, on the way back from a shop dedicated to rocking horses. We've just taken a rocking horse we rode when we were little to be restored. The proprietor of the shop didn't think the model was worth 'refurbishment' – it wasn't a 'golden age' rocking horse – but my mother wants it for her new grandson. Moreover, it was given to us by my father's sister Mildred, who's now dead, so it seems a pity to lose all that rocking-horse history. Personally, I wish we didn't live in a world where even rocking horses remember.

During the drive home, I ask my mother about her 'courtship' with my father: 'How did you meet? We thought you bumped into each other on some station, and Dad chatted you up.'

For years we'd been fed the grandparents' story – that my mother and father did a *Brief Encounter*, bumping into each other out of the blue on a steamy railway station. Only after my father's death did my mother put on that semi-smile which portends some revelation, some hesitant contradiction of received truths. The revelation always starts with a drawn out 'Well . . .' and continues with a statement to the effect of 'actually, that's not *strictly* true' with heavy emphasis on 'strictly'. 'Well . . . actually it's not *strictly* true that a right angle has eighty-nine degrees.' 'Well . . . I know we *told* you the Battle of Waterloo was in 1816. But that doesn't mean it actually was.'

On this occasion, my mother says: 'Well . . . *Brief Encounter* isn't *strictly* true. We used the story about bumping into each other for your grandma and grandpa. We thought they didn't need to know everything.'

'So how did you and Dad meet?'

'Dad was in the classifieds. I think it was in a magazine called *The Teacher*. It was at the back – and caught my eye because no one advertised like that in those days. There was no such thing as lonely hearts in the 1960s.

'I'd made a mistake in moving back home after university. I was lonely, back in the Devon sticks, in a place called Kingston. After four years away, there I was at home again, not allowed out except for work. Even if I had been allowed out, there was nowhere to go, no one to meet, no other young people. We didn't go to pubs or nightclubs then – it wasn't done. At the school where I was working, there were only older teachers. The countryside was beautiful, of course. But it was so . . . empty.

'So when I came across it, the advert got me because the advertiser was lonely too. I can't remember the wording, but it was something about an 'attractive, intelligent, lonely man seeks female company'. Typical Dad, a bit vain. But I liked the sound of him. I wrote to him, and we arranged to meet on King's Cross station.'

I wonder (though I don't say so aloud) if my father had many responses – and, if so, why he chose my mother. Perhaps he'd met others beneath the clock at King's Cross, with a mac over his arm, before my mother. Perhaps there are other universes where my father ended up with the 'wrong' woman; universes where the Plymouth to Paddington train was late, where my father forgot his mac, where 1930s Germany didn't vote in Hitler, where a butterfly flapped its wings differently in Rio.

'After the first King's Cross day we met up every weekend. Right from the start we were comfortable in each other's company. We did lots of things. We went to see *Goldfinger* in a London cinema, *The Sound of Music* in Plymouth. We went to London Zoo and sat on the grass in Regent's Park and walked hand-in-hand round the British Museum. I visited Dad's tiny bedsit in Peckham. He had a Polish landlady who talked a lot, and we cooked pork chops on his little gas ring. We had a day in Exeter, visiting the cathedral, sitting on a bench outside. That afternoon was spoilt by an angry woman telling us off for kissing in public.

'There were a few weekends when I didn't see him. He *said* he was going to see his parents up in Oldham. I assume that's where he was going, but I never pressed him.'

My father proposed on the morning after New Year's, 1966. He was standing with my mother on Reni's doorstep. I like to think it was snowing. My mother said yes; she didn't know then that my father was married to someone else in this very same universe.

'I remember . . . I remember the elation when he asked me to marry him, keeping it a secret for a few weeks, choosing the

engagement ring from Samuel's in Plymouth, day-dreaming
about the future . . .'

'How long was it before Dad told you he was married
already?'

'After we'd been engaged a couple of months, I asked *him*
what he'd been up to all those missing years. Why hadn't some
prettier girl snapped him up in that time? He'd said he was ten
years older than me, give or take. If I'd known in the first place
that he was actually fourteen years older, I might not have
started it. And if I'd known that *and* about him being married,
well . . .

'Fourteen years' difference is a long time when you're 23. At
one point, your grandparents hunted out one of Dad's aunts in
Oldham. Quite how they did it, I don't know – real detection
work. This aunt told your grandparents that Dad was older than
what he'd told me. I didn't believe it – thought it was a ploy.
Your dad was such a good pretender, and was willing to go to
any lengths. It even says he was 35, not 38 on the marriage certificate.'

'Another forged document!'

'I suppose so, but better not print that – it might be illegal.'

She laughs, 'You never know, perhaps it means we were
never *legally* married after all. It doesn't matter now. It'd just be
funny. The final joke.'

I look hard at my mother's face, and wonder how hysterical
she'd find the joke if it turned out true. Suddenly, I'm scared
by my own research. There are things one doesn't want to find
out.

As I'm writing, I have some of the documents laid out in
front of me. There is the marriage certificate which reads '35
years old' next to John Taylor, and which suggests that he was
born in 1931. There is the visitor's passport from August 1966,

which likewise gives Dad's date of birth as '5 Aug. 1931', as does a copy birth certificate, seemingly issued in 1946 (after he was adopted). It's not really from 1946, though. The issue date is doctored; '1946' is written over a deleted '1966', which is just visible from the other side of the paper. Perhaps he thought it might look a bit suspect if all his documents were issued anew in mid-1966. After all, not only did he get a new birth certificate and passport, but also a new NHS medical card. This again states '5.8.1931' as his date of birth. A later medical card, however, has the date of birth scratched out, and written over with '5.8.28'. Another visitor's passport, issued in 1982, has '5.8.1928', as does a certificate of adoption. For some reason, the latter is torn lengthways, in a way that hardly looks accidental.

Between contradictions, scratchings out and deliberate tears, I can't arrange these papers into a pattern, into any likeness of my father. Papers like these can't answer the questions I want to ask of them, questions like: can you *really* misplace three or four years of your life? And if not, why pretend? Was he so worried about his age – and my mother's reaction to it – that he was willing to commit 'identity fraud'? This hardly squares with the Dad I knew, who was so terrified of the law that he thought Sergeant Flowers would come a-knocking when I taped songs off the radio. Perhaps there were other reasons for the two different birthdays. Were the missing few years too painful and he wanted to lose them? Or did divorce, a nervous breakdown and Electric Convulsive Treatment lose them for him?

When I've talked about the conflicting documents people have suggested: 'Perhaps he was with MI5, CIA, KGB. There couldn't have been many people back then fluent in French, German, Italian, Spanish and, of course, *Russian*. Think about it: *Russian*, if you know what I mean.'

In fact, my father himself said he was approached by MI5 after university. Quite how they 'approached' him is not known – one can only imagine the scene as James Bond parody, accompanied by a Shirley Bassey soundtrack. Perhaps he accepted: he never told my mother what his answer was. Presumably, she was meant to assume that he said no. But . . . perhaps perhaps perhaps – perhapses rocking backwards and forwards, forwards and backwards. Can you imagine the state you've reached where you hesitate, even for a second, over whether your father, a headmaster and respectable suburb-dweller, could once – for three or four years? – have been an Oldhamian Roger Moore, an Oldhamian Old Ham?

We're meant to assume that the '1928' dates are the correct ones. When we contacted the registry, it's what they said. So the most benign explanation is that, in 1966, he obtained a new birth certificate showing a different date of birth (1931 instead of 1928); he back-dated this certificate by altering the issue date to 1946; he then got a new passport using the new birth certificate; he told whoppers on his marriage certifi-cate . . . and all to keep up a lie about his age which had got out of hand. Quite how he managed to pull off this self-identity fraud, we'll never know. For my father, summer 1966 must have been hard work.

'He must have got entangled by the age lie he told when we first met. Gosh, I was so uncurious. Even when the three years gradually reappeared, a long time after we were married, I never wondered where they'd been.'

I imagine the missing years slinking back on to forms and documents, into conversations and memories, pretending they'd never been away. 'It's seems so strange now that I never got round to asking about these things.'

What she *did* get round to asking about was what my father

had been doing during the missing fourteen-minus-three-years.

'We were leaving the beach as the sun was setting. I asked: "What've you been doing all these years?" I can remember the shocked expression on his face as if it's close up. He coughed and said, "Well, I've been being married." He looked shocked that I didn't know already. Perhaps he'd tried to let slip before.

'But how was I meant to guess – I lived in Devon! There weren't any divorces where I came from. As a child, I wasn't let out to play with friends, even though it was the middle of nowhere. Then I was sent to an all-girls' grammar school where boys and sex didn't exist. Even when I went away to Leicester University I was just a mouse – having coffees and chats with girlfriends. There wasn't any of the drinking and drugs and "free love" everyone now associates with the 60s – or at least, not in Leicester. Bit of a disappointment, really.

'When Dad told me he was married, the implications of divorce and second marriages flooded into my head. I was horrified. All those Sundays at church made sure of that. A few weeks later, I broke off the engagement and gave the ring back. But it was already too late. It was probably too late a couple of hours after we'd met. And Dad was so persuasive when he wanted to be. He went on and on at me, wouldn't let me alone, till I gave in.

'It just wasn't done to have anything to do with married or divorced men. In the 60s divorcees were like homosexuals . . . except no one had heard of them, so it wasn't like that either. Maybe in London or Liverpool it was different, but Grandma and Grandpa lived in Devon. And they weren't exceptions. Even when we were married, people would cross streets in front of us, refuse to share pews with us in church.

'We didn't tell your grandparents till one weekend at Easter, when Dad came to visit and told them. It was ghastly beyond anything I'd imagined. There was a huge row. Your grandma and grandpa wouldn't speak to me for a week. They went from room to room in furious silence.

'By June, Dad was banned from the house. The rows were too much. Though they were mainly on one side. Dad was quiet, patient. He only once lost his temper, and had a go back. But that once,' she pauses, breathes in, 'was terrifying . . .

'Between me and them, the rows never stopped. They used to say: "Why don't you talk it over with us? You never talk to us any more!" But they didn't *really* want to talk about it. They wanted an opportunity to shout me down, persuade me it wasn't the right thing. Talking ended in rowing, like everything else we did.

'It all got so vicious, painful. There was no escape because, as I said, I wasn't allowed out. For months, it was two against one, without a break. What I remember more than anything is the guilt. When your grandpa was sitting at the dinner table – when Grandma had left the room to fetch the salt – and it was quiet, he'd say: "You do know that you're making your mother ill with this business?" Your grandma would totter back into the room with the salt, and I'd see what I was told to see – that she was thin and pale. Of course, I can see now that she was making *herself* ill. But back then I felt I was wrecking their lives and their health in one go. It seemed like my engagement was the end of the world to them.

'I never meant to cause all this trouble, to be a rebel. I wasn't into all of that 60s teenage rebellion scene – I preferred Brahms to the Beatles. I was a rebel by accident.

'The problem was your grandma and grandpa had such high standards. They had a kind of readymade "knitting pattern" for a daughter. I didn't match the pattern, so I was a disappointment. I was no good at practical things like knitting, wood-turning, or baking cakes – the things Grandma and Grandpa rated. I only did well academically, which was tenth best. I just wasn't their kind of daughter. And your dad was certainly not their kind of son. He was an intellectual from the city, and used to take an hour to wire a plug. He could barely be bothered to bang a nail in a wall and call it a hanger.'

I look in the side mirror, and wonder if I'd have been my father's 'kind of son' if he hadn't had Parkinson's, Capgras, dementia; I wonder if I'd have been my father's kind of son more than I was my father's Parkinson's kind of son. You never know: he might have been proud of the time it takes me to put up slanting shelves.

My mother continues: 'No doubt your grandparents were so nasty because they loved me. They were worried. Eventually, though, all the "end-of-the-world" rows succeeded in making me more determined, not less. I wonder what would have happened if they'd been all right, accepting about it. There're many moments where things could have gone other ways. You have to wonder "what would have happened if" such and such had been slightly different.'

Sometimes, I think that my mother's memory has been trapped in a 'what-would-have-happened-if' maze ever since he died: 'What would have happened if Grandma and Grandpa had accepted him?' 'What would have happened if Reni hadn't been around?' and, most importantly, 'What would have happened if he had never got Parkinson's?'

The wedding 'what-ifs' include a disorientating one about my father's divorce papers. My mother explains: 'Dad's decree nisi came through in April 1966. The document certifying the decree absolute for the divorce came through on the 1st of September

1966 . . . or so he said. Actually, I never saw the decree absolute, and haven't been able to find it. What if it never came through? What if he fibbed about the decree absolute, like he did about his age on the wedding certificate? That'd mean we weren't legally married. In the 60s, it would have been awful to think such a thing. But to find out now – well, it'd be the ironic icing on the wedding cake, wouldn't it? Very funny.'

As before, there's nothing in my mother's expression to suggest whether or not she really would find it a good joke. She's studying the road ahead.

'Things did get better when I left home, late that summer. I got a job in an East End school and moved to London. I started enjoying myself, seeing Dad every evening and weekend. I felt more confident. Two friends at the school colluded to make sure I didn't talk to anyone who didn't approve of me.

'We went to see Dad's vicar at Camberwell about the wedding. He was very kind, though divorcees couldn't get married in his Church of England church. He sent us to the Congregational church down the road. Everyone was welcoming there.

'Dad never asked me to choose between Grandma and Grandpa and himself. He did all he could to arrange the "fairy tale" wedding I wanted. He arranged a honeymoon in Oxford and a new home near Basingstoke – where he would carry me over the threshold in traditional style.

'Whilst he was arranging these things, Grandma finally decided for herself that there was no hope for us, no turning back. When she realized this, what was odd – but characteristic – was the way she took over all the organization, the guest list, the catering and so on. She ended up organizing almost everything.

'No doubt, when your grandma and grandpa saw they

couldn't reverse the situation, they decided they'd control it instead. That's the word all those self-help psychologists on TV would use: they were "controlling". They were "controlling" before and after the wedding. It's amazing how patient your father was with them. After we were married, he never said no, I couldn't visit them. We used to drive down to Devon two or three times a year. The one thing he wouldn't allow was for me to visit them on my own. Grandma hated that, said it was her right to see her daughter on her own.

'Though the fuss died down as the years passed, there were sudden moments when I realized it was still lurking under the surface. All those attitudes, all that anger didn't just evaporate. Now and then, I'd come face to face with them again, and I'd still be at a loss how to react. For instance, it was Christmas 1988 when I first told Grandma about Dad's Parkinson's. They'd come up to stay, and you'd gone to bed. I told her about the diagnosis. She turned to me and said: "Whatever you two've done in the past, even you don't deserve that." I didn't answer.'

No wonder, I think, that my father didn't want her to visit her parents alone. Nonetheless, as he became iller, she did start going to see them, for a few days at a time, leaving him with me. He'd stand up and jab his index finger (in the vague direction of Devon?) and shout: 'Why's she gone down there? They've always had it in for me!' If he was feeling particularly bad, a few 'bitches' might be thrown in for good measure. Only then did I begin to understand that there were family tensions beyond those involving myself.

Both my grandma and grandpa are now dead. Perhaps what counts is that, after everything that happened, Grandpa cried, head down, at my father's funeral. It hardly matters if it wasn't for my father.

Back in the car, my mother's still in 1966 – or, rather, 1966 filtered through 2003 chat shows: 'Yes, that's the right word for them and what they did: "controlling". Of course, I didn't realize they were "controlling" at the time. I couldn't know because there wasn't a word for it then. And there were no self-help books or programmes either. It made it worse that I couldn't put into words what they were doing. You see, whatever *you* think of it, perhaps this self-help psychology stuff *can* be a good thing! It would have done me good.'

We've driven past the Wrekin in Shropshire, through a village called Little Wenlock, and have stopped in Much Wenlock to have a quick look between showers, before we head home. 'We used to come here lots with Daddy,' my mother says. 'He loved this part of Shropshire.' There's a small abbey – which is shut – and a Tudorish main street. We meander down it, avoiding groups of bored teenagers. There's a tiny market-place which is padlocked, and a couple of bookshops. Browsing through one of them, I find a complete set of Thomas De Quincey's works. I waste mental energy debating whether or not I can afford the set, and haggling with the bookseller.

Not that I really think I will buy the books. It's just a way of diverting my thoughts from what's really bothering me: that I don't remember what I've seen of Much Wenlock, don't remember Little Wenlock, don't recognize the part of the Wrekin we drove round. My father loved visiting these places, but they don't mean anything to my memory now.

'I suppose it was before you happened, or when you were little, that we saw a lot of Shropshire,' my mother says. 'When we first came to Stoke we were so unhappy we had to get away in the evenings. So we'd take your brother and sister to the country – to the Mayr Hills, Ludlow or "the Cave".'

'The Cave' was somewhere in Staffordshire or Shropshire or

Derbyshire. It was a walk down a steep path under bluebells, across a pat-ridden meadow, past a brook and finally to a picnic beneath a slate cliff. It was somewhere I loved as a child. But none of us could ever remember how to get there after my father lost his memory; 'the Cave' isn't marked on any maps. And anyway, would I know it if I saw it again, if I don't recognize Much Wenlock?

'I suppose Much Wenlock was before you happened, or when you were little.' So often, listening to my mother talking about the past, I feel that I came on the scene too late. I missed the past that mattered to her and my father, and am part of what came after. My elder brother and sister can recapture some of it, but I was either too young or not there. Perhaps it's part of being a son or daughter, and particularly a younger child: by definition, you're on the scene too late, coming after the great events of your parents' youth, after their King's Crosses, after their domestic revolutions, after their evening trips back from Much Wenlock, after they were well enough to walk down steep paths to picnics in caves.

By the time a younger child like myself appears on the scene, the revolutions have often given way to limbos, the King's Crosses to Stoke-on-Trents. I grew up watching my father slowing down, giving up work, giving up everything, dozing off to *Cagney & Lacey*. Witnessing this limbo, I wasn't even sure – believe it or not – if my parents really loved each other. Whereas my grandparents held hands, my parents didn't. Instead, all I saw were angry-looking hair curlers, rows about Devon, ever-worsening shakes. It was only when he died that I understood how much my mother loved my father. It was only when he died that I came to know what history they'd been through, pre-me, pre-*Cagney & Lacey*. Only then. 'All is in retrospect,' says Katherine Mansfield. It seems especially true when you're a third-born or (according to my new calculation) fifth-born child.

On the way home from Much Wenlock, we drive through Wellington, near Shrewsbury. My father lived here for a while with his first wife. From the road, it looks like a collection of roundabouts.

WHSmith's, St Pancras Station

Hegel remarks somewhere that all great world-historic facts
and personages appear [in history] . . . twice. He forgot to
add: the first time as tragedy, the second as farce.

(Karl Marx, 'The Eighteenth Brumaire of Louis Bonaparte')

Still, if I can't remember their Much Wenlocks, their
Wellingtons, their King's Crosses, at least I have my own
London St Pancras. My St Pancras doesn't seem as romantic as
their King's Cross, but that might just be because I was there.

It's thirty-two years since 1965. I'm meeting a girl in
WHSmith's on St Pancras station, across the road from King's
Cross and its clock. At this time, of course, I'm not aware that
there is a clock on King's Cross worth knowing about. I know
nothing and (to be frank) think nothing about how my parents
met, or who they were before me. All I know is that there
should be a girl on St Pancras who will recognize me, mac or no
mac – a girl I can only meet here, since her home in East Acton
is strictly off-limits.

She'll recognize me because, unlike my parents' encounter
on King's Cross, this isn't our first meeting. That took place a

few months before, at Warwick University Students' Union. It was Valentine's Day, 1997, and, in true romantic style, a few friends and I were drunkenly leering at freshers.

My future date at St Pancras was hanging round the dance floor. I fell in love with her legs at first sight, and the rest of her piecemeal. I stared at her legs and – to my surprise – she started staring back.

After half an hour of squinting and winking, I stumbled over to her, and shouted at her face: 'Do you want a drink?' She shouted at my face: 'Maria.' I shouted at her face: 'Do you want a drink?' She shouted back: 'No, I don't dance, but a drink would be nice.' I shouted: 'I'm a poor postgraduate student.' She shouted back: 'I'll pay for my own Snakebite and Black if necessary.'

So I bought her a drink with her own money and we sat down in the 'chill-out' area. I said it was very chilly in the chill-out area, she said it wasn't, but I put my arm round her anyway, just in case. Then I kissed her.

An hour later, Maria put on her duffle coat and said, 'Take me home.' So I did.

To return to WHSmith's on St Pancras station. It's July 1997, and Maria and I have been seeing each other for five months. We're meeting here because, during the holidays, she lives in London with her mother and father.

She appears from behind a pillar. She's wearing her duffle coat, even though it's a hot summer's day. We kiss and go on the tube for an 'all you can eat' lunch at a Chinese restaurant near Leicester Square. Then we walk and walk and walk. She takes me round China Town and Soho – we have a nose round a couple of sex shops – then to Green Park. We laze around for a bit before going to see Buckingham Palace. She stands outside the railings and shakes her fist at the monarchy ('Let them eat cake indeed!'). We walk down Oxford Street, but don't look in any of the shops; we have a beer in a Notting Hill pub and buy some second-hand De Quincey. We walk everywhere, hardly stopping. By the end of the afternoon, my feet ache and ache. But it's now five o'clock, and she's getting nervous about her parents. They don't like her out after tea time – don't really like her out at all – and certainly wouldn't like her out with me.

To be honest, they barely know I exist in 1997. I am a hanger-on at the edge of consciousness, a minor bother, a 'nose-frog' to attempt a rough translation of their Greek substitute for 'Jonathan'. Being a nose-frog isn't that bad – metaphorically speaking, it just means you're an inconvenience who gets in the way a bit, attaching yourself to unsuspecting noses.

Maria's parents, Anna and Dimitrios, are from Cyprus – Anna from a village in the Turkish-occupied north, Dimitrios from a wealthy town in the south – and that is where they are always about to return to, leaving this 'rabbeesh' place called London. We'll go, they say, we'll go tomorrow . . . well, or next year . . . or when Maria's finished school . . . or as soon as she's finished university . . . or when we've unpacked the suitcases so we can pack them again. Over there we've got a beautiful house that's getting overgrown, whilst here we've got a council flat with 70s wallpaper and curtains made of rags. Why bother to decorate, why bother to unpack, why bother to mend the washing machine or fix the heating when we're about to leave for good?

Going, going, but never gone. Perhaps that's what it's like to be in exile. After all, her mother can't go back to her village, and hasn't been able to since the Turkish army annexed the northern half of the island. She cries (often) and tells Maria that the night before the Turkish invasion of 1974 she dreamt that one of the icons in her village church fell apart in her hands. Over and again, she kept trying to put the pieces back together. Over and again, thinking she'd managed it, she'd look down to see the Turkish flag in her hands, not the Virgin and Child. Since that dream, there's been a green line separating her from her past, and she can only squint at unfocused photos of it that Maria finds on the internet – pictures of a village populated by rubble, a chapel stripped of its icons, a churchyard of dug-up skeletons robbed of their jewellery.

If it's difficult for Maria's mother to find her home amongst these images – to recognize her place of origin in them – she's strangely willing to find it almost everywhere else. Exiled from the one place she loves, anywhere that's got a hint of green and that's not a council flat in West London has become a likeness of it. Memories of rural Nottinghamshire where she and her husband first lived together, postcards from the Lake District, photos of holidays spent by others in Austria, even Hanging Rock in *Picnic at Hanging Rock*, a film we once watched with her – all of them elicit an excited, 'That eez jast like-n my home villeege.' If the plot and dialogue of *Picnic at Hanging Rock* were incomprehensible to her, the film was still an aesthetic success because the Australian outback seemed interchangeable with northern Cyprus. For Maria's mother, everywhere has become a poor substitute for a place which no longer really exists, or at least not as she half-remembers it.

By contrast, Maria's father, Dimitrios, *could* go back to his place of origin; he has a house and large family in southern, unoccupied Cyprus. Indeed, he's been declaring his intention to move back with his wife and daughter for twenty-five years. Now and then he starts packing Maria's suitcase for her, shouting that she is the one 'stoopeed' reason he has stayed, and that the whole mess is to be sorted by forcing her back to Cyprus and marrying her off to whatever man is 'stoopeed' enough to take her. His rage doesn't carry him past a few layers of socks and blouses, though – and certainly not to his daughter's under-wear drawer. Eventually, he wanders off, swearing under his breath that they'll go soon, swearing that he'll vote for the BNP at the next election. They've put a leaflet under the door saying that they'd pay £60,000 to immigrants if they return to their own countries. He doesn't care if he's the only non-Anglo-Saxon, Greek Cypriot in the country voting for them; he wants to be 'sent back to where he comes from'. 'Pleezen send me back,' he seems to be saying, 'Pleezen send me back becoz I cannot send myself.'

No, Dimitrios cannot send himself, and instead he lives in limbo, West Acton. There are many forms of exile, and his is as terrible as any, self-imposed or not. In limbo, he and his wife are trapped in a world of endless debates about forty-year-old matchmakings, love affairs and weddings, and more recent schizophrenias, cancers and deaths – as if no one has fallen in love or married since the 1960s, only gone mad or died.

Dimitrios does sometimes take extended holidays from limbo, visiting Cyprus and his family. But he always comes back a few weeks later, to a country which was partly responsible for his island's agony, a country where no more than a handful of people know him, a country of ragged curtains and broken washing machines. Who knows why – he probably doesn't, whatever he says about everything being Maria's fault. I suppose at least here he's popular in the local William Hill, where his unerring instinct for old nags has never failed him yet; at least here he has the freedom to swear and gnash his teeth to his heart's content, without upsetting any elderly matriarchs; at least here he can vent his unending fury on the country, his wife, his daughter, the Turks, the British Empire, the

Americans, Henry Kissinger, the National Lottery, utility bills, fake door-to-door salespersons on *Crimewatch*, those (and I translate) 'Jeweesh whores' who present the BBC news, neighbours, old nags that lose, old nags that win on which he was going to bet but didn't and old curtains which should have been replaced but haven't. I ring Maria when she's staying in London and hear in the background a constant white noise of high-pitched hysteria (her mother) and baritonal fury (her father) – all in Greek Cypriot dialect, except for the odd phrase which rises to the surface: 'Tony Blair', 'George W Bush', 'Maria', 'Breeteesh Gas', 'dabble-glazeeng', 'Anna Ford', '2.40 at Uttoxeter'.

Oh, yes, and the word for nose-frogs, which I've also learnt to recognize. Gradually, as the years pass and I persist on the edge of Dimitrios's consciousness, I evolve from mere nose-frog to some species of Mediterranean hedgehog, to other, increasingly nefarious creatures, most of which are untranslatable. Eventually, by dint of lingering long enough, I qualify as a human being – or, to be more specific, 'a long-haired Eengleesh gay-puff' – and someone worthy of grown-up swearing. 'Gay-puff': sounds kind of nice, like something you'd powder your nose with. Still, I think I preferred the lily-pads and croaking – even being mistaken for Humphrey Bogart by my father was better. Having said that, I do have an illustrious, fellow 'Eengleesh gay-puff' in George Michael, according to Maria's father. He refuses to admit that he used to extol George Michael as a marvellous example of the *Cypriot* race – that is, before an alleged incident in some public lavatories apparently changed the singer's nationality (and sexual orientation) forever.

I, on the other hand, risk being changed into a cushion. That was what happened to Maria's first 'husband' – a blue teddy bear with heart-shaped paws. When she was five, she and Blue Teddy watched a schools' programme which told them all they needed to know about reproduction. Subsequently, they decided to put theory into practice. She donned a veil, dressed Blue Teddy in one of her father's bow-ties, said 'I do' for herself, said 'I do' for Blue Teddy, sprinkled shredded paper over the newly-weds, and then retired to the cupboard under the stairs for the wedding night. Her mother discovered them; horrified, she sent Maria to bed without any feta and crackers. Back from school the next day, Maria couldn't find her new husband any-where, search as she might – under the stairs, in the laundry basket, on top of wardrobes. But there was a brand-new blue cushion perched suspiciously at one end of the sofa. This was the fate of my predecessor. And this is the terror I am con-fronted with every day: the terror of waking one morning to find myself staring out at people's bottoms, encased for eternity in a soft furnishing.

Like Blue Teddy before me, I am not Greek. I am not Greek Cypriot. I am not Greek Cypriot and Orthodox Christian. I am not Greek Cypriot, Orthodox Christian and am certainly no 'levendi' ('macho lad'). I am not Greek Cypriot, Orthodox Christian, a *levendi* and – again like Blue Teddy – I have no experience of hard labour, whether in factories, coal mines or on village farms. I am a middle-class, lapsed-Protestant, untidy-haired Eengleesh boy, who gets paid for something which is incomprehensible to them (and largely to me as well). But more than this, *I* am not *them*. That's what really counts. *I* am not *them*. I don't mean 'them' in a general sense, as in '*like* them' (Greek, Orthodox, Cypriot and so on). I mean 'them' specifically, as in not Dimitrios or Anna, not her father or mother. They talk about arranged marriages, but nothing gets past a few threats and half-hearted introductions – like returning to Cyprus, it's all about going, going, but never gone – because they want her there, in her room, in the flat forever, never growing up.

Perhaps most parents are unconsciously like this, but with Maria's parents the unconscious is almost conscious: when Maria was younger, Anna used to slip a curtain ring on to her daughter's finger and declare that, sometime in the future, they would be married. No wonder Blue Teddy copped it, getting in the way like he did.

Dimitrios and Anna are lonely, and Maria is the daughter of their exile. She is the only person who connects them to the present, the only person who is at home in their home *and* in their exile. She's also the only person who can fill in their Council Tax forms. There was another, but this never-to-be-born elder sibling is buried in an unmarked plot on the Yorkshire moors, a grave that will be forever Cyprus – and a constant reminder to Maria that she was her parents' only child to reach a world of exile and Council Tax forms. This is what I am taking from them. Like Capgras syndrome incarnate, I am guiltily, stealthily bodysnatching an only daughter who they thought was shut up in her bedroom; I am guiltily, stealthily replacing her with someone they don't recognize.

This new Maria is a 'whore' (though not *yet* a 'Jeweesh' one like those on the BBC), 'worthless', 'a fucking beetch', 'no daughter of mine', and 'a disgrace to my dead mother who rolls about in her grave' – especially since moving in with the 'Eengleesh homosexual' a couple of years ago. Quite how she can be a 'whore' by living with a 'gay-puff' is beyond me. The logic doesn't matter. I sometimes wonder if, for all the swearing and spluttering anger, it's just that Dimitrios doesn't have the language to express the furious love he has for his daughter. Perhaps that was the case for my father too (how can I know?): whether pidgin Greek or Parkinsonian English, the languages we have fail to express the love and rage of father-hood.

'Tuna! (pronounced 'Choona!'),' Maria's father bawled on the phone one day. 'Fucking tuna! Bladdy bladdy tuna!' After a minute or two of this, she put the receiver down. It took a few minutes to work out what Dimitrios was trying to say – that he was rather concerned about her diet now she'd moved away from them. He was worried that all she was eating, whilst living with the 'Eengleesh gay-puff', was tinned fish. 'Bladdy tuna' is part of the vocabulary of anxiety-ridden fatherhood.

As far as anxiety-ridden motherhood is concerned, Maria's mother cries and cries, declaring that she will die soon, killed off by what she's been put through by her daughter, her hus-band, the Turks, leaving everyone in peace. 'You know-n you making me eel? You know-n I'm eel wiv all thees business wiv that Eengleesh boy? My blood pressure, eet goez ap and ap and ap. I going to die.' Going, going, but never gone . . . thank God. Over dinner, during one short-lived visit to the flat, Dimitrios shouts at his daughter: 'You bladdy making your mother bladdy eel, you know!' And Anna totters back into the room with the salt, seeming much thinner and paler.

All this is why, back in 1997 and for many years afterwards, Maria and I don't meet at her flat in West London. Instead, we wander 'in secret' round the British Museum, the Natural History Museum, the Science Museum, the National Gallery, the Tower, Oxford Street, Bond Street, Acton High Street (a bit warily, being so close to home), Regent's Park, Holland Park, car parks, music shops, bookshops, sex shops, friends' houses and friends of friends' houses. Like my parents, we too had our Renis with whom we stayed – a friend in Harrow and two cousins of Maria's who'd run away from their parents, leaving behind fatherly fury for a life of pyjamas, daytime TV and self-help psychology.

There are so many points of contact between my mother's King's Cross story and my St Pancras that she sometimes cries when I talk to her about it. Both include brief encounters on stations, days out in London, parents who disapprove, parents who are 'controlling', self-imposed illnesses, Renis who help, friends who turn away, fury, love, salt . . . It doesn't matter to me if these repeats, these echoes in our histories are a matter of perception, of order imposed retrospectively on the past.

Otherwise, I don't know why I'm writing about my St Pancras, in an account of Mr John Taylor and his disease. I suppose none of it's separable in my mind. I can't talk about my father and my relationship with him without also talking about girlfriends, siblings, half-siblings, aunties, adoptive aunties, aunties who aren't aunties, the Holocaust, butterflies in Rio and so forth. Digressions are inevitable. Still, you might think it's a bit of a lame excuse, and I'll stop now.

Except . . .

Except . . .

Except for one more thing, to paraphrase Columbo.

Put it this way. This book is about my father and the past. But there are times when words aren't just descriptive or retrospective. There are times when they do things to the here and now. An example might be the 'I wills' spoken by my father and mother in a Congregationalist church in Camberwell, on the afternoon of 17 December 1966.

Another example might be: 'Maria, will you marry me?'

Tyrol

Rarely, rarely comest thou,
Spirit of Delight!

(Percy Bysshe Shelley, 'Song')

My mother's letter – the one about how she and my father met – goes on to talk about their first holiday together:

Our first holiday was in Austria, August 1966. It was Dad's suggestion to have a holiday abroad, and he booked it. It was a late booking, so the Austrian Tyrol was the only holiday with spaces left. Though Dad had his own single room, I had to share with another girl, who turned out to be rather odd and difficult to get on with (it was 1966 remember!).

I wonder if the parenthetical remark refers back to the room-mate's oddness or to the necessity for separate rooms – whether my mother is claiming that people were more likely to be peculiar in 1966, or that, because of an oppressive sense of morality, unmarried couples were often stuck with eccentric chaperones. Whichever it may be, I recall this particular guardian of moral values being discussed before, as a young woman in thick spectacles, who was known to tiptoe after men into the Gents. My mother's letter continues:

> We went with Galleon (a 1960s travel company) by
> overnight coach, with a flight over the channel to Ostend,
> and we stayed in the Gasthof-Pension Post in Sautens in the
> Oetz Valley.
>   I had never seen such beautiful scenery. We had a
> wonderful holiday: sightseeing trips to the glacier, to Merano
> (Italy) and to Innsbruck. In Innsbruck, Dad brought me a
> silver friendship ring; it had edelweiss round it. We did a lot
> of walking and used the local Postbus. One day we swam in
> the lake, it was very cold, and Dad said lake waters were
> always the same temperature – true? He seemed to know
> everything. We joined a local festival procession and danced
> on a wooden stage erected in the woods. We drank vodka in
> a café in the afternoon and ate apple strudels. At the
> Tyrolean evening at the end of the week, Dad got quite
> jealous of one of the young local Austrian performers.
>   All the people in our party looked up to him because he
> spoke fluent German and French. He translated the menus
> for everyone and ordered for them. I was very proud of
> him!
>   Love, Mum xxx

Many summers later, my parents returned to the Tyrol, chaperoned now by teenagers, children and wheelchairs. We had a number of holidays in Austria in the later 1980s and early 90s. Perhaps my mother was trying to recapture that exquisite, vodka-in-the-afternoon, dancing-on-a-stage-in-the-woods, strudel-and-lakes kind of joy which the brasher joys and agonies of families drown out. It's another case of children necessarily being on the scene too late.

After all, whenever I'd exclaim at the sublimity of the Salzkammergut or the Inn Valley, she'd say, well, yes, they were wonderful, but the Oetztal . . . now that was something else. Why didn't we go there then, I asked? Because there were no travel companies going that way any more, no package tours, she said. It was wild and isolated and steep and quiet. And I thought: a beautiful valley denied to package holidaymakers must be special, like a Sleeping Beauty too good for non-princes from Stoke.

One day, we did go there. In the late 80s, we were on holiday in a nearby valley. Four of us – my mother, father, sister and I – took a train into Innsbruck, and then a bus out towards the Oetztal. Meadows rose into cliffs which fell back into meadows. We reached Sautens and stepped off the bus. Looking round, the scenery did seem to me wilder, more darkly baroque than the other valleys we'd been through.

We walked down the road from the stop. Sautens was empty of people. It was just us and the rows of maize, the cowbells, the crickets, the Alpenblumen, the potentilla, the Alpine carnation, the mealy primrose, the auricula – and all those other flowers my mother picked illegally.

We found Gasthof-Pension Post, where my mother and father had once stayed. We stood in front of it for a minute. I took my father's hand, and led him up the steps. My mother murmured something about just wanting to see it, not go inside. But I said we should knock and find out if the original owners were still there. 'They won't be here after all these years,' said my mother. But they were.

I knocked and Frau Schmidt answered, a stocky woman with curly black hair. Funny, there was no need of introductions. My

mother stammered something about having stayed there in
1966. Before she'd finished the sentence – something like 'we
thought we'd come and see where we stayed a long time ago,
before we were married, we were Taylor and Kelly then' – the
woman was beaming, nodding, saying, 'Ah, yes, Herr Taylor,
who liked the strudel. And these are your beautiful children.'

Frau Schmidt led us through the hotel and on to a veranda,
which looked out to one end of the valley. We sat at a table and
she brought us apple strudel, Coke and schnapps. She didn't sit
with us. She expressed her welcome not so much in words but
in swirls of cream. Over the strudel, we discussed whether Frau
Schmidt truly recognized my mother and father. The question
boiled down to whether or not she'd heard my mother say
'Taylor' before she exclaimed 'Ah, yes, Herr Taylor.'

'But she knew Dad liked apple strudel.'

'That's a fair bet, isn't it? It's such a long time ago.'

Tyrolean quiet.

'If nothing else, she might be pleased that her hotel is
remembered. And, who knows, she might have remembered
Dad. He used to speak for everyone.'

Dad said nothing this visit, English or German. I thanked
Frau Schmidt for the food, and my mother tried and failed to
press payment on her. She beamed at my father, and shook his
trembling hand. We wandered back to the bus stop.

Waiting for the bus back to Innsbruck, all I could do was ask
her, with a smirk: 'Surely it was a bit scandalous, you and Dad
going on holiday together before you were married, if you know
what I mean?'

She turned away. 'No. We had separate rooms. Of course.'

I immediately felt terrible for asking, as if I'd borrowed my
mother's memories and returned them scratched and smeared.

Public Toilets in Venice

Gradually, progressively, our holidays were infected by disease.

In 1981, we went on a package holiday to Malgrat de Mar, Spain. Above and beyond the usual early-80s mix-up with over-booked hotels and building sites; above and beyond having to endure a two-day coach tour with four children and (on the return leg) a life-size plastic donkey who insisted on taking his seat; above and beyond the worries about who was dancing with his elder daughter to the then-ubiquitous 'Birdie Song'; above and beyond all this, the story my father returned to most often over Sunday lunch involved losing his younger daughter.

We were on the beach. Helen was only three, and had trundled off while my father's back and mind were turned. For a moment, he'd forgotten she was meant to be with him – and when he remembered again, she wasn't. I can still see the helpless panic on his face as it appeared above my sandcastle. After an hour of horrors and trampled sandcastles, my sister finally turned up round the corner of a hotel, swinging a spade and laughing at 'silly Daddy with silly lined face'. It took a while for the 'silly lined face' to reshape itself, to go back to normal. The memory of that face reminds me of a face from the same year, when my father forgot Helen's name at our 'Explorers' club, and reached over to ask me what it was. It's possible that neither memories, neither faces mean anything. Or perhaps the face above my sandcastle, and the same face at the Explorers, was already losing its elasticity, becoming petrified in the anxiety-mask of Parkinson's. And, at the same time, perhaps his youngest child's image, name, whereabouts were already being touched by the dementia associated with Parkinson's – a dementia which would gradually black us out, one by one.

It's often said that Parkinson's might be developing for as much as a decade before it's diagnosed. The disease destroys cells in the 'substantia nigra' section of the brain which produce a chemical called dopamine. Dopamine is a neurotransmitter, used by parts of the brain to transmit messages. And because of what Parkinson's does to the substantia nigra, there's a shortage of dopamine in parts of the brain such as the 'basal ganglia' and the 'pedunculi' which supervise bodily movements and control. It's thought that the basal ganglia doesn't initiate movements, but it modifies them, fills in their details in terms of speed, distance and fluidity. So with a shortage of dopamine, movements can't be fine-tuned or controlled properly. This results in clumsiness, rigidity and even random movements like tremors. In this way, Parkinson's destroys communication routes between mind and body, brain and nerves, the mental and the physical. The disease can only be diagnosed by trying out the medication and seeing if it alleviates the physical symptoms. By this time, it's often the case that up to four-fifths of the dopamine-producing cells have been killed off.

This pre-diagnostic, cellular genocide is surpassed by the dementia closely associated with Parkinson's – Dementia with Lewy bodies (DLB). Lewy bodies are microscopic, round deposits in damaged brain cells. They occur in the brainstem nerve-cells of all Parkinson's patients, but are much more virulent in those who develop dementia. Dementia with Lewy bodies can only be conclusively diagnosed by dissection, by opening up the brain *post-mortem*. Both Dementia with Lewy bodies and Parkinson's are strangely retrospective diseases: one can only be diagnosed after the patient's death, the other only after the necessary medication has been administered, in a peculiar reversal of normal practice. It's rather apt that I'd never heard of DLB till *after* my father's death – as if, since then, I've been able to see the Lewy bodies inside his brain.

Dementia affects about a fifth of those with Parkinson's, and Dementia with Lewy bodies is the second largest form of dementia in the UK. Well over 120,000 people have Parkinson's in the UK, and more than 1.5 million in the USA. No doubt there are many more who don't, as yet, suspect what's happening inside their brains. How do we know Parkinson's or Dementia with Lewy bodies are not happening to us whilst I'm writing, whilst you're reading? Parkinson's, Dementia with Lewy bodies: these are diseases which are quietly petrifying, fossilizing your mind until one day you reach for an image, a memory, a movement, a daughter and touch cold rock instead . . .

Links between Parkinson's and palaeontology: an unpleasant slang term for an old person is 'fossil', and Parkinson's is often an old person's disease. Links between Parkinson's and palaeontology: my father's bones became all too visible underneath his skin, like a skeleton in rock, by the late 90s. From a 1998 holiday to Denmark, there's a photograph of him in his wheelchair, looking out at the North Sea. Behind him is a row of four concrete statues doing the same. My father's face, turned to stone by Parkinson's, is the same colour as their concrete.

Links between Parkinson's and fossils: well, the great James Parkinson (1755–1824) – the doctor who first described the eponymous disease – also made an important contribution to palaeontology. He didn't just write the classic 'An Essay on the Shaking Palsy' (1817), in which the tremors and tribulations of Parkinson's were first diagnosed; he was also a founding member of the Geological Society and wrote the beautifully titled *Organic Remains of a Former World: An Examination of the Mineralised Remains of the Vegetables and Animals of the Antediluvian World, Generally Termed Extraneous Fossils* (1804–11). The book describes an 'oryctological holiday' around England, during which the narrator finds out about fossils. My father would have understood. On holiday, he too used to chip away at Manx coves and Spanish beaches for ammonites and trilobites. He'd show us them proudly and tell us 'facts' about them – and I'd say a dutiful 'Oh.' I was more interested in Spanish girls and plastic donkeys, whilst my father saw holidays as educational experiences, involving guide books, bird-spotting books, fossil-spotting books, binoculars, museums, abbeys, old churches.

The problem was that, as time went by, he was fighting not only an ignorant son but an ignorant disease, neither of which had any respect for fossil facts or church histories. As early as 1983, for instance, he realized a life-long ambition to visit Venice for a day. But I sulked all day because I wanted to be back at our resort: what was all this sinking grandeur to the hotel pool and a girl from Doncaster? And my father moaned all day because of Venice's lack of public conveniences. He spent the entire afternoon searching through the labyrinthine streets not for a beautiful, blond boy (like Gustav von Aschenbach in *Death in Venice*), nor for a lost daughter in a red coat (as in Du Maurier's *Don't Look Now*), but for the Gents.

The Rialto Bridge, the Bridge of Sighs, St Mark's: all were stop-off points on the way to the lavatory.

Post-Venice, the Toilet Visit gradually came to occupy centre-stage when away from home. Trips out became structured around the peremptory demands of the Toilet Visit. The Toilet Visit: put in capitals, it looks rather aristocratic, like a version of the Grand Tour.

The nature of the Grand Tour developed over some years. It started when Dad and I used to catch the bus to go shopping in Newcastle-under-Lyme. I'd say to my father, 'I'll see you in a couple of hours, 2.45 by the Gents on such-and-such a street,' and wander off. As years went by, though, I'd have to wait longer and longer outside the Gents. It'd get to 2.50 or 2.55 or 3.00 and he wouldn't have turned up. I'd walk round town again, and find him on a bench, clutching a plastic bag and scrunching it up with every heavy breath. 'Sorry. I was . . . Sorry. I was about to come. I got a bit tired and needed a sit down.' Or he'd come as we'd planned at 2.45, and announce his need for the toilets, since we were next to them. Holding on to the banister, he'd take the steps one at a time into the dank depths of Stoke's Victorian conveniences. Five minutes later, he'd re-emerge – but by the time we reached the bus station (a hundred yards away), he'd announce the need to go again. This time, he'd not come back.

I'd hang around at the top of the stairs, pacing backwards and forwards, wondering if anyone was looking at me in a suspicious manner. After all, there'd inevitably be something about gay bashing written on one of the walls, and my father was always convinced that my long hair was 'asking for trouble' in this respect. Eventually, I'd huff and puff and walk down the stairs and into the Gents.

'Dad!' I'd shout from outside the cubicles. 'Dad! Are you in there?' – hoping I wouldn't receive an answer from an unrecognized voice to the effect of: 'Yes, of course, come and join me, do. No objection to your fond, if kinky, paternal appellation either.' But no. Instead, a whimper would answer me from one of the cubicles. I'd push open the door, and find my father crashed on the unmopped floor with his trousers round his ankles. Standing over him, I'd try and pull him up, followed by his trousers. Meanwhile, the men standing at the wall opposite would turn their heads to stare – wondering what was going on between that hippy and the old guy, who looked like he was fighting the former off.

Sometimes he was, pushing me away as I was trying to zip up his fly, shouting, 'Get away from me. You, you're "funny", you are. I don't want you touching me. You're "funny", I tell you!' He didn't mean funny ha-ha, and nor did the square-cut blokes eyeing me from the urinals. 'Shh, Dad. You'll get us into trouble.' 'Don't you go shushing me. I'm not going to be shushed by you, when you're . . . messing around with me. I don't trust you. It's . . . disgusting.' And it was clear that the thought was shared by others in the Gents.

I was threatened at least once by a fist attached to a tattooed arm attached to a man with a very unhappy moustache. 'What you fucking doing with that old man, eh? Eh?' Explaining to the fist that 'the old guy' was my father just made matters worse. 'He's no son of mine,' said my father, mis-recognizing me at precisely the wrong moment. I thought all was lost. But then my father added, 'No, he's not my son. He's pretending. He's a teacher at school. And . . . what are these children doing in the staff toilets? Round them up for lessons now!'

The fist looked at us both in disgust for a second, and then walked off, saying to his mates: 'One's queer, one's a fucking pisshead. Not coming to these fucking bogs again with weirdos like that around.'

So we went to Venice, Barcelona, Salzburg, Paris, the Italian Lakes, the Dolomites, Spain, Denmark, the Austrian Tyrol. And we saw toilets. Care, I suppose, is a kind of progressive myopia: toilets in the foreground become more focused than the mountains behind. Care is obsession with details – especially toilet details – at the expense of anything more grand. On holidays and days out, the details breed. Details are a bit like the tribbles on *Star Trek*: the tribbles are a race of fluffy pets which breed at an exponential rate. Though they seem innocuous, soon there are millions of them all over the SS *Enterprise*, uncontrollable, unherdable. Our holidays were like that. We went boldly where we'd never been before, but the tiniest of details started to get in the way. Given the encroachment of bladder problems, bowel problems, pill schedules, paranoia, immobility and so on, small inconveniences like missing coaches or late flights bred like tribbles.

In your own home, you have some control. You can police the tribbles into some kind of order. When I used to look after my father, my mother would leave Post-it Notes all over the house of dos and don'ts: how to heat up the spaghetti, which pack of pads to use for the inside of his Y-fronts, who to ring if Social Services forgot to turn up, what not to put on the worktop in the kitchen, what would be delivered on such and such a day, the precise ritual of going to bed broken up into thirty-second portions, and so on. She even arranged the pills into empty egg boxes for me, one egg box per day, each egg compartment containing the relevant tablets and labelled with a time.

So if I dwell on details and toilets and egg boxes, perhaps that's because anyone who's been even the most part-time of carers knows the overwhelming vastness of the apparently insignificant. In *Awakenings*, Oliver Sacks claims that Parkinsonism, with its micro-ambulation, micro-graphia, micro-tics, is all about a loss of a sense of scale, or – to put it another way – the development of new and bizarre kinds of scale. But this spreads to the carer as well, as details which are minute to others blow up into uncontrollable aliens.

Two of the worst species of tribble in this respect were called paranoia and paramnesia. Paranoia is easy to ignore when everyone conspires to recognize it as such. Away from home, however, people weren't in on the conspiracy, and took my father's horror stories seriously.

Austria, 1993, for example, and we're sitting outside a hotel ordering Tyrolean beer and fish and chips from a waitress in a frilly apron. My father is on the bench next to me, his hand tremoring, his head darting from side to side, his eyes paranoid-wide. I'm not taking any notice because the waitress has long eyelashes, and I'm wondering how to chat her up. My father notices my lack of notice, or notices my notice of her eyelashes, because he suddenly makes a grab at the waitress's dress. He shouts at her: 'Take me back. They've kidnapped me. Take me home. I want to go home. Home. Home.' He repeats this half a dozen times, in English and German: 'Heim. Heim. They've kidnapped me. Him. I don't know who he is. But he's in charge. They've taken me away.'

The waitress looks down at him and his hold on her apron, and all I can think is, damn, that's blown that one. Goodbye, eyelashes.

I prise his hand away from her bottom, and try to laugh it off. I can't explain to her what's happening, because she doesn't have enough English and I don't have any German. At least there's one advantage to this: she doesn't have enough English to understand 'kidnapped' and get me arrested. 'Sorry', I say.

When she brings the fish and chips, she plonks it down on the table at arm's length. My father makes another grab at her, but she's out of reach. She reports us to the manager for sexual harassment, and he asks us to eat our food and leave. 'That's exactly what I wanted to do all along,' says my father.

An afternoon a week later, and we're sitting in the backyard of my parents' house in Stoke, sipping remnants of the Tyrolean beer. My mother brings out Heinz soup to go with it. He grabs her arm as she tries to put it down on the garden table. 'Take me home. He's kidnapped me. I want to go home. Take me home!' 'Shut up, Dad,' I say. From the kitchen, I can hear my younger sister, Helen, singing 'Take Me Home, Country Roads'.

Many years later, I find that my father's 'Take Me Home, Country Roads' paranoia has a technical name. 'Reduplicative paramnesia' is a syndrome in which it becomes difficult to recognize your surroundings, to the point where you believe that a familiar place like your home has been duplicated – sometimes over and over. Everywhere is home, but nowhere is the *real* home. There are only copies, fakes. You go on holiday only to find yourself in a duplicate home, and you stay at home only to find yourself, in a sense, on holiday. It's all rather like the paramnesia of package holidays: you go abroad and find a home that is more like home than home itself, with fish and chips for breakfast, lunch and dinner.

My father's paramnesia and paranoia got worse. In 1995, on a boat trip around the Italian Lakes, his eyes almost pop out with paranoiac paramnesia: 'Where are you taking me? Why have you kidnapped me? What ransom do you want?' He gets distracted for a second by some peacocks squawking at the boat from a nearby island: 'And what do those peacocks want?'

'What do you mean "what do the peacocks want"? Do you think they've had a hand in kidnapping you too?'

'Don't laugh at me. Tell me where we're going! What have you done with home? What have you done with my son?'

'I am your son.'

'No you're not. I can see right through you. You're a con. What have you done with . . . with Jonathan?' Full-scale Capgras: 'You're a fraud, pretending to be him. Where are you taking me on this wreck, fraud?'

'But you like boats, darling,' says my mother.

'Not this bloody one. We're going to drown. It'll be your fault. Taking us sailing on a wreck.'

'Don't be silly.'

'Yes, stop being silly. It's embarrassing,' says my sister, whose teenage cool is being dented by his shouting. She starts humming 'We are Sailing' to herself, and hides under her hat to avoid a scene. Wise move. My father's voice is getting louder, his head swivelling from side to side.

'Take me home! Look at him – he looks like the devil. He's laughing at me. And . . . what do you think you're staring at?' I'm not sure whether this last comment is addressed to the peacocks on the shore, or the other passengers. Many of the latter are certainly staring at and listening to us – as if my father's paranoia is a stand-in for a tour guide's commentary.

I say: 'Dad, shut up. Everyone's listening.'

'Good! They'll all hear I've been kidnapped. Kidnapped!'

'Please.'

'Help, police! Les gendarmes, die Polizei, polizia, whatever-you-call-them! Get me away from these mad people! Help me!' No one's even pretending to look out of the windows now; they're all eyeing my mother and me up and down. Admittedly, we don't look like organized criminals, with my rainbow T-shirt, my copy of *Middlemarch*, and her Laura Ashley handbag, but then you never really know, do you?

Certainly, people here are increasingly unsure if we're villains or not. I smile pacifyingly, tapping my head to reassure them: 'He's ill, you know, can't move properly, doesn't know what he's saying, it's a shame, but what can you do?' Then I turn to him and shout a whisper: 'For Christ's sake, Dad. Shut up!'

Nonetheless, the 'he's-ill-you-know-what-a-shame' smile is undermined when we dock in Locarno, Switzerland – and my father springs to his feet, and is the first prancing along the gangplank. 'Where now?' he asks breezily, 'Ooh, look at those amazing clocks. Splendido, as they say!'

My father and I on the boat to Locarno

It's one of the most bewildering symptoms of Parkinsonism and its medication (at least to outsiders) that sufferers switch so quickly from what are called 'off' states to 'on' states. Off states might consist of paralytic rigidity, uncontrollable tremors, even catalepsy; on states are the return to normality, control and fluidity of movement. Parkinsonians can switch from an off to an on state – from shakes as mechanical as Swiss clocks to Tyrolean dancing – within a few seconds. Within a few seconds, my father could switch from paranoia to forgetting that there was anything to be paranoid about. Off, on, now you see it, now you don't: an agonizing shake that's lasted for hours suddenly disappears; someone who's been rigid all afternoon is now waltzing to Johann Strauss.

This 'on-off' effect is exaggerated by L-Dopa or levodopa (sometimes known as Sinemet), the usual medication for Parkinson's. L-Dopa works by artificially boosting dopamine levels in the brain. Once absorbed, the patient's Parkinsonian symptoms suddenly disappear. As the medication wears off, however, the symptoms return. Take the next dose of L-Dopa, and soon the patient is in control again. Take too much L-Dopa, and symptoms such as tremoring, ticcing and rigidity return with increased force. Take too little L-Dopa, and the off-symptoms also return with increased force. Take just enough, and in time it won't be enough, or it'll be too much. The off states get worse, the ons get more like parodic versions of the offs. Change the dosage again, space out the drugs again. But now the ons are too violent, the offs too paralytic. Change the dosage again and again, move the pill timings around the day, the changes becoming smaller and smaller in ever-decreasing spirals, the on-off effects becoming increasingly uncontrollable. Not only care but Parkinsonian medication is all about minute details, tiny changes in pill regimes which have drastic effects – exacerbating the difference between ons and offs, collapsing ons and offs into each other, never stabilizing for long.

In *Awakenings*, Oliver Sacks illustrates the extremities of the on-offness of Parkinson's by citing one of the great Parkinsonian Urban Myths. According to the myth, a wheelchair-bound sufferer was parked by the sea shore one day. In the sea, a swimmer was getting into trouble. Suddenly, the Parkinsonian came to life, dived into the sea and saved the swimmer from drowning – only to return to his customary off state afterwards.

The problem is, other passengers on our boat trip to Locarno don't seem to know any Parkinsonian Urban Myths. A burly Italian grips my arm as I'm trying to follow my father off the boat. The Italian's growl roughly translates as: 'What the hell are you doing with that nice old gentleman?'

I don't know what to answer. So I just smile, 'Kidnapping him,' and walk briskly away.

Whether he understands me or not, I don't know. He doesn't come after us, and probably puts us down as lunatics. Suddenly, pushing an empty wheelchair into Locarno with my father tottering ahead, I feel an acute sense of foreignness. I look around and see Alpine health everywhere: burliness, rosiness, fleshiness, out-dooriness. Everyone is darting around, laughing, calling, blooming. We, on the other hand, are visibly out of place, illegal visitors from the land of the ill. No wheelchairs here, thank you, no paramnesia, no Capgras, no Shaking Paralysis. No one else seems handicapped in the Aryan Tyrol or Lakes. From this moment on, holidays make me feel that disability and illness are exclusive to Midland towns – like sleet, oatcakes and potbanks. Or, worse still, perhaps they are exclusive just to us. Maybe we're foreign everywhere, even in Stoke.

Which is not to say that sometimes we couldn't pass for normal-foreign rather than extra-foreign. The on-off effect of my father's Parkinson's was often polarized on holidays, and sometimes the ons were so pronounced that we almost felt at home. An example: it's 1997 and we're in Austria, sitting in the hotel bar after dinner. Someone in the corner is playing the theme from *The Third Man* (over and over) on a zither. My mother has gone up to her bedroom to get changed; my father is sitting across from us in his wheelchair, staring at the doilies; I'm laughing with my younger sister about the lake we've been swimming in today. Only afterwards, when climbing the hill and looking back, had we noticed that the lake was infested by vast water snakes – snakes which were twisting patterns in the fertilizer being pumped into the lake at the far side. 'I just hope it won't make us sick as a doggy dog,' says my sister. As usual, our conversation doesn't need my father, who's leaning ever closer to the doilies he's scrutinizing.

A waitress comes over and asks what drinks we'd like. She directs the question straight at my father. I start to speak for him, but my father suddenly pulls himself up from the doilies, and talks over his son . . . in fluent German. Up till now, my father's linguistic skills have been a matter of family myth: 'Oh, yes, he knew French and German fluently, Latin, and a lot of Russian, Italian, Spanish. He was trying to teach himself Chinese.' But here I am, as an adult, confronted by the reality of myth.

Just as my sister and I have been making jokes with references he can't follow, now we listen uncomprehendingly to a conversation full of laughter, questions, answers, even – no, surely not – *flirtations*. He wriggles in the wheelchair and his face loses ten years. Eventually, the waitress goes off to get the drinks he's ordered (whatever they are), muttering 'reizend, charmant' under her breath. I assume these are swear words, having no real faith in my father. Or perhaps I'm just jealous, refusing to admit that he's been more successful with a long-lashed Austrian waitress than I ever am.

My mother appears, straightening her dress, smiling at us,

asking us if he's 'behaved himself'. And his face regains the ten years, his wheelchair slouch returns, and he's once more absorbed by the doilies.

The next evening I start shivering, then there's vomiting, diarrhoea. I can't move from the bed for twenty-four hours. Whether it's fertilizer, water snakes or the drinks he ordered, I don't know, but a day later, my sister is sick too. Another day, and my mother is starting to shiver. Meanwhile, I feel just well enough to sip the odd cup of tea, but there's my father to think of . . .

I ask the holiday rep at the hotel what we can do: 'I think my mother needs a doctor.'

'No, she'll be okay. You got better, so she'll be okay.'

'But she says she's never felt so awful in her life.'

'Don't worry. You don't need a doctor.'

'But . . . but what can we do with my father?'

'You can look after him till she gets better.'

'But I can barely walk. And my father is starting to show symptoms himself.'

'He'll get over it too. Everyone in the hotel is getting over it. It's just some bug someone's brought over from England.'

The tea swirling in my stomach doesn't agree that it's nothing, and I want to go and ask the snakes in the fertilizer if they think it's nothing. But I can hardly bring myself to speak: 'He's disabled.' I don't know what to say. 'What if he . . . doesn't get over it?'

'He will. Nothing's wrong.'

Next morning, I'm being sick in the sink after wiping my father's diarrhoea off the floor and trying to pull him out of it – and I decide I'd like to introduce the rep to my friends the snakes. My father and I are in the hotel toilets. Someone else comes in, looks at us, mutters 'Ach Gott!' and leaves. I sit on the toilet seat for a second, sweat pouring off me in globules. 'Ach Gott,' I say. I pull my dazed father off the floor, and wipe the shit off his trousers with one hand, whilst trying to stop him falling with the other. 'Ach Gott,' I say. He goes down again, this time hitting his head on a sink. 'Ach Gott,' and I'm crying, as I fall back on to the toilet seat. Another try. I pull him up with main force. He's bruised and distressed and eerily dyskinetic. He's looking everywhere wildly – the ceiling, the mirrors, the strip lighting – everywhere, that is, except where I want him to go. I pull him out of the door and into the corridor.

'Look at the patterns on the carpet, Dad,' I say, trying to pull him along. The patterns on the carpet look like snakes trapped in diamonds; I'm hoping they'll provide a useful regularity for his footsteps: 'One two one two one two.' He walks a few diamonds, but the paces get smaller and smaller, quicker and quicker. This is 'festination', I'm told: he's hurrying but getting nowhere, his upper body dangerously ahead of his feet.

'Come on, Dad, one two one two.' But it's no use, and we come to a precarious standstill, and he wants the toilet again, and I want the toilet too, and sweat and tears and dizziness are taking over, and he's starting to fall, and I wish my mother was better, and I wish the rep was swallowed by the snakes and . . . And suddenly my father is scooped up and carried off by a huge German couple, one on each arm. They carry him with his feet dangling above the carpet to a nearby chair. Then they get one for me too, and bring me a Coke from the bar, and pat my arm, and everything is okay . . . for a while.

So the last major holiday we had together ended with the tribbles taking over. We didn't go on another big holiday again; there were too many variables, too many tribbles-in-waiting.

'Perhaps we tried to do too much with him,' my mother says. But it necessarily became a smaller and smaller too much after

1997. By 2001, he couldn't walk at all, and we could only go to places suitable for wheels, not legs. We went for a drive along the West Cumbrian coast. Driving for miles, we finally came across a strange, isolated resort called Silloth. We got out and wheeled my father round a town of corrugated-iron holiday camps, peeling guest houses, market stalls where they sold second-hand pants and a beach of angry dogs. I bought a kite from one of the shops, but it didn't fly, despite a strong wind. Someone swore at me for scraping her ankle with the wheel-chair. My father said: 'Take me home.' And, this time, we did.

Mahler in Stafford

Another holiday, this time in a house in Scotland, 1984. I'm eleven and I'm allowed to stay up later than I used to. One night, my father says to me: 'We have a coffee at night. Why don't you have one too, boy? In fact, why don't you help make it?' Each night after that, we go into the kitchen at 10.30 pm. I spoon out instant coffee and different amounts of sugar into the cups; he measures out milk into a saucepan; I watch it as it boils; and I pour it into the mugs. This is the first time I've been allowed near a cooker, and there's an exciting danger in it. My father wipes up the milk I spill on the worktop. 'That's a good boy. When we get home, this can be your job.' Oddly enough, I'm pleased to be given a daily chore – especially one which involves the danger of burns and therefore the possibility of days off school.

When we come back from Scotland, I continue making evening coffee for myself, my mother and father. Or, at least, I do for a couple of weeks. Gradually, disappointment sets in at the lack of unintentional burns. The coffee starts getting a bit later – 10.35, 10.45, 10.50. At 10.30, there's a computer game I want to finish, a chapter I want to read, a TV programme that will last another quarter of an hour. My father pops his head round the door: 'Are you ready to make the coffee?' and I say, 'Just a sec.' A few minutes later, his head appears again: 'Do you want me to make it?' and I say, 'No, it's all right. Give me a minute.' A minute and four more pass. 'Do you want me to make coffee tonight, boy?' My father called me 'boy' after 'Boy' in the old Johnny Weissmuller *Tarzan* films; he thought I looked like him, and was disappointed when I didn't live up to my prototype.

'Come on, boy.' 'I've told you. Just give me a minute.' And I'd sit there for another three game overs, pretending not to hear the clink of coffee cups from the kitchen, the wheeze of the fridge door, the milk being poured into the saucepan. After one last game over, I'd saunter into the kitchen and find my father standing over the cooker. With mock outrage, I'd exclaim: 'I said I'd only be a minute.' 'But I waited and waited.' 'You didn't. I was only a minute or two.' 'You can take over now, boy.' 'Hmph. There's only a bit more to do. I wanted to do it all. It's *my* job.'

As the years passed and I became bored with coffee making, I'd have more game overs, until the coffee was finished and being carried into the living room. Then I'd rush out: 'Dad! I can't believe you've made it.' 'I waited, but it's getting late.' 'It's not. I said I'd do it.' Mum: 'Why didn't you let him do it, darling?' Dad: 'You always side with him.' Mum: 'No I don't, darling. But why can't you wait if he wants to do it?' Dad: 'But can't you see, he doesn't? He waits till I've nearly done it so he can be cross at me.' Me: 'What rubbish!' Mum: 'You're being silly, darling.'

I'm sure most father–son, mother–daughter relationships are shot through with these trivial micro-battles over coffee making, bathroom tidying, car cleaning. The problem for me, though, was that, as my father's illness encroached, I started winning all the time. Bit of a pushover, you might say, lapping someone with Parkinson's, who spends most of the day asleep in an armchair.

Take the washing up. By the time I was sixteen, I was offering to wash up after tea to please my mother. Such a good boy. I'd fill the bowl with soapy water whilst my father cleared the table. Often, the clink of the plates would merge with a lecture about Charles XII of Sweden or Louis XIV of France. I was studying A level history, and he was trying to persuade me it wasn't a big yawn: 'When I get you talking about it, boy, you chatter away enthusiastically. So I don't understand why you complain about it.' 'I'm not the one chattering about it,' I mutter. 'Pardon?' 'Nothing. Just bring me the stuff off the table, will you? I've had enough of Charles XII for one day.' That was how I treated and ended some of the last, extended conversations we ever had. He knew everything (or so it seems to me now) and I talked to him about nothing.

Reduced to silence, he'd bring a pile of cups from the table and slide them into the washing-up bowl in front of me. 'Dad!' 'What?' 'I've told you not to put the stuff straight into the bowl.' 'It doesn't matter.' 'I've told you before. I rinse the food off the plates first.' Pause. Some of the stew rises to the top with the bubbles. 'Look what you've . . . Dad!' He's done it again, sliding dishes with bits of banana jelly straight into the water. There are bubbles of beef jelly and banana stew in front of me.

'I can't believe it. I told you this second. And you've done it again. You did it on purpose,' – this is quite possible. 'I forgot,' he says – and this is, of course, even more possible. 'You can do the washing up now.' My mother comes into the kitchen: 'What's the noise for? What have you done, darling?' Me: 'He put the dirty washing up straight in the bowl.' Mum: 'Darling.

You know the others don't like washing up, with it all swimming in a big mess.' Me: 'I'd told him once and he did it again.' Dad: 'I forgot.' Mum: 'For goodness sake, darling. Can't you do anything right?' Me: 'He can finish it. I'm not doing it like that.' I storm out the room, hearing my mother behind me: 'Look what you've done. You've upset him again.' My father, defeated, shouts: 'Don't you see? It's just his excuse to get angry at me and not do the job he's meant to do.' Mum: 'Don't be silly, darling. You're so cynical about him.'

I confess. I confess that my father's cynical 'silliness' about me, about the washing up, about the coffee making, about a million other, tiny things was right. I confess my teenage laziness and point scoring: I did just want an excuse to get angry with him to get out of the washing up. I did want an excuse which made me look like the injured party, and made my mother side with me over him.

I could resort to another excuse to excuse these past excuses. I could point out that it wasn't easy, growing up while my father was growing down with Parkinson's. But no. Some of it was all too easy, especially the point scoring. I will confess without excuses: growing up was a million micro-battles which I kept winning. My father was the opposition, my mother kept the score.

In a different form, the point scoring continued into my twenties, when I started looking after him in my mother's absence. 'Wait till Mum gets home' (as opposed to the more familiar 'Wait till your father gets home') was the threat I used if he was 'playing up'. When Mum did get home, I would rehearse his failings that day in gory detail. She would ask: 'Oh dear, what has he done today?' and I would answer: 'What *hasn't* he done today? He kept shouting and trying to fall out of his chair. He threw a cup of tea on the floor. Then he fell on the broken pieces. The cuts are his fault, not mine. When I'd cleaned him up, he went to the toilet a thousand times. Then he *really* started annoying me.'

One girlfriend, who overheard me talk like this, told me I was a bastard. I was supposed to be looking after him, not scoring goals against him, she said. And your mother doesn't want to hear it. You're just making her feel guilty for leaving him with you.

I agreed, but tried to explain that I needed someone to register every tiny detail of the day. Otherwise, what happened between my father and me was effectively non-existent; after all, he couldn't remember it, one minute to the next. I tried to explain that I needed to justify my exhaustion, and – if things got out of hand – my tyrannical fury to someone. In return, I needed that someone to exclaim gratefully, 'There, there, never mind, you tried your best, thank you.' For me, that someone could only be my mother; it was impossible to describe what went on to anyone else – and certainly anyone outside the family. No one else could understand the exhaustion, the frustration, the tyrannical fury of care. Carers are meant to be selfless, infinitely patient martyrs. No one understands anything short of that ideal.

'But he hit me,' my father would say, after being subjected to my recital of his misdemeanours.

'I don't blame him. He says you've been playing up, darling. This won't do.'

'Lies! All bloody lies! He's just scoring points by listing lies. It's him. He did those things, not me!'

'Come on, darling. You can't keep behaving like this.'

He pauses, and glances between us with wide eyes: 'I see. You both. In a conspiracy together, you and your . . . your . . . fancy man here!'

I laugh, embarrassed. Now I want to give back the points I've scored. My mother shoves him into his chair and snaps: 'Be quiet, darling. You're paranoiac. It's time for your pills.'

'I . . . he . . . you together . . . conspiracy . . .' He trails off, losing the thread of his paranoia, his mouth stuffed with tablets.

Paranoia. Odd word, that. It implies that the paranoiac is necessarily wrong or even mad; etymologically, the word comes from the Greek, via Latin, for 'madness' and, aptly enough, 'demented'. I'm sure a lot of people who live with a paranoiac, however, feel quietly guilty, concerned that the paranoiac is more right than mad. In this sense, paranoia is a contagious disease: the carer gradually becomes paranoid that the paranoiac isn't paranoid, but has got a point. I for one became paranoid that my father's paranoia was a bit close to the mark – that he recognized me all too well for the Oedipal point scorer I was.

Conversely, I can't help worrying that my behaviour shaped his paranoia. I can't help worrying that the micro-battles and point scoring somehow caused the paranoia. On the one hand, there was his (frequently correct) cynicism about me: he saw through my coffee-making and washing-up scams, whilst my mother didn't. On the other hand, he must have felt terribly frustrated by his decreasing ability to make his opinion count for anything but 'silliness': 'Don't be silly, darling. It's just the disease speaking.' Did the frustration compound the cynicism over and over? Did cynicism become paranoia? And did paranoia become misidentification, transforming me into that arch-villain, Mr Gil-Martin? Is there a graph I could draw, an equation I could formulate, to express the gradual transformation from son to Gil-Martin? Cynicism + frustration, both raised to the power of 1 million micro-battles = paranoia + Capgras misidentification.

Certainly, by the time I was nineteen, we weren't having

conversations about Charles XII any longer. In fact, we weren't having conversations about much at all. My mother had gone back to full-time teaching, and my father and I would sit over a lunch of meatballs and tinned potatoes, letting the television do the talking between us. Any conversation we tried to have ourselves was only ever a couple of links away from various explosive topics – from recurring arguments neither of us could find the end of. Often, after a *Neighbours*-filled silence of twenty minutes, he'd suddenly launch into one of the arguments, as if it had been going on all the while – which, in a sense, it had, in our minds. It'd start with taboo questions such as: (1) Why was I disgracing him by signing on for unemployment benefit? (2) Why was I disgracing myself by sponging off him? (3) Why was I disgracing him and myself with long hair? (4) Why was I evading this new Poll Tax? Was I doing it on purpose to get him in trouble with the police again? Well, he was going to pre-empt any such trouble by reporting me to the dreaded Sergeant Flowers this very afternoon.

We never found the end of these rows. It's as if they're still going on, somewhere in the ether, in an alternative, argument universe, far far away. I'm still coming up with responses, with posthumous repartees. And if he were here, my father would probably threaten me with Flowers again.

Mental illness does strange things with time. It replaces chronology with total synchrony: rows, holidays, Poll Taxes, everything is happening now, nothing is in the past. As the disease took hold, my father would spontaneously resume an argument from five years before. Or he'd relive a playground incident from Willfield High School. Or he'd burst out laughing at a sausage which reminded him of a long ago joke: 'Dad, what are you laughing at?' 'A joke about a sausage where a vicar goes up to a . . .' 'Goes where?' 'Where a sausage goes up to a . . .' 'Goes where?' 'I'm not sure. It's funny, though.'

This was frustrating. But there were certain things I dreaded him bringing up – things that, ten years on, he seemed to think had happened today. His dementia trapped us all in his syn-chronic universe – and this meant being trapped in our mistakes. Rather than a straightforward process of forgetting, my father's dementia was also a remembering of things others would forgive, forget or repress; it was a remembering of grudges, of faults and stupidities from the past, as if they were still current. Ten years after the event, he'd bring up something both he and my reddening cheeks seemed to think had hap-pened an hour ago.

One of the most ludicrous examples of this dated back to when I was eighteen. I'd snogged a girl at a party, and rang her up the next day – unaware that my father was in the bathroom with the door ajar, listening. (He called it 'overhearing'.) The girl seemed shy, and the conversation became a one-sided stream of consciousness. I asked her what music she liked, she said 'Dunno.' I asked her what subjects she did at college, she said 'Dunno.' I asked her what her hobbies were, she said – sur-prisingly – 'Dunno.' Out of things to say, desperate, I told her what my hobbies were: 'J. S. Bach, Edgar Allan Poe and mas-turbation.' I laughed, she didn't; she just said she didn't know what 'Edward Allan Poo' was. My father didn't laugh either – despite knowing Poe's work well.

That night, he asked me downstairs as I was getting ready for bed. He and my mother were sitting on the sofa, my mother clearly uncomfortable. 'I don't think we should be doing this,' she was whispering to him. He ignored her, and just jabbed an accusing finger at me and said, 'I tell you. I was in the bath-room. He said he liked "masturbation". He said that. He told the girl it was one of his hobbies. He said he liked Bach, Poe *and* masturbation.' Repeated like that, all three sound like iniq‑uities: masturbation, Bach *and* Poe? Disgusting. 'Bach, Poe and masturbation – that's what you said to her, isn't it?!' Infected by the kind of mortification known only to teenagers, I told him where to stick Poe's *Tales of Mystery and Imagination*, and rushed upstairs.

From then on, I lived in terror of his bringing up the incident again – precisely because he did, all too often, as his mental state degenerated. Years on, and the incident was still happen‑ing in his head. Years on, and my hobbies were still the *Six O'Clock News* at tea. I'd be grinding the pepper over his food, he'd push it out of the way, jab a finger straight at me, and shout: 'I tell you. I was . . . in the bathroom. And I heard . . .'

By this point, I'd already be red as a teenager again, knowing what was coming (so to speak). And I'd have a horrible feeling my mother knew what was coming too. 'Be quiet, Dad. No one's listening.'

'And . . . I tell you. I was in the bathroom . . . he was on the phone. I heard him. He said . . . his hobbies.'

'Be quiet, darling, and eat the broccoli.' My mother would try to stuff some greens into his mouth. But his head would twitch from side to side, in a Parkinsonian form of evasive manoeuvres. He'd jab his finger again, this time in a generalized way at the cauliflower cheese. I'd hope this wasn't some unpleasant double‑entendre about my hobbies.

'No. You don't know. Well, I'll tell you. You've got to hear this. Unbelievable. He said . . . to her . . .' Maybe the story was going to fizzle out like the sausage and vicar jokes . . . but no, it's too late: 'He said to her: "My hobbies are Bach, something and masturbation." That's what he said. Him there. Masturbation. Your . . . your son. That's what he likes. Mastur . . .'

'Just open your mouth for the broccoli. Darling, the food's going cold.'

'You're trying to shut me . . .'

'Damn right I am.'

Shutting him up with food was the only recourse when he started the story in front of visitors. It was bad enough that my family heard it over and over. My younger sister was subjected to it on at least four occasions. She learnt to stick her fingers in her ears and sing 'Food, Glorious Food' to herself.

The girl on the phone didn't like Bach or Poe, but I started seeing her all the same. Back from university for the summer break, I visited her every day.

'You see Sarah every day,' says my mother one evening, as I'm putting my shoes on. 'I thought you might come out with us tonight for a change.' She's in the kitchen, mopping the floor around my father. He's doing the washing up from lunch, in a bowl swimming with remains. I've refused to do it, and it's been left three hours to congeal.

'I'm going to see Sarah. We've got a video out.'

'You've seen her already. Come on, it's Dad's birthday tomorrow.'

'Tomorrow's tomorrow.'

'I thought we'd go out tonight. As a family.'

'Oh, let him go,' says my father from the kitchen. 'I told you this'd be his answer. Doesn't want to be seen with us.'

'Look, you can ask Sarah to come.'

'We've already paid for the film.'

'It's your father's birthday.' Whisper: 'You know he's been ill lately. Make an effort for him.'

'That's emotional blackmail. I'm going out.'

My father's washing up is getting louder: 'If he doesn't want to come, I don't want him there.'

'You spend every minute of the day with her. You used to be different. You've changed into an angry young man.'

'I don't spend every minute with her and I haven't changed. It's you lot who've changed.'

My mother is starting to cry.

To my mother: 'I'll come out tomorrow, when it's Dad's *actual* birthday.' In the general direction of my father: 'He's not the queen, you know.'

I go to get my coat from under the stairs. From behind the door, I hear the row escalating – now between the two of them.

'I told you so,' shouts my father. 'He just comes home to see her, not you.'

'Darling, stop it.'

'It's true. He doesn't give two hoots about you or my birthday or my Parkinson's . . . And . . . you know what he and that Sarah do together, don't you? When I was at university, you knew the people who were up to . . . and . . . He's capable of anything. Remember what he said on the phone that day? Do you?'

'Stop it. It's silliness you're talking. And he can hear.'

'I don't care,' he slams the plates on to the draining board. '*That's* your favourite. *That's* what your favourite's really like.'

'I don't have favourites. It's you who has favourites.'

'No. You do everything for him, give him my money, let him get drunk every night. He walks all over us! Walk, walk, walk. Yes, he does.' I can see him through the crack between the door and the door frame. He's shaking and is repeating himself strangely. 'He does. I told you told you told you so.'

'Stop this, darling. I wanted us to go out together. As a family.' Sobbing.

'Tell *him* that. Not me. It's not my fault – I mean, it's my birthday he's wrecking. I'm not wrecking it. It's him. Wrecking.

Tell *him*. Not me. Him. Your favourite. Him. Him.' By 1993, my father's repetitive pronouns are drifting towards vagueness, a nebulous world where 'he' and 'him' might equally refer to his son or to his old deputy headmaster. He uses the names 'Jonathan' and 'Boy' less and less. 'I told you so, told you about *him*. Told you.'

'Please. Stop.'

'Sometimes I don't know him any more. I don't know who he is. He even looks like someone else.'

I back out into the hall, having found my coat – and he's there, pointing at me. His face is barely recognizable with fury. 'He's the one that causes the trouble. Him. Don't you see?'

I'm frightened but I laugh.

'You bloody . . . bloody . . .' He can't find the noun.

'I'm going and I'm not coming back.'

'You bloody . . . bloody . . .' In his anomic rage, nouns like 'sod', 'devil', 'bastard' and 'Jonathan' have gone, magicked away – just as, a couple of years later, he'll forget the word for cushion.

'I'm going out, and you can fuck off. You were right before: I don't care about your fucking birthday or your fucking Parkinson's if you're going to talk to me like that.'

I stride outside, slam the door for added effect, and almost run the mile to Sarah's house.

Once there, Sarah sits me down with a bottle of gin. I'm shaking. She yawns. 'Never mind. Let's get drunk and watch this video.' We help ourselves to her parents' drinks' cabinet. She puts on *Psycho 2*.

An hour or two passes. As I get drunker, my shakes subside – but now Sarah seems to be catching them.

'What's wrong?'

'It's that house,' she whispers.

I glance around. 'What house?'

'The *Psycho* house, stupid.'

I've not been taking notice of the film, distracted as I am by Sarah's bra strap. I glance back at the screen, where Anthony Perkins's house is silhouetted atop a hill. The façade looks like your average American haunted house.

'What's wrong with it?' I ask.

Her breathing's quickening: 'In shadow like that, it looks like the things I see sometimes – the spiders. There's something wrong about that shape. It can't be just me if it's been made into a film.'

'A crap film.'

'That doesn't make any difference.'

She's crying and has hidden her head in her hands.

'Hey.'

She screams and throws herself on the floor. 'Turn it off off off! Did you put it on on purpose? Please, turn it off!'

I do so, as a corpse is discovered buried in the coal bunker. Perkins has gone mad again.

Sarah calms down, and I drunkenly take her upstairs to lie on the bed. I think the scare is over. She's been having more and more of these peculiar 'turns', hearing things, seeing things, reliving the violence of long-lost memories. At least my father sees benign goats on the piano; Sarah's hallucinations are sending her the way of Anthony Perkins.

'I see spiders,' she said to me one day, a couple of months before *Psycho 2*, 'even when they're not there. I hate them.' 'Why do you hate them so much?' 'I don't know. It's something to do with what happened when I was six. When that boy did things to me. You know.' 'Why don't you let it all out. It'll make things better if you talk the spiders through. It always does.' Of course.

Rather than making everything better, the spiders had got worse and worse. The hallucinations started to turn up all over the place, crawling into every evening we spent together. Crawling over her body whilst she slept. Crawling into her mouth when she ate. Crawling on to videos we watched. She started cutting herself again, making herself sick, breaking mirrors where she saw spidery reflections.

She's lying on the bed. I'm leaning over her, kissing her. But these are spider kisses. She shrieks again and starts hyperventilating. She scratches my face and punches me so hard that I fall back on the floor. I get up, and she's writhing on the bed. Her pupils could almost be spider shaped for all they see of the real world. I try and hold her still, but this makes things worse. She flings me off again, warding things away that aren't there. She throws things around, punches the mirror, cuts herself, falls over and whimpers, 'Help help help help help.'

I'm holding her on the floor now. She's quieter but still twitching and crying. Ten minutes have passed and the bedroom is a mess. She tells me that when I leant over her in the bed, I was in silhouette – like a tarantula, like the *Psycho* house, like blacked-out memories of a boy she once knew. She thought I was a giant creature feeding off her. Gradually, the blackness of the creature's face was peeling away. And a boy's face was there, and she knew who it was. She recognized it as the boy who raped her when she was five, six, seven, eight.

And I listen and wonder what can of spiders I've opened by playing the role of caring boyfriend who wants to help and 'talk things through'. I wonder if you can ever empty a can like that, get to the bottom of it. 'I think you need to see someone,' I say.

'Who?'

'Just someone professional. Someone who knows about these things.'

She looks up at me. She touches my face and there's a bit of blood.

'I've not got schizophrenia.'

'I didn't say you had.'

'That's what you meant.'

My head is spinning like a spider's web. 'It's not. I don't understand.'

'You said I'm a schizo. You did. And you should leave now.'

'Look . . .'

'I don't want to be diagnosed by you. I'm not schizophrenic. Or paranoid. I'm not anything.'

'This argument's getting weird . . .'

'And you're going to say it's my fault it's getting weird. You should go home. Leave me alone . . . The spiders weren't there before you. Go away. Away away away.'

I leave her crumpled on the floor, mumbling, 'Away away away away.'

Drunk and dazed, I stagger out of the house and down the road, swerving from side to side like a Parkinsonian. It's late and I'm tired and there's no one around and I'm tired and my head hurts and I'm tired and it seems such a long way home. I can't go back to Sarah's where I get mistaken for a spider. I don't want to go home where I'm mistaken for a 'him' who could be any-him. So instead, I lie down on the pavement and pass out.

I don't know how long I'm asleep. Eventually I wake up and find where upright is again. Leaning forwards, I start shuffling home.

And then a shout and footsteps and a sharp, hard feeling against the cheek where I was scratched earlier. I look up and see four figures coming at me. I shout 'What?' and wait for an answer. When one doesn't come, I start running. One of the figures has got hold of my sleeve, but I wrench it away. I'm sprinting towards the street where home is. It's cold at this speed, and I feel I'm getting away by inches.

But I sprint too fast and take a stride for which my legs are too short. I fall on the road, fifty yards from home.

And four figures are standing above me, kicking me in the face, in the head, on the body, on the legs. A part of me each.

The figures are blacked out above me . . . like the house in *Psycho 2* . . . like the black widow in Sarah's bedroom . . . like prosopagnosia, when the facial processing system in the right hemisphere of your brain is impaired, and everyone looks the same.

Suddenly, I remember to scream and I'm screaming: 'Help help help help help,' – like my father, but this time someone's listening.

Within seconds, a tiny woman who lives at the top of the street is standing in her front door, waving her broom. She's shouting that she knows who the silhouettes are and has already phoned the police. Naturally, the four silhouettes are scared of the tiny woman and her broom, so they swear and run away.

My father comes out of our house and shouts at their backs. He helps me inside because I can't walk on my own. I'm bleeding and crying on him. I'm crying that I love the tiny woman with the broom, that I love the ambulance woman who's checking me over, that I love the policeman (not called Flowers) who's come to see what's happened . . . and that I love my father. For this moment, I'm happy to be any pronoun he wants me to be.

The following afternoon, after a second painful bath and a second round of plasters and TCP, I go to Stafford with my parents and hobble round the shops. In WHSmith's, I flick through the CDs. Eventually, I pick one out. It's a new recording of Mahler's Seventh Symphony, with a beautiful illustration by Charles Rennie Macintosh called 'The Harvest Moon' on the cover. My father's at my elbow.

'Looks good, doesn't it?' I say.

'Hmm. I don't go for this Mahler chap like you do. It's a fad, if you ask me, like flares.' He pauses, as if he's forgotten what he was saying but has remembered something more important. 'Boy, do you want that?'

'What?'

'Do you want it, boy? I'll get that Mahler for you.' His fingers have closed round the other side of 'The Harvest Moon' from mine. He's not looking at his hand, though, because he doesn't need to; at present, it's performing its function on its own, smoothly and unconsciously. He's looking straight at me. His other hand is in his pocket, searching for his Visa card.

He can't find the words to say he knows what's happened with Sarah and what happened outside the house last night and what's happening when he answers the door and sees a stranger instead of me. 'He never spoke much,' my mother says, 'but it got worse with Parkinson's. He had less and less words left to speak with, less and less of a voice that wasn't a mumbly-whisper kind of thing.' But here he is in WHSmith's, trying to recover something from the 'mumbly-whisper'. Here he is, trying to express himself, even if it's only through the language of Visa, his 'flexible friend'. If he can't find the words to convey that he knows I'm his son – and he knows his son likes Mahler – at least his Visa can.

Minutes, months and years later, my sinking feeling understands his Visa language. But at the precise second it's happening, I miss one of his last acts of generosity. Instead, my reflex action is to say: 'No, it's okay. You mustn't,' and I take

'The Harvest Moon' from him and return it to the shelf. Perhaps I'm hoping he'll argue the point, but he doesn't respond at all – he grunts and wanders off, the shaking starting again, the WHSmith's moment lost.

There's a section of your brain, some scientists believe, that is devoted to empathy. Empathy and sympathy are biological processes, in what's known as the brain's 'mind-reading' faculty. The mind-reading faculty allows us to recognize, experience and sympathize with other people's emotions and personalities. We exist to other people only as the sum total of the cells devoted to us in their amygdalas, superior temporal sulci, medial-frontal and orbitofrontal cortices – just as they exist to us only in ours. You might open up someone else's brain and find a miniature version of yourself in there. But then again, you might not recognize the you that's imprinted on that person's grey matter. In his later years, I certainly wouldn't have recognized my imprint in my father's mind-reading faculty, given Capgras syndrome. And, I dare say, vice versa too. I didn't have the excuse of Capgras, but it's said that some people – people with autism, for example – have damaged mind-reading modules, which means they can't empathize or identify with others properly.

For years, I felt that my brain's mind-reading capacity must be damaged or under-developed. Empathy's running low, I hear the scientists tut. Maybe other faculties annexed empathy cells for their own purposes – the how-to-get-out-of-chores faculty, for instance, or the nightmares-about-spiders faculty. On many occasions during his illness, I realized after the event that he and his Visa had been trying to say or do something fatherish ('Let me buy you this CD as a present'). But I always missed these moments because they were camouflaged amongst 10,000 'Help help helps', 'Who are yous?' and 'I told you sos'. There were so many times when he tried his best to recognize me, and I was the one who ruined it with the wrong response.

Maybe, I'd feel afterwards, if I'd answered correctly, he'd have answered me – and we would have had a proper conversation. Perhaps, by finding the right answer at the right time, he'd have forgotten his dementia, forgotten his forgetfulness, forgotten his tremors and terrors. But no. My empathy cells only worked in retrospect, after each opportunity had vanished.

Trentham Park

L et's remember a world before Parkinson's. Let's talk about . . . Toros and Lumps and Trees and Sledging.

Toros was a game we played as soon as we could walk. Whistling Bizet, Dad would hold a towel for us as we climbed out of the bath. One by one, we'd snort, paw threateningly at the ground, raise our index fingers to the sides of our heads – and charge at the towel. Dad would cry '*Olé! Olé!*' and swish the towel to one side, catching us in it, scooping us off the floor, drying us furiously.

Another after-bath game was Lumps, which was in lieu of Toros, when my father was too busy for the latter – too busy meaning he was downstairs reading the *Guardian* or my *Beano* (when no one was looking). Though my father was a head teacher, I don't have any memories of him working at home in the evenings. His day job was invisible to us as children. The busiest I remember him was polishing shoes or washing up or fiddling with the television because everyone on it was green. Only during certain weeks of the summer holidays did he spread out papers across the dining room table and shut himself away. He was marking exam papers – worth 1p a paper he said – in

order to pay for our holiday. We weren't allowed to disturb him
for a couple of weeks; he'd come out of the dining room at odd
times and disappear again after a snack. And I kept thinking,
it's like my favourite film, *Chitty Chitty Bang Bang*, where
Caractacus Potts disappears into his work shed for weeks. The
children have to be looked after by their grandpa, Lionel
Jeffries. All they can hear from the work shed are hammerings
and chuggings and bangs. Until, one fine morning, Caractacus
Potts emerges with the car and a famous song. Admittedly, my
father didn't have a car or a song to show for his efforts. He was
supremely impractical – taking an hour to change a plug – and
had a very indifferent sense of pitch. So cars and songs weren't
an option. But, after weeks in the dining room, he did have a
neat stack of CSE French papers and money for a new holiday.

To return to the subject of Lumps. After we'd had a bath,
we'd sneak downstairs and peep through the doors into the
living room. With luck, Dad wouldn't be in there. We'd tiptoe
in and crouch on the rug in front of the fire. Scrunching ourselves into a ball – head on the floor, arms and legs
underneath – we'd pull the towels over us, so we resembled
white or pink 'Lumps'. I'd make an inch-wide slit at the bottom
of the towel, in order to see what was going on outside.

Then we'd wait. Sometimes, we waited so long we got bored
and my father would walk in on Lumps beating each other up.
More usually, a minute would pass, the door would open, and
I'd see his slippers coming into the room. 'Hmm,' he'd say to
himself, 'I wonder why the room looks different tonight?' He'd
sit in his chair and pretend to look at the newspaper, and we'd
giggle. 'Hmm, what's that noise?' he'd ask, putting the newspaper down. He'd stand up again and pace round the room:
'There's definitely something different about the place.' Then,
he'd kick his toe (gently) against one of the Lumps and look

down. 'My goodness. What's going on here?' He'd bend down to inspect. 'Well I never. A Lump. There's a Lump on the floor. That wasn't here before. There are other Lumps too. Where do they come from, I wonder?'

Raising his voice, he'd call Mum: 'Darling, come quick! There are Lumps in the lounge.' Mum would come in, wiping her hands on a tea towel. 'Look!' 'My goodness. Lumps. All different sizes and shapes.' 'What shall we do with them?' 'We could try tickling one of them to see what happens.' And they'd prod and tickle one of us through the towel.

'Ooh, the Lumps make noises,' Mum would say, 'like squealing piglets. We don't want Lumps that make noises like that in the house, do we?' 'But what can we do with them?' 'We could throw them in the dustbin.' 'That sounds like a plan. The dustmen come tomorrow. They'll take the Lumps away.' 'You get hold of that end, I'll get hold of this, and we'll carry them out, one by one.' And Dad would bend down and scoop one of us Lumps off the floor.

Whoever was inside would then roll out of the towel on to the floor. 'Ooh, look, it's some kind of abandoned child. Hiding inside the Lump.' 'We can't throw that away. It might be diseased. We'd get in trouble with the dustmen.' 'We could keep it instead, I s'pose.' 'Or we could tickle it.' And whoever the Lump-Child was would be tickled till they were crying, and rubbed with the towel till they were dry. Then Dad would look around and exclaim: 'Look at the other Lumps. They're moving. We'd better sort them out before they take over the world.' And so it would continue, until we were all dry.

That was Lumps. Trees was a game I claimed as my own. Trees was simpler, less ritualized than Lumps, and generally consisted of my shouting 'Silver birch! Silver birch in a force-ten gale!' The game involved standing on my father's lap, whilst he gripped my ankles. He'd rock me from side to side, making wind noises. I was the tree, my father the wind. Together, the type of tree and the strength of the wind would determine how fast and far I bent from side to side. If, for instance, I was an oak and the wind a mere breeze, I was almost still. If, however, I was a 'silver birch like the ones in Trentham Park which I peel the bark off' and Trentham Park had been strangely hit by a tropical typhoon, then I'd be swung from side to side so far my treetop almost brushed the sofa. Sometimes I'd go so fast I had to cover my eyes with my branches. Before lunch, I'd have been every single tree I could name: oak, ash, palm, monkey puzzle, fir, apple, elm.

If lunch were delayed, the game became increasingly nuanced. It started taking into account whether I was deciduous or evergreen. If I were evergreen, I would be less affected by autumn gales than if I were deciduous; deciduous trees had to be shaken about violently in order for them to lose their leaves. Then there was the added question of geographical location: was I an elm in Trentham Park or Siberia? By the time lunch was ready, the game had become so complex that I was a 'wych elm in the Scottish Highlands enduring an eighty-mile-an-hour blizzard with an advanced case of Dutch elm disease'. Dutch elm disease being incurable, this was normally the end of Trees and the beginning of lunch.

If Trees is personal to me, Sledging is something all my siblings remember. Years later, writing the eulogy for my father's funeral, my brother asked each of us to write down a list of 'Dad memories' he might refer to. All four of us headed our lists with those sledging nights of long ago. As Parkinson's took hold the sledging nights stopped, and the deep snow we'd known as children dried up. But from before that time, we all recall those moments of delight when Dad, with no warning except snow, would ceremoniously emerge from the garage, dragging the old, wooden sledge behind him – as close as he ever got to Caractacus Potts emerging at the wheel of Chitty Chitty Bang Bang.

My mother would dress us up in five layers of clothes, two pairs of socks, two pairs of gloves, wellingtons, Stoke City scarves and bobble hats. The wardrobe emptied, we'd run into the snow and the three (later four) of us would pounce in a heap on the sledge:

'I'm going on it.'

'No, I am.'

'Get off, who's oldest?'

'Get off yourself, who's youngest? I need to be pulled along.'

'Are you a baby who can't walk?'

'Shut up both of you and get off. *Actually*, it's my turn.'

'How can it *actually* be your turn? We haven't even started yet.'

'Because *actually* you had the last go last time.'

'But this is the first sledging this year.'

'Yeah, but I remember that last year you had the last go. *Actually*.'

And so on and so forth. My father tries to pull three or four of us along at once and almost puts his back out. 'Right, two at a time. Youngest first, then we'll swap half way.'

'Ha! Geroff, you heard Dad!'

'Baby.'

My father pulls us and the sledge by the rope. We get as far as the top of the street, about thirty yards from home. The snow is deep here and is coming on to the sledge: 'My bottom's getting snowy.'

'Moaning mini. It's your fault for wanting to be on it first.'

'Dad, I want to get off the sledge.'

'You were desperate to be on it before.'

'But my bottom's getting wet.'

'Okay, Karen, it's your turn.'

'I don't want to go on it if my bottom's going to get wet. Jonathan can stay on.'

'But I don't want to. It's your turn.'

'No it's not – you have to stay on and your bottom will get frostbite and fall off. Ha ha.'

And so on and so forth. Within another thirty yards, of course, the argument has been inverted again to: 'It's my turn,' 'No, it's not,' 'Yes, it is.' And so on and so forth. Reading these arguments back now – with their repetitions, circularities, automaticities – I can't help thinking that childhood has symptoms in common with dementia.

My father drags us down the road, past the graveyard, past the silhouette of the Wedgwood Mausoleum, across the main road, across our favourite 'pooh-sticks bridge', past my mother's church – and into Trentham Park, where there are dozens of people careering down the hill on sledges, boxes and dustbin liners. There's even a dog on one of the sledges; he doesn't know what's happening, but is clearly enjoying the cold wind on his tongue, which is trailing behind him. I recognise the dog as Dr Crippen, a stupidly docile Alsatian from next door. He isn't in control of his tongue or his sledge, and is spinning round and round, and is now hurtling backwards. He disappears into a nearby drift, only to emerge a few seconds later, shaking snow over Dad. He bounds up the slope towards his owner, woofing wildly. Sledging is far better fun than burying your wife in the cellar, Crippen seems to be saying.

I want to copy Dr Crippen, so I jump off the sledge, take the rope from my father and start pulling it up the slope. I manage five yards and come to a halt: 'Dad, will you take the sledge up the hill for me?' Dad: 'Of course, boy.' My sister: 'If you can't pull the thing up to the top, you can't ride it down to the bottom.' Me: 'But Crippen can't and he does.' 'He's a dog.' 'So are you.' Dad: 'Stop it.' Me: 'But she started it.' And so on and so forth till we reach the top.

I get on the sledge, but Robin pounds me with snowballs till I fall off: 'Oldest first,' he shouts. Meanwhile, Karen takes advantage of Robin's distraction and climbs aboard. She shoves herself off; Robin pelts her with snowballs as she whizzes past, waving like the queen. Helen starts making a tiny snowbear, knowing that she doesn't stand a chance against her older siblings until Dad intervenes on her behalf. She's singing a medley of carols to herself. I find an abandoned dustbin liner and slide away on that.

A few minutes later I'm at the top again, and Dad is on the sledge. He pulls me down in front of him, and we're off with a sound like Mum sharpening kitchen knives and Dad's steering with his boots and laughing and pulling the rope this way and that to avoid Dr Crippen and there's another boy in front of us who we miss at the last second and then we hit the flat ground and he slows the sledge with his boots and I wish I wish I could remember this moment more clearly.

We carry on till we're wet through from purposely falling off. We carry on till we're freezing cold from Robin's snowballs. We carry on till we're exhausted from pulling the sledge a quarter of the way up the hill each time and then calling Dad to pull it the rest of the way.

Dr Crippen never seems to tire, and is still burying himself (rather than his wife) in snow drifts as we leave. We wander home, recapping the arguments we had on the outward journey between yawns and moans about wet toes and Robin's snow-balls. After a snowball in the face, even Dad gets exasperated and mutters something under his breath about a guy called 'Gordon Bennett'.

Back home, the house smells of fruits made of marzipan. 'Yuck,' I say. Mum makes us leave our boots and outer clothes at the front door. Helen is crying with the cold. Robin is throwing snowballs at the windows for want of any other target. Karen and I rush to the fire to toast our fingers and toes. 'It's my fire.' 'It's mine.' 'Don't hog it, you.' 'You're the one who's hogging it. My fingers are colder than yours.' 'How can you tell?'

Mum comes in: 'Don't stand so close to the fire. You'll get chilblains.' 'What are chilblains?' 'They're terrible, sore things on your fingers. You get them when your hands are freezing one minute and too hot the next.' 'Your fingers fall off,' says my brother, 'and then your head. There's lots of blood. And then your legs break too and you can't walk. You're paralysed from the neck down. And then we laugh at you. Ha ha.' 'Be quiet,' says my father, sinking into the armchair with a selection of marzipan fruits. 'That's enough chilblains for one night.'

Chilblains, Dutch elm disease – so many childhood games ended with the threat of illness or injury. Toros might impale you. Bottoms might get frostbite. Dr Crippen was sledging in our local park. The word 'Lumps' is infected with disturbing connotations now, given what happened to aunties we loved.

Still, I think about those games. I think about Sledging and Lumps and Toros and surprise trips to see *Chitty Chitty Bang Bang*, and I think: Dad, my dad, you were a wonderful father.

(Dementia with Lewy bodies, Parkinson's, Capgras, you were not.)

Bottom of the Bookcase

Every disease is a musical problem. Every cure is a musical solution.

(Novalis, *Encyclopaedia*)

In remembering my father, I can't help also remembering things which aren't him, which are inadequate substitutes for the real person. I can't help remembering books, records, films which have survived him, and now stand in his place. I can't help remembering . . .

(1)   David Lean and Noël Coward, *Brief Encounter* . . . because my parents also met on a station; because my father also had a mac; because he was married; because, though I never guessed it whilst he was alive, my parents really did love each other.

Still, however apt in some respects, *Brief Encounter* is only good for the beginning of my parents' relationship. It doesn't tell you what would have happened if Celia Johnson and Trevor Howard had stayed together. Besides which, my mother says there weren't any steam engines in 1965 – just 'those nice, new unsmoky diesels'.

(2)   Gustav Mahler, Symphony No. 6 . . . not because my father liked Mahler, but because I want him to be the hero of the first and last movements; because, in the Andante, I hear distant cowbells from my parents' first holiday; because, in the Scherzo, a faltering, little tune keeps popping up amidst the horror – a tune that's marked 'old fatherly' (to translate the German *altväter-isch* literally), and that is eventually reduced to shadow. Mainly, though, I choose this piece because the finale (according to Mahler's wife) depicts a 'hero, on whom fall three blows of fate, the last of which fells him as a tree is felled'. In 1907, a couple of years after completing the symphony, Mahler himself suffered three blows of fate: the death of a daughter, his resignation from the Vienna Opera and the diagnosis of heart disease. It's impossible, I think, to listen to such ultra-Romantic music with a rationalist's hat on, denying the prophetic, the superstitious, the *ir*rational elements of the finale. The prophecy was true in retrospect. And I listen to the piece now and hear in it – retrospectively – a prophecy of my father's later life. Three blows of fate: not the death of a daughter, but abandonment by a disaffected son; not resignation from the Vienna Opera, but early retirement from headship of Willfield High; not the diagnosis of heart disease, but the diagnosis of head disease.

(3)   Rimsky-Korsakov, *Scheherazade* . . . I want to mention that piece, along with Beethoven's Seventh Symphony,

Sibelius's Second, Tchaikovsky's Fourth Symphony and First Piano Concerto, Strauss's *Blue Danube*, just because my father loved them. The list could go on.

At the beginning of high school, he helped me with a project on Johann Strauss, playing the pieces over and over on the new stereo, even cutting out pictures of nineteenth-century waltzers for me. Whenever we had homework to do, he'd say, 'Let's look it up.' He'd lift down a volume from his set of green encyclopaedias and dictate from it, as if he were reading from his own mind – as if the twelve volumes embodied the storehouse of his brain. They seemed to contain anything you could want to know on any subject. Or, at least, anything you could want to know up till circa 1928, when they were published: for years, I went around thinking the League of Nations had never been dissolved and Einstein was still alive. When I was a child, human knowledge ended in 1928.

Despite their datedness, I was grateful to my father's encyclopaedias; they furnished me with many a plagiarized B+ assignment – including the one about Strauss and waltzes. 'It says here that the waltz was risqué at the time.' 'What's risqué?' I'd ask, faux naif, enjoying my father's discomfort. 'You know. It was thought too . . . *familiar*.' 'What's too familiar?' 'Erm, yes, well, touching a woman and holding her body close. And all that. It was seen as, ahem, sexy. Something that the Mary Whitehouses of the day might have complained about. Like disco dancing, but sexy in a nineteenth-century kind of way. If you see what I mean. Ooh, look, it's dinner time.' 'Oh,' I nodded, transcribing every word he said straight on to the page.

(4)   Another Beethoven work – the 'Egmont Overture' . . .
       because he told me this was the only seventy-eight he
       had when he first lived in London. He used to play it all
       the time, until his bedsit was burgled one day. Burglars, it
       seems, used to steal Beethoven in the 1940s.

(5)   Talking of the 1940s, Glenn Miller's music does not fea-
       ture amongst the things I associate with my father . . .
       though I know he loved Miller's music as much as
       Beethoven's or Tchaikovsky's.
           In this respect, I was often accused of dictating my
       father's musical tastes when he was unable to express
       them himself: 'You don't want to listen to that Miller rub-
       bish, you want to listen to this record of mine.' I have to
       confess that, sometimes, I'd offer him a choice of two LPs,
       he'd point at one of them, and I'd go off and play the one
       I wanted anyway.

(6)   Like Glenn Miller, Shakespeare was another of my
       father's passions I purposely disavowed as a teenager.
       Unlike Glenn Miller, my attitude has changed since, and
       I want to include here a text by Shakespeare. To be spe-
       cific, I want to mention the half-hackneyed speech from
       As You Like It – you know, the one about all the world
       being a stage, etc – as featured in the green, hard-bound
       copy of *The Complete Works* kept at the bottom of the
       bookcase, next to the two carved owls, halfway up the
       stairs, in my parents' house, Stoke. My father would read
       me this passage when, in my early teens, I used to pro-
       claim that Mr William Shakespeare was 'out-of-date
       cwap' (without having read any, naturally). As far as I
       was concerned, the green, hard-bound copy of *The*

Complete Works could rot at the bottom of the bookcase, next to the two carved owls, halfway up the stairs forever.

By contrast, as a much younger, illiterate child, I was obsessed with the mysterious, green book. Sitting on the stairs, I used to take the tome off the bookshelf, lay it in front of me, stroke it and pretend to read it to the two owls. I thought the book must be important because it was the biggest volume in the bookcase, and because I couldn't imagine ever being able to read it. I couldn't read till I was eight; I used to sit in the library corner at school, petting the books, staring wonderingly and stupidly at them. Perhaps that's why I now find incomprehensible the general disdain for books amongst literary academics, amongst people who study and teach them for a living. I went through childhood thinking heavy, dusty volumes would remain forever a prohibited, adult pleasure like sex (whatever that was) and instant coffee; and that feeling has lingered into literate adulthood. When I was seven, my father politely enquired of my teacher if I might be – to quote – 'a retard?' But nice Mrs Newman was of the opinion that petting books was almost as good as reading, particularly if the books petted were *The Complete Works*: 'Patience, Mr Taylor. We're not into the forcing method here. More the stroking method. Jonathan's learning through stroking. Like osmosis.' They didn't have SATS then. As my mother points out: 'Gosh, imagine if you were born now. Imagine the files they'd have on you all: Robin was hyperactive, getting bored every second; Karen didn't speak and ate nothing but beef spread for three years; people thought Helen was spoilt; and you had "learning difficulties". You stroked books for hours.'

By the time I was thirteen, though, I had learnt to read without stroking, and had made up my mind that the only thing *The Complete Works* contained was a load of old cobblers. This conclusion was based on the premise that a girl at school, whose ankles I thought highly of, said so. On overhearing my informed criticism, my father seemed concerned for Shakespeare's reputation. So he took out the green book from the bottom of the book-case, halfway up the stairs, next to the carved owls, and leafed through it till he found:

All the world's a stage,
And all the men and women merely players;
They have their exits and their entrances;
And one man in his time plays many parts,
His acts being seven ages. At first the infant,
Mewling and puking in the nurse's arms;
And then the whining school-boy, with his satchel
And shining morning face, creeping like snail
Unwillingly to school. And then the lover,
Sighing like furnace, with a woeful ballad
Made to his mistress' eyebrow. Then a soldier,
Full of strange oaths, and bearded like the pard,
Jealous in honour, sudden and quick in quarrel,
Seeking the bubble reputation
Even in the cannon's mouth. And then the justice,
In fair round belly with good capon lin'd,
With eyes severe and beard of formal cut,
Full of wise saws and modern instances;
And so he plays his part. The sixth age shifts
Into the lean and slipper'd pantaloon,
With spectacles on nose and pouch on side,

His youthful hose, well sav'd, a world too wide
For his shrunk shank; and his big manly voice,
Turning again toward childish treble, pipes
And whistles in his sound. Last scene of all,
That ends this strange eventful history,
Is second childishness and mere oblivion;
Sans teeth, sans eyes, sans taste, sans everything.

My father would read me the whole passage in an attempt to prove Shakespeare's 'universal relevance' – an assumption literary academics of a later generation are bravely combating. My father brought me up to think that there was a point to studying literature, that there was truth and beauty in it: 'Books are the peak of civilization, boy, not TV. Remember that.' I've tried to remember it, Dad, but a lot of other teachers, academics and educationalists haven't. Over time, I've discovered that those whose lives are meant to be devoted to the study of literature are really devoted to the study of why *not* to study literature. Academics are generally people who think they have *transcended* blind faith in literature. In reality, they've just regressed to the attitude of the early teen, whereby Shakespeare is once again a load of 'cwap'. I know of specialists in Renaissance drama who refuse to teach Shakespeare on account of his out-dated sexist and racist attitudes. Personally, I'd have thought that to accuse Shakespeare of sexism and racism is to affirm, not refute his timeless relevance.

'Look at Shakespeare's timeless relevance,' my father would say. 'See how many of these descriptions fit you or me or other people we know. The "whining school-boy, with his satchel" who creeps "like snail" to school – I

wonder who that is?' 'Dunno.' 'It's you, of course. You're
"like snail" every morning.' My father made the point
that the missing 'a' between the words 'like snail' makes
a lot of the difference to the simile. Shakespeare, he said,
is self-consciously aiming at timeless relevance in the
whole speech; and this universality works not only on a
general level ('All the world's a stage') but also in terms
of minute details. By leaving out the 'a' before snail,
Shakespeare is de-particularizing the snail and, by associ-
ation, the boy. This is not 'a' snail – it is the universal
concept of snail and snail-ness; this is not 'a' school-boy –
it is 'the' school-boy who is everybody's school-boy-ness,
regardless of time. No doubt my father was thinking it
was his school-boy-ness as well as mine. Perhaps he was
also thinking it was his first son's school-boy-ness too.
Back then, of course, I didn't know my father had a first
son. I didn't understand any of what my father was saying
while a school-boy myself.

Many years later, it was this very passage, from the
same copy of The Complete Works – still kept at the
bottom of the bookcase, halfway up the stairs, next to the
two carved owls – that I read during my father's funeral
service. Except that I censored it as brutally as some
Stalinist apparatchik. I kept the school-boy and the soldier and the judge, but came to a halt at the line 'And so
he plays his part'. I didn't want to mention the 'lean and
slipper'd pantaloon' with his 'shrunk shank' or the
'second childishness . . . sans teeth, sans taste, sans everything.' I thought we'd had enough of oblivion; so I made
the passage sans 'sans everything'. In turn, this also meant
excising an earlier line, 'his acts being seven ages', in a
futile effort to disguise the missing two stages.

And the effort was futile: whether or not they knew the passage, the people listening must have noticed the gap where nothing ('sans everything') should have been. The speech describes a man growing up and older, so most people would expect it to end with old age and 'second childishness'. But in the new, improved, optimistic, Socialist Realist version at my father's funeral, there was no decrepitude, no senility and no oblivion. It ended instead with the man at the peak of his career as the 'justice'. And most people in the church that day must have known that I was reading a lie, as false as Stalinist theatre. I wish I hadn't done it now. My father wouldn't have approved of bowdlerizing Shakespeare. It's just that the last two 'acts' in the passage seemed all *too* apt, *too* relevant. And my father never warned me when I was younger that relevance can be horrifying as well as wonderful.

(7)   Long before his funeral, the horror of relevance was why an increasing number of books, records and films were banned from the house. They were suppressed, one by one, because of the associations they evoked. It got to the point where I thought we'd eventually run out of records we were allowed to play, books we were allowed to read, videos we could watch.

Purged works included the video of the Rodgers and Hammerstein musical, *Carousel*, because it reminded my father of Willfield High School. The school had put on a performance of *Carousel* in the late 1970s. I was taken to it – there are vague memories of colours and songs. Come the 1990s, because of its associations with his old, dreaded work place, my father used to watch *Carousel* as a horror movie: 'This is horrible! Horrible!' So we stopped putting it on, and sent the video on a one-way ticket to the attic.

Another purged work was Igor Stravinsky's *Rite of Spring* – and particularly its incarnation in Walt Disney's film, *Fantasia*. Disney famously misappropriates Stravinsky's music to illustrate early evolution and the age of the dinosaurs. For the life of me, I can't think of any relevance, timeless or otherwise, that could have been painful to my father in this film. Perhaps there were no associations, and he just found *Fantasia* scary. But that doesn't explain the vehemence of his aversion. If *Fantasia* was on television, he'd sit with his eyes screwed up whimpering: 'Turn it off, please. Turn it offoffoffoff.' He'd start whimpering even before the film got to the Stravinsky section, when there were only dancing toadstools on the screen. And he would continue to whimper when we'd finally turned the film off out of frustration.

Asked why he hated it so much, he'd say: 'It's the dinosaurs. There's something about them. Something like nightmares.' This would have been understandable, but for the fact that he loved dinosaurs, generally speaking. He enjoyed more 'realistic' portrayals of dinosaurs on BBC documentaries, or in books. One of the best Christmasses I ever had was the year before he died; I gave him a huge book about dinosaurs, and he sat for days, book on lap, new bobble-hat on head, staring at different species, fumbling with the pages. I was happy: I'd managed to find something which engrossed him more than the inside of his eyelids. But when I tried to put *Fantasia* on again, the eyelids reasserted themselves: 'Turn it off. Offoffoffoffoffoff.' There must have been something about Disney's *cartoon* dinosaurs which disturbed him. Somehow, they were more horrifying by being less 'realistic' than the pseudo-photos in the book.

Then, of course, there's the peculiarly un-Disneyesque music itself. The last time I played the *Rite of Spring* complete within his earshot was August 1995. We were on holiday in Italy; I was in my bedroom, and he was in a room across the corridor. Both doors were shut between us – I don't know how he heard it. I sometimes wondered if he had a radar which could sense the piece within a certain radius. Whatever the case, halfway through 'The Adoration of the Earth' he burst through my door and shouted: 'You're playing that on purpose! You've put it on because you want to give me dinosaur nightmares again!' My mother followed him in and told him he was disturbing everyone in the hotel, and that he should be quiet with his silly paranoia.

The confession I want to make is that my father's 'silly paranoia' was (once again) justified. He was right, in that I did sometimes play snippets of the *Rite of Spring* 'on purpose'. Whilst he dozed, I'd put the record on – ever-so-quietly – to see if he recognized it subliminally. Scientific curiosity, I thought, watching him twitch in his sleep.

(8) Certain comedies also made him twitch in his sleep, if in a different way. These included *Fawlty Towers*, *Blackadder 4*, *Last of the Summer Wine*, *The Seven Year Itch* and the *Police Academy* films. A rather miscellaneous list, I grant you, but all of them made my father guffaw, even in his last years. We'd think he was asleep. He'd be slouched

in his chair, chin on his chest, eyes screwed shut, drool pending . . . And then, suddenly, he'd be muttering the lines back at the telly and heaving with laughter. Laughter which made his body bounce in the chair. Laughter which cracked the Parkinsonian mask. Laughter which seemed to issue from a long-hidden self.

When he was laughing, he'd never open his eyes. In fact, he was often at his most catatonic when the rumblings started. I suppose the comedies must have worked for him on a purely aural level, however visual some of the humour seems. Or maybe he was playing them out on some stage deep inside.

(9)   From inside laughter back to outside horror, and *The Haunting*, a 1960s film which (as far as I know) my father never saw. Here is a film which knows about the horror of care, the horror of hearing knocking on walls at night – and the horror of *not* hearing them.

At the start of the film, there's a girl who grows up and grows old in the nursery, located at the top of the house. Bedridden in her last years, the woman is looked after by a nurse, whom she summons by hitting the wall with a stick. One night, the nurse is too busy 'carrying on' with a man from the village to hear the summons. The stick falls from the old woman's hand, and she dies. Thereafter, the nurse is condemned to live in the house, haunted by mysterious bangings on walls . . . until she hangs herself. Years later, another woman comes to stay in the house, and hears the knockings and shufflings again. This woman has also been a carer, looking after her sick mother for twenty years. It's gradually revealed that she herself is haunted by one night when she didn't respond to her mother's bangs for help – and her mother died.

Only this film knows what it's like to sleep in a house where there's only you and someone who's dependent on you. Only this film knows what it's like to wake up in the middle of the night to hear shufflings, mutterings and scratchings from the next room. To wake up and hear someone calling 'Help help help' to the dark. To wake up and hear tears and crashes, and find a bedroom turned upside down, the bed shredded in pieces. To wake up, convinced you can hear your father gasping for breath in the next room, because he's swallowed his false teeth. To wake up and not hear this, convinced the teeth have already choked him to death. Or to wake up and hear your father shrieking about nightmares full of cartoon dinosaurs.

(10) *The Haunting* understands these night terrors. But they are all it knows about: it doesn't understand or encompass anything beyond the terrors of care. *The Haunting* doesn't know what the 'Intermezzo' from Franz Schmidt's *Notre Dame* knows (and vice versa). This miniature, slightly kitschy piece knows what happened to my father and me on Sunday 22 April 2001. It knows what happened one day in a forgotten room, down a long corridor, in a dilapidated hospital. It knows that there was one moment when my father seemed to know me, and I him. It was the only witness present, and I return to it now and then to be reassured that the moment did actually happen.

Of course, none of these works quite work. None of the texts listed above manage to understand my father entirely. They don't even understand my understanding of him.

If these texts can't understand *him*, I wonder if there are any which understand his disease? Well, I suppose there are odd pieces of music which come close, which I hear as Parkinson's Symphonies, Dementia Concertos. I'm thinking in particular of certain late twentieth-century Russian pieces, such as Shostakovich's Fifteenth Symphony and Alfred Schnittke's Concerto Grosso No. 1. Here is the music of Parkinson's: the musical tics that won't go away, the palilalia, the tremoring, the paralytic stasis, the festination. Here too is the music of dementia: the horror, the paranoia, the inability to pursue trains of thought, to piece together coherence from disconnected cells. But here too are fleeting moments of joy you don't notice till after they've gone: musical echolalias of long-ago symphonies, of tangos-gone-by, of William Tells that my father might have been.

PART THREE

What I Knew

When did I know what I know now?

When I was five, my father came from Oldham, and he had an unspecified number of sisters.

When I was ten, my father came from Oldham, and he had an unspecified number of sisters. At the same time, he somehow came from the Isle of Man too, where there was an auntie who wasn't his sister, and an uncle who was dead.

When I was seventeen, my father came from Oldham, and he had an unspecified number of sisters, and maybe or maybe not some brothers. At the same time, he came from the Isle of Man too, where there was an auntie who wasn't an auntie, and an uncle who was dead. And, frankly, being seventeen, I couldn't have cared less.

When I was twenty, my father came from Oldham, where he had an unspecified number of sisters, and maybe some brothers. He came from the Isle of Man too, where there was an auntie who was old and forgot things. There was also an unmarked grave where a Mrs Margaret Taylor was buried. Somehow, Mrs Taylor was simultaneously my father's mother and not my father's mother. It seemed too complicated to go into, especially since there was a Mary from Oldham who wasn't my father's mother either, and an unidentified dead woman in an old photograph. There was talk of fostering, selling and a long gap in his life – between leaving university and meeting my mother – all of which seemed irrelevant to the here-and-now of his encroaching illness. If he was losing the ability to recognize me in the present, how could I expect him to explain all the different people, sisters, aunties and mothers in his past?

When I was twenty-five, however, a letter came from the Salvation Army which initiated the long process of explaining these people and his past for him.

Isle of Man

Ghost-like I paced round the haunts of my childhood,
Earth seem'd a desert I was bound to traverse,
Seeking to find the old familiar faces.

(Charles Lamb, 'The Old Familiar Faces')

'When I was young, I lived for a bit in the Isle of Man, and went to school. The school was knocked down, but it was roundabout hereish.' We all remember my father saying that, gesturing loosely towards a car park in Castletown, on the Isle of Man.

But when I trace one of my father's supposed 'relatives' on the island, she declares: 'Oh no. He never lived here. An auntie had a house in Castletown, where the car park is now. Maybe he was thinking of that. But Jackie never lived on the island or went to school here. Jackie just came for holidays.'

I get sidetracked: 'Who's Jackie?'

'Your dad, of course. When I first got your letter, I thought, hmm, John Taylor. That dings an old dong. And then it came to me: you mean *Jackie* Taylor.'

'I thought Jackie was a girl's name?' My father's gender

hovers worryingly in the indeterminate space between my question and her answer. I've got to the point where anything is thinkable.

'Not then. Jackie: that was who he was to us. Gosh, never thought I'd hear that name again. Jackie.' She says the name as if it's a secret between her and history.

I return to what I was asking before: 'So, he never lived here? Never lived on the Isle of Man?'

'Nope.'

'Never went to school here?'

'Nope.'

'*Definitely* never went to school here?'

'Definitely not. Jackie never went to school here.'

I can't help trying one more time: 'And you couldn't possibly be . . . wrong about it?'

The old woman doesn't deign to answer, just snorts and looks out of the car window. So I appeal to my mother instead: 'You remember him saying he lived here, don't you?'

'I *remember* him saying that, yes. I must be remembering wrongly.'

'But I remember him saying it too, and so does everyone.'

'Then perhaps everyone's remembering wrongly.'

'How can we *all* remember the same wrong thing? And *all* forget the right thing?'

The conversation continues in this way for a while, headbanging itself against a stark choice: that either my father lied about his early life, or my mother, my siblings and I have all misremembered something we desperately wanted to remember. We'd clung to the streak of Manxness across our past to temper the bleak Stokeness of the present. Of the places we knew best as children, my parents never hid their distaste for Stoke-on-Trent, or, for that matter, Torquay; and Oldham was just another Stoke, with less pottery, more relatives. So the Isle of Man was the one place which we unreservedly loved. It had been our father's home in the past – or so we thought – and we hoped it would be ours in the future. At different times, my two sisters moved to the island . . . and then moved away because of winter gales (which, of course, we never experienced on summer holidays), the dogfish (it's a long story) and the lack of a good hairdresser's.

'He definitely, certainly, absolutely never lived on the Isle of Man, definitely, certainly never went to the school in Castletown.' In a trice, we're exiled from our family's imaginary past, exiled from a homeland that was never ours in the first place. We're relegated to common Stoke tourists; no green, faery isle for us.

The Isle of Man had meant so much to us, consciously and unconsciously as well. For years, I had recurring dreams about travelling to the island. As I got older, the journey in my dreams became more complex. Maybe I missed the boat. Or boarded the boat and realized I'd forgotten something. Or got the wrong boat. Or my father's car wouldn't get up the ramp. Or a thousand other variants in which it became harder and harder to reach our holidays.

Nowadays, my dreams have changed, and they're all about trying to get away *from* the island. It's getting dark, and we're driving round in circles, searching for Douglas port. Eventually, my father takes a wrong turn up a treacherous cliff, where night and sea are coming on to the road.

Before such nightmares, I used to love the journey to and from the Isle of Man. In the 1970s and early 80s, we'd arrive at the port in Liverpool or Heysham and there'd be queues of cars with suitcases on their roofs for a half a mile. We'd jump out of the car and run to the harbour wall to see which ships were in.

There were quite a few coming and going then: *Manx Maid II*, the *Viking* which ran aground, *Ben-My-Chree V* which had a stepped front where crowds sunbathed on deckchairs, and the *Lady of Mann*.

The *Lady of Mann* was my favourite, partly because the name sounded sexy, partly because I won my first ever bet on it. One morning before going to the island, I bet my father 10p that the boat taking us there would be the *Lady of Mann*; he said, no, he thought it would be *Ben-My-Chree*. I was right, and I duly received 10p. When my mother found out, she was furious: 'This is terrible,' she said, near tears. 'You're encouraging gambling when you know what I think of it.' 'Gambling?! It was 10p!' 'You start off with 10p on the *Lady of Mann*, and you end up addicted. Like one of those waifs on television.'

My mother's protestations, however, didn't put an end to the 'gambling'. It just made it more covert. When she was in the kitchen, my father, my siblings and I would surreptitiously pick names of boats out of a hat and pledge 10p each for the next trip. Everything was conducted in whispers. Even then, we knew that Dad wouldn't betray the conspiracy to Mum; even as children, we knew my father was adept at keeping secrets, whether his own or others'. Still, you'd have thought my mother would have guessed what was going on – given the way that, on sailing days, we waifs-in-waiting rushed to the harbour wall, and were either jubilant or crestfallen depending on what we saw.

If queuing for the Isle of Man boat was exciting, the actual voyage was positively C. S. Lewisesque – or, at least, it was for children brought up in the (apparently) un-C. S. Lewisesque world of 70s Stoke and unexceptional wardrobes. 'Let's play on deck, in the ropes!' we'd yell, pulling Dad's sleeve until he surrendered his flask of coffee. We'd run round the ship, shouting in the quiet rooms, making crocodiles on the screen in the cinema room, trying to break portholes to see if water would come in – and then on to the deck to point at jellyfish as big as chandeliers.

This was the time to 'Play in the ropes!' The ropes were huge, immovable coils on the bow, coils into which you could lower yourself, or (if you were small like me) be lowered by Dad. Playing in the ropes consisted of various games – pretending to be a drowning sailor, pretending to be a cobra charmed out of a basket, pretending to be a giant squid attacking the ship's crew, pretending to be a deadly jellyfish, expressing deadliness in various ways. If there were a few coils nearby, we could play the cattle-market game. We'd each climb into a different coil, or 'pen'. Then we'd declare what farm animal we were: pig, calf, chicken, warthog, camel, tadpole or Care Bear (being brought up in suburbia meant that we had a rather nebulous idea of farm livestock). An auction would follow, in which Dad would take bids for each pig, calf, Care Bear, etc. The auction usually ended with the last game, the pretending-to-forget-about-the-piggy-called-Jonathan-and-leaving-him-in-the-rope-coil-so-he-can't-get-out game. For me, this game wasn't funny, just long and tedious. Forgetting games usually are.

We're averaging seventy miles an hour round the TT course on the Isle of Man. There's an eighty-year-old woman in the passenger seat, who's shouting 'Faster! Go faster!' and reaching for the gear stick. The TT, or 'Tourist Trophy', course is a treacherously twisty, thirty-eight-mile circuit of the island's A roads, on which there have been motorcycle races since 1907 – usually resulting in someone's death. It's especially dangerous when it's foggy like today. That's the context in which the eighty-year-old woman's 'Faster! Go faster!' and her reaching for the gear stick should be understood.

Helen gets there first and floors the accelerator. The old woman claps her hands and looks round at my mother and me on the back seat. She's grinning and her white hair is standing on end: 'Your sister's good, isn't she? This is what the TT's for.'

The old woman is Cath Q., the 'relative' who has just blithely announced that my father 'certainly, definitely' never lived on the Isle of Man – that we have no claim to Manx pedigree, only Stoke mongreldom. It's August 2003, and this is the first time we've met her. We're driving her from south to north of the island, in order to meet up with other members of her family. It feels more like she's driving us, though: 'Faster!' she shrieks. My sister takes one corner, where bikes have been known to shoot off the course, in fourth gear. The clapped-out Peugeot's on two wheels, pretending it's a Norton or Velocette from the glory days of the TT.

A few minutes before, we'd been late turning up at Cath's house. She'd emerged from the mists before I reached her front door. 'Silly boy!' – these were the first words she ever said to me in person – 'Silly boy! I told you we had to get through before six-thirty.' It's racing season, and the roads were closing for TT practice in fifteen minutes. 'We'll never get through now, and I so wanted you to meet the others. It takes at least half an hour to get up to Ballaugh.' She stamped her arthritic foot. I led her to the car. 'You're late,' she told my mother.

'Sorry,' said my mother from the back seat.

Cath climbed into the passenger seat and shut the door. 'You're Helen, I suppose, and you're late too.'

Helen nodded.

'Do you think we can make it through?'

Helen nodded again, and the car's wheels spun. Then, we were off.

The roads were almost empty as we leapt over the mini-roundabouts at Ballasalla. Cath was gripping the dashboard as we shot up Foxdale road. I was feeling sick as we went through red lights at Ballacraine crossroads, on to the official TT track.

Now we've taken the Glen Helen bend. Cath suddenly shouts: 'Ooh, look, there's a policeman in that lay-by. Stop! We'll ask him whether we can get through before the road closes. Helen! Stop here!'

Helen, thinking there's an emergency of some sort, swerves into the lay-by. We're still going at a fair speed when Cath opens her door. I shriek: 'You can't do that . . .' convinced that our new-found elderly cousin is crazed – and is trying to take out the policeman with the car door.

For a moment, I can't help wondering if opening car doors at 70 mph runs in the family. After all, my father often used to do this, especially when my mother was driving. We'd be on the M6, where he had a terrifying propensity for vehicular paranoia: 'Why are you stealing me? Take me home.'

My mother would shout at him: 'For goodness sake, darling, be quiet. And get your hand off that gear stick.' The gears crunch, the car swerves from middle lane into left-hand lane. Someone who was behind us is now in front of us, hooting wildly.

'You can't do that, Dad. Bloody stop it.'

'You've stolen me!' He's winding down the window so he can call for help from other cars zooming past.

'Please stop it.'

'Stop it!' he repeats echolalically, 'Stopit stopit stopit. Please please please.' His eyes are paranoia-wide, and he reaches for the seatbelt, trying to press the release button. Thankfully, his co-ordination isn't quite up to it; I smack his hand and put it back on his lap. He tries again, I smack again. Try, smack, try, smack.

He's twitching backwards and forwards in the seat, rocking the car's suspension with him. 'Stop it, Dad, please.'

'Help help help – they're stealing me!'

'Kidnapping, you mean,' my younger sister corrects him from the backseat. 'The word's kidnapping, not stealing.' She yawns and stares out of the window, abstracting herself from the drama. 'It's as bad as squares instead of cushions.'

'*Kidnapping* then! They're *kidnapping* me!' He taps at the window to his left, gesticulating at a car that's under-taking us: 'Hello there! I'm being kidnapped! You there! It's me! Hello! Look over here! I've been kidnapped! Hello! Hello!' The people in the car wave back at him, and Helen starts humming Lionel Ritchie ('Hello, is it me you're looking for?').

'Help help!' My mother stuffs a gobstopper into his mouth. It performs its self-proclaimed function.

We think that's paranoia over – and I look away: 'Yes, Dad, honest, we're taking you to a secret location, cos there are *so* many millionaires who're willing to pay a ransom for you.'

Whilst I'm saying this, it's suddenly too late. His 'Help help helps' have morphed into the telltale danger signal: 'Let me out!' The danger signal is followed by a click – and, yes, he's found the handle and opened the car door. He's even moving his left leg towards the space where the door was, and where now there's tarmac whizzing underneath.

My mother shrieks. I swear. Helen looks up, tuts and yawns. The car swerves on to the hard shoulder and off again. A van behind curves round us and hoots. My father reaches calmly for the seatbelt release, as if getting out on the M6, Junction 11, at 65 mph is much like getting out for a picnic. As if we're 'there' and he's keen to get out and explore. As if the kidnapping, the paranoia, the paramnesia have been forgotten, and now he can step out into the ultimate 'there', death.

The car swerves once more as my mother reaches over his lap and slams the door shut. 'Thank God,' I say. Helen tuts again, and turns up her personal stereo.

A few years later, on the Isle of Man, Cath Q. is already leaning out of the car as we screech to a halt in the lay-by: 'Come along, you,' she calls to the policeman. 'Come along. You're going to tell us if we can get through to Ballaugh before the road closes, Sid.' She obviously knows him – most people know most people on the Isle of Man – and doesn't want to kill him after all.

'If you step on it you might,' the policeman grins, clearly excited by the prospect of speeding.

So we're off again, past Cronk-y-Voddy, through Kirk Michael, past the Bishop's Court, and up towards Ballaugh. Meanwhile, my mother and I are almost crying with relief that we're not accessories to the murder of a Manx policeman. 'Come on,' says Cath to Helen. 'Go faster!'

Cath is our long-lost, adoptive first cousin, once removed. As children, the only relative we knew on the island was an 'Auntie' Molly. This is already confusing, because – as I've mentioned before – most relatives in our family were called 'auntie', except for uncles. In actual fact, Auntie Molly was my father's adoptive first cousin, being the daughter of my father's adoptive mother's sister. If you see what I mean.

Every holiday, we'd visit Auntie Molly in her house near Douglas. She'd make me play the disused piano in her front room, and I'd plonk out a Mozart sonata on yellowing keys. The notes all sounded the same, as if the instrument had forgotten the difference between C and G. At the end, she'd clap her hands and slip me a fiver. Given that the piano had musical dementia and that my Mozart memory was also rubbish, I wondered if Molly would have been as pleased, in a financially remunerative sense, if I'd played Karlheinz Stockhausen. Whatever the case, as soon as my mother discovered the crisp note I'd been paid for my crap notes, she'd try and give the former back for me. 'He doesn't want this, Molly.' No, of course I don't. How silly.

In the past, my father was close to Molly and her husband. They'd looked after him in the aftermath of his disastrous first marriage. They probably knew more than anyone else about that trauma, as well as my father's early life in general. But Molly's husband died when I was three; and Molly took her knowledge with her into a nursing home, Alzheimer's and, in 1997, her grave. By the time I knew what questions to ask about my father – by the time I knew there were questions to ask – the answers were beyond my reach.

By the mid-90s, Molly's conversation had been reduced to a merry-go-round: 'Nice place this. The last home was horrid, got closed down. My son lives in Jamaica now. Can't visit much. Your father, you know, he . . . Nice place this. The last home was horrid, got closed down. My son lives in Jamaica now. Can't visit much. Your father, you know, he . . . Nice place this,' and so on, never filling in the gap after 'Your father, you know, he . . .' He what?!?

Auntie Molly is buried in a beautiful graveyard near Douglas. The grasses are overgrown, and bees, hoverflies, butterflies are everywhere, hovering above graves like multicoloured memories. But they're just teasing me. They can't answer direct questions about my father any more than Molly could when she was in the nursing home. Much like her, all they can do is repeat the same fluttery phrases or buzzing noises over and again.

Giving up on the Red Admirals and Camberwell Beauties above Molly's grave, I wrote to her son R., in Jamaica. Dear R., do you remember anything about my father, anything about his links with the Isle of Man, anything at all? R. wasn't interested in my interest, though, and it was his wife who wrote back:

As regards your request, we can't help much. We spend very little time on the Isle of Man and hardly know anyone there. The only parent we have there is my mother who is 96 and lives in a home. She doesn't recognize my voice on the phone any more . . . Sorry we cannot be more helpful.

R.'s wife did, however, give me the name and address of someone who might be able to help. I wrote to this someone next. She knew nothing, but gave me the name and address of someone else. Someone else was friendly, but knew nothing too, and a lengthy phone call got me a pleasant nowhere. Finally, after a long list of someones who knew nothing, I was given the address of someone called E. H. She sounded prom-ising, so I sent her a letter. I was writing to the dead, though: E. H. had died in an immolation of osteoporosis three years before. The letter languished on the dead woman's 'welcome' mat until it was picked up by her daughter. She thought it was an imaginative scam. Just in case it wasn't, she checked with her surviving aunt, Catherine Q., sister of E. H.: 'John Taylor. Hmm. John Taylor . . . Oh, you mean Jackie! Jackie Taylor.' Another name, another identity. 'Jackie Taylor, never thought I'd hear that name again.' And, one Sunday afternoon, Cath Q. rang me up to tell me about her moment of recognition.

Suddenly, the someones I'd been talking to, whom I didn't

know, who didn't know me, who knew nothing about my
father, became names I recognized and could hang on a family
tree. E. H., it turned out, was my adoptive first cousin, once
removed, being the daughter of my father's adoptive mother's
sister. Simple as that. Likewise, E. H.'s daughter is my adoptive
second cousin, being granddaughter of my father's adoptive
mother's sister. Cath Q., as I say, is my adoptive first cousin
once removed. And Molly's son, R., is an adoptive second
cousin, being son of my adoptive first cousin once removed,
Molly. I'd try and draw a family tree to explain it better – but,
what with my father's real family (both sides), my father's adoptive family (both sides), my father's own first family, my father's
second family (us), the faux-aunties who may be friends, and, of
course, my mother's family (both sides), it'd have to be on a
multi-dimensional plane. I could produce a pop-up version of
this book; only then might it be possible to model my family
properly.

A pop-up book might also be the best way to simulate our first
meeting with Cath. Pull a tab and see how the car wheels leave
the road as we bounce over Ballaugh's humpback bridge. Pull
another tab, and see Cath's hair stand on end, her hands clap
with delight. Pull a final tab and see us skidding off the main
road.

   The police seal the road behind us. Crowds are gathering.
The buzzing of bikes is audible from a distance. We stop outside
a whitewashed house, overshadowed by a huge Three Legs of
Man flag. The door opens and cats and cousins pour out to
greet us. My adoptive first cousin once removed, Cath, is still
trembling from the journey, as I help her out of the car: 'Phew,
what a ride.'

   Soon, we're sitting awkwardly round a table of party-size

sausage rolls, cheese and pineapple on sticks, and crustless egg-and-cress sandwiches. There's E. H.'s daughter (the one who found the letter), her husband and her brother; it turns out they're all second cousins. My mother sits stiffly in the corner, nibbling a quarter-sandwich. Helen looks bored. I'm recovering from carsickness. Only Cath looks at ease in this peculiar family reunion, this one-generation-late reunion, this reunion of cousins and pseudo-aunts who never met in the first place. Cath is enjoying herself, capriciously doling out fragments of the past with the cheese sticks.

'Pass the tongue sandwiches, will you? The last time I saw Jackie, by the by, was 1945. Never saw him again. The conversation we had that last time was funny. Hmm, yes, funny.' She laughs to herself, takes a bite of a sandwich, and turns to the hostess: 'Good tongue, this. Did you get it from the butcher's in Kirk Michael's?'

'Yes, Auntie.'

'Good butcher's that. You can't get quality tongue in Ballasalla these days. Co-op's pretty poor.'

'And . . .?' I ask.

'And what, dear?'

'And the last time you met my father?' Pause. Cath is busy buttering a slice of bread. 'In 1945? You said it was funny. The conversation you had.'

'Oh, yes, it was 1945. We didn't see him again. When I got married, we moved away from the island for a long time.'

I know this already, and want to get back to 1945: 'What happened when you saw him?'

'Who?'

'Jackie. My dad.'

'What about him?'

I can't help wondering how deliberate this obtuseness is on

her part. She's the centre of attention because she's in control of the knowledge, and she's not intending on giving up that privilege too quickly – if ever. She's not senile by any stretch of the imagination: dementia is the opposite of what she is, what she's doing. Dementia is an incontinence of memory; Cath, by contrast, is in total control of the past, teasing us with it, dispensing it in bits and pieces when she sees fit. Here is a woman who is enjoying old age, enjoying the privileges it brings – privileges which include sole proprietorship of the distant past. When she leaves the room to go to the toilet, moaning about her ageing joints, one of the others whispers to me: 'Don't listen to her groans. She's got weller as she's got older. She'll be bright as a button by the time she's a hundred.'

She sits back down. 'What happened when you last saw my dad in 1945?'

'Oh, that. He was seventeenish then. Funny thing. He told me, "You know what, Cath, when I'm older, I'm never going to get married. It's a waste of time from what I can see."'

'What irony,' exclaims my mother, forcing a laugh through the quiche.

'It was only three years afterwards that he married for the first time, wasn't it? I remember something about the Taylors and Molly not approving. I never saw Jackie again. I didn't know he got married a second time.'

It's a tiny fragment, but at least I've discovered one person who remembers my father from his early life. We talk for a few minutes about my job, the book, the TT, the Manx cheese and biscuits. During this time, Cath is silent, no doubt mulling over what historical fragment to break off and divide amongst her audience next – like Christ at the Feeding of the Five Thousand, but with Jacob's Crackers instead of loaves, crab sandwiches instead of fishes, and my father's past instead of parables. Suddenly, she interrupts her nephew mid-sentence:

'I never saw Jackie again. But my sister, E. H., did.'

'I thought he only kept in touch with Molly.'

'It must have been the mid-1970s. I got a phone call from her one day. She said, "You'll never guess who's been to visit this afternoon, Cath," and I said, "No, who?" and she said, "You'll never guess," and I said, "I can't," and she said, "Someone from a long time ago," and I said, "Who?," and she said, "Jackie Taylor," and I said, "Gosh, after all those years," and she said, "After all these years."'

We're perched on the edge of our chairs by this point, almost bobbing up and down, willing the story to continue. Cath's pause goes on for so long, though, that we realize she's reached the end of the anecdote. Our bobbing grinds to an anticlimactic halt. I say, 'Oh,' and there's another pause.

But my mother is thinking. 'The mid-70s. I remember. We were on holiday here. One afternoon, out of nowhere, Dad said to me, "I'm going looking for people." He said he wanted to find some of the family he'd lost touch with. He took our first son, Robin, and they disappeared for hours. Odd, really: when he came back, he never told me he'd found anyone. Just talked about a higgledy-piggledy bookshop they'd stumbled across in the fog, under the Witches' Mountain – you know, the one near St John's, in the middle of the island. Typical Dad that, ending up in a bookshop. And typical, too, that he didn't mention the important part of the day, that he'd found your sister, his cousin.'

Years later, my father used to drive us round and round the Witches' Mountain, trying to rediscover that higgledy-piggledy bookshop. Trying, that is, to find the bookshop again, not the relatives. My father found it far easier to keep in touch with books than he did with family members. There are so many people he lost for long periods of his life, or forever: most of his relatives on the Isle of Man, his sisters, nieces and nephews from Oldham, his first son and daughter, his 'real' father, the best man at his second wedding, all his friends and colleagues. And finally there was me: like all those others, I was lost and forgotten, in a Caprasian sense. It's almost *too* easy to trace a continuity between my father's life-long tendency to mislay loved ones, and the forgetting illnesses of his last years. Misplacing family and friends became an ingrained habit his brain turned into a disease.

The symptoms and causes of his proto-dementia, proto-Capgras are rather common. My father was never a great letter-writer and, like many men, he saw the phone as an unpleasant necessity to be passed to someone else as soon as possible: 'Hello?' 'Hello, Dad.' 'Hello.' 'How are you?' 'I'll get Mum. Darling? It's Jonathan, I think.' Presumably, he felt Mum could answer how he was better than he could himself.

But there are lots of people who aren't good on the phone and who don't write letters. That doesn't mean they lose family members at the astonishing rate my father did. On a psychological level, perhaps this propensity to misplace loved ones was a symptom of his first and terribly premature parting at the age of three – when his mother died, and he was gradually given away, bit by bit, piece by piece, to his adoptive-parents-to-be, the Taylors. Perhaps this first agony lurked beneath everything, undermining his ability to maintain permanent relationships, making subsequent partings seem all too easy.

Partings were second nature to my father. He seems to have led a picaresque, Don Juan-becomes-Don Quixote kind of life, drifting from episode to episode without taking as much as a wife, a son or a Sancho Panza with him. When he moved in with my mother he brought with him one tiny suitcase containing two shirts, a photo of his younger self and an old fork. Everything else and everybody else were left behind, in the previous episode. Perhaps this kind of thing was more common in the past. Given world wars, great depressions, social mobility, disease, starvation, it might be the case that Europeans from the first half of the twentieth century tended to have more picaresque, episodic, adventurous lives than we do.

My father reached adulthood as the Second World War was ending; he was part of that moment when anything seemed possible, when many people thought we might build Jerusalem in England's green and pleasant land – to quote the hymn we sang at his funeral. He was part of that ambitious generation which tried to leave the past behind; that generation which voted in Clement Attlee's government, which set up the Welfare State and the NHS, which sought a classless society. He rose out of the slums of Oldham to be the first in his family to go to university. He became a teacher, shot up the career ladder and attained a headmastership.

But he also embodied the failures and defeats of post-war utopianism. Like everyone else, he compromised the utopian ideal of getting rid of classes, allowing it to morph into the more personal ambition of rising between classes. In his success in this respect, he was haunted by terrible insecurity: he hoarded up money against disaster; he had recurrent mental problems and breakdowns; he detected class prejudice everywhere (often with justification); his children seemed from an alien world; and, finally, there was illness, old age and death waiting at the end. One of the biggest costs was the past. In his social mobility, in his quest for middle-class security, he kept leaving people from the past behind. Kept leaving love behind. With each episode of his life, he 'rose' a step higher, so that each episode invalidated the last. Each episode was effaced by the next one, and that included the people involved.

After his last visit to E. H. in the 70s, my father's Manx family was largely effaced. So was the higgledy-piggledy book-shop, though he did at least try to find that again. 'I suppose you can't accidentally stumble across something a second time,' he'd sigh. 'There are Manx fairy tales about things appearing and disappearing in the island's mist. They say that whenever the queen comes to visit, the island hides itself from her with a thick fog. We got lost in the mists by the Witches' Mountain and stumbled across the higgledy-piggledy bookshop. To find it again, we'd have to get lost in the same fog. Suddenly, it'd be there.'

Settling down into an armchair and a large sherry, later that evening Cath says, 'The first time I met your father, he must have been seven. That'd make it 1935. Jackie and the Taylors would come over on holiday for Wakes Week – the holidays the cotton workers had. My mother and her two sisters – including Maggie Taylor, your dad's adoptive mum – they'd arranged to meet up in Yates's Wine Lodge in Douglas. It was my mother's birthday. They wouldn't let me in. I was young back then. Auntie Maggie said, there's Jackie over there, in the boating pool on the prom. Go and introduce yourself and play with him, whilst we have a couple of drinks. So, for an hour or two, I paddled with Jackie and sank his model yacht. Ha ha.'

She's told me this before, but I can't interrupt a memory I already love. Fifty years later, my dad used to take me to sail my model yacht on this same boating pool – the one in the sunken gardens on Loch Promenade, Douglas. After a while, he'd become restless, snapping: 'You're not doing it right. You'll sink it.' He'd self-righteously take over from me, setting the rudder and sails himself. Lowering it back into the water, watching it catch the wind and glide away, he'd smile dreamily when he thought no one was looking.

The boating pool was more or less deserted by the time I came to sail my boat on it in the 1970s. In 1935, though, it was one of the prom's main attractions. I'm told that there'd often be dozens of children round it, floating a convoy of white yachts and clockwork speedboats. Now and then, a boy would be sure to provide further entertainment by falling in, face first. The crowd of children-captains would send up a cheer whenever this occurred.

You can't reanimate memories like this, and the cheers were reduced to one by the time I tried to fall in, at the age of ten. Even later, in the late 1990s, my elder sister bought my father a model yacht. But, as with the higgledy-piggledy bookshop, we drove round for hours, unable to find the boating pool again. Finally, we realized it had been concreted over. Not much call for boating pools nowadays.

'I remember the boating pool, I just don't remember Jackie Taylor,' says one of the other cousins, when Cath has finished her story. Nods go round the room: apart from Cath, they all share a concrete space where my father should have been. 'I even remember visiting the Taylors, Auntie Maggie and Uncle Jim, in Castletown – but not Jackie.'

'Do you remember the tortoise, though?'

'Of course I do.' Jackie was one thing, but how could one not remember the tortoise?

'You mean the Taylor tortoise?'

'Yes.'

'I remember him too. Huge, he was.' He evidently loomed larger than my father. 'Lived in the back garden of their house on Springfield Terrace.'

'I went round to the Taylors' house when I was seventeen.

When I got there, they told me to "go and play with the tortoise round the back". I'd never seen one before. Very exciting.'

'They always said that to me too: "Go and play with the tortoise round the back."'

I ask everyone what the tortoise's name was, but that memory has gone the way of Jackie Taylor. Afterwards, I try and find out what happened to the tortoise after his keepers, Maggie and James Taylor, died. Tortoises can live for 150 years, so he's probably strolling around somewhere as I speak, mulling over his memories of 'playing' with my father – memories he keeps under his shell. A tortoise would be a real artefact, something hard I could touch from the lost past. There are so few of such artefacts left, which can tell me with Cath that, 'Yes, your father was alive. He did exist before Parkinson's, before you were born. He was this person, not that person, and his history was this history, not that history.' Cath is one of very few people who can tell me these things, who can tell me she remembers my father when he was young. The others here have only indirect memories; unlike Cath, the second cousins have only second-hand memories of a tortoise who might have memories of my father.

And then I get worried that I'm going mad: if I'm searching for the Taylors' tortoise, why stop there? Why not try and find the tortoise's offspring?

As I've mentioned before, Oliver Sacks says that Parkinsonism is about a loss of representative and socially accepted kinds of scale. Thus, the sufferer often performs functions on a much larger or smaller scale than is 'normal' – for example, repeating things a thousand times or writing in a miniscule hand. Sacks comes up with a Chaos Theory of Parkinson's. With both Chaos Theory and Parkinson's, he says, tiny causes can blow up into huge effects. It's impossible, for example, to achieve the ideal dosage of levodopa for sufferers, because an almost infinitely small difference in quantity can have a dramatic effect. Likewise, other, seemingly minute factors contribute to the drug's efficacy as well: a fluttering finger may spiral into a bodily tornado, a breeze through the curtains might cause a bone-shattering fall. I have seen it happen.

To write a family history of someone's Parkinson's, then, is also to write an impossible, Parkinsonian kind of history, where breezes, fluttering fingers, butterflies, tortoises, micro-battles and minute changes in medication are of the utmost importance. In writing such a history, the historian must him- or herself necessarily become infected with Parkinsonism and its loss of any 'normal' sense of scale.

That loss of scale works both ways, of course. Not only does the Parkinsonian historian get caught up in tracing the effects of minute causes on the individual case; he or she also needs to trace the effects of worldwide events on the apparently-insignificant-to-anyone-else subject of the study. In particular, I'm thinking here of the Second World War, and its effect on my father's holidays on the Isle of Man. I ask Cath: 'Did my father stop coming to the island during the war, between when he was about eleven and seventeen? Do you remember seeing him then?'

'Why?' asks Cath. What a peculiar non-answer.

'Wasn't the island sealed off from visitors?'

'Why?'

'Because parts of it were turned into some kind of prison camp.'

'That's right.'

'So he couldn't have come over?'

'I suppose not.'

'But you did say something about Saturday nights, going with him on the trams to the dances in Douglas?'

'Yes, I did.'

'But that wasn't during the war years?'

'It couldn't have been if the island was sealed off, could it?'

My repertoire of available questions exhausted, I sip my sherry, feeling that I don't know any more than I did two minutes before; I've just had my own implied answers repeated back at me. And I think, why should I be surprised at this? She's the same generation as my father and others who were happy to live and die amongst half-truths, mists, myths and forged birth certificates. What is this self-helpish urge my generation has to say everything, to confess all, except a reaction against a previous generation happy to say very little?

Once back in our holiday flat, I flick through an old book of my father's. It's called *Island of Barbed Wire* by Connery Chappell, and it tells the story of the Isle of Man during the Second World War. I find that my assumptions and Cath's echolalic responses were wrong – that my father might well have had holidays on the island during the war years. Despite a slump at the start of the war, the number of holiday-makers soon picked up again. In summer 1941, there were so many tourists that the ships had to leave people behind. Maybe Cath can't remember any of this. Or maybe, there are some memories, big or small, that she doesn't feel the need to reveal – memories destined to turn into butterflies in overgrown graveyards.

If, as I think probable, my father *did* visit the island during the war years, the surreality of the place must have made his childhood memories far more complex than my own. Large sections of Douglas's promenade, Onchan, Port St Mary with its black sands, Peel with its fish-and-chip shops, Laxey with its waterwheel, Port Erin with its jellyfish-infested beach – all of these places were also infested with barbed wire. This was because large areas were being used as camps to intern thousands of 'enemy aliens'. At one point, there were as many as 14,000 people sent on compulsory holidays to the island. These included many 'enemy aliens' who were neither enemies nor aliens; the camps indiscriminately mixed together Jews and Nazis, blackshirts and Anglo-Italians who owned restaurants in Stockport.

My father would have seen some of this as a boy, whilst sailing his yacht in Douglas boating pool. A few yards away, opposite the pool, were the fences, the barbed wire and the internees staring out from Metropole Camp. Shut up behind the wire in requisitioned hotels – a kind of bizarre, Orwellian Butlin's – the internees could shout self-righteously at my father: 'You're not doing it right! You'll sink it!' But they were absolutely excluded from taking over.

It's possible my father would have heard other sounds from the camps as well. Marching and crying, no doubt; but also singing, debating, Schubert's *Death and the Maiden* Quartet. Two of the founding members of the Amadeus Quartet were interned in the Douglas camp, as well as many other musicians who put on concerts. There were also well-known artists and painters such as Kurt Schwitters, writers, doctors, philosophers . . . and my father just beyond them, sailing his model yacht, obliviously surrounded by other histories.

There comes a moment, though, when you grow up and realize that these other histories aren't oblivious to you and your yacht – when you realize they aren't always behind a barbed wire, excluded from taking over. J. B. Priestley tells us he experienced such a moment of 'romantic recognition' in 1914, when he glimpsed the elderly Empress Eugenie of France: 'Young and loutish as I was in those days, nevertheless there flared about me then, most delightfully, all the splendour and idiocy of the Second Empire, and I knew that we, every man Jack of us, were in history, and knew it once and for all.' I can't tell you when my father's moment of romantic recognition was; perhaps National Service, a few years after he'd stopped sailing his yacht on Loch Promenade. Mine was when I realized that The Towers Hotel in Port Erin, Isle of Man – where we'd spent many holidays when I was young, where we'd gone round and round in the revolving doors till we were sick, where we'd cheated other children at 'Behind the Curtains' on the lawn, where I'd given my father a tiny boat in a bottle for his fifty-second birthday present, where we'd stayed one last time in the late 1980s, and the place was suddenly shabby and empty, where now there's only concrete, and I can only return to the hotel in dreams – when I realized that this pebble-dashed, Manx Manderley had been used in the Second World War to house pro-Nazi couples.

There are many places on the island which are now criss-crossed with other meanings, other people's histories – places where once there had only been my simple history of boating pools and revolving doors. Where once there was Castletown beach and fossil combing, now there are long-lost Taylors, tortoises, holidays infected with Parkinson's, schools Dad never went to. Where once there was Peel, sandcastles and fish-and-chip shops, now there are also internees, prison riots, underground tunnels. Where once there was just us, playing jellyfish in the *Lady of Mann*'s ropes, now we are haunted by previous children from my father's first marriage, who also played in ships' ropes . . . who also bet on which boat would take them on holiday . . . who also flew kites at the Point of Ayre . . . who also saw the ugly walrus at the wildlife park . . .

who also turned the waterwheel of the old carousel at Silverdale . . . just as my father had done before them.

Where once there was a windswept space we didn't know, now there is Malew Church cemetery, a legendary vampire, my father's grave.

I first visited Malew Church cemetery on a holiday in 1993, when my mother told my sister and I that we were going for a 'short detour'. My father wriggled in the passenger seat and said nothing. I thought we were on our way to laugh at the walrus in the zoo. But my mother pulled up next to a boarded-up church in the middle of nowhere. She turned off the engine, sat for a moment with her hands on the steering wheel, stared in front, and announced: 'I've brought you here because this is where we will be buried' – as if it were happening today. 'Somewhere here is Daddy's mother's grave. That's where Daddy and I will be buried in the future, when we both die.' What had been a blank space on the map was suddenly being coloured in.

My elder sister Karen tried to stop my mother's macabre matter-of-factness. She said: 'This is horrid,' and put her hands over her ears. I nodded politely and thought about lunch.

'You need to know that here is going to be important. It's bound to happen some time that we die. The arrangements have been made beforehand, so it'll be easier for you. Our bodies will come over by boat and be buried here.' I wondered if Dad had even started bets on which boat it would be.

As if it were an everyday stretching-legs stop, we climbed out of the car and had a look around. Only my sister stayed put. In particular, we were looking for my father's adoptive mother's grave – 'plot no. H24 in the 1935 yard' according to the records. My father had finally got round to tracing it, thirty years after her death. One might wonder why it'd taken him thirty years to hunt it out, given how close they were. I suppose he found the dead as easy to lose touch with as the living. Eventually, after walking to and fro for half an hour, we found plot no. H24, an anonymous lump between two well-kept graves.

Since then, a stone has been put there. It's covered with tiny fossils, like the ones we used to find on Castletown beach. It reads: 'In Loving Memory Margaret Alice Taylor 1881–1963 and John Taylor 1928–2001.' The stone has a space reserved at the bottom for a future 'and' – the dreadful future my mother threatened in 1993.

In between 1993 and the future, there was another morning, in November 2001, when we returned to Malew Church cemetery. As my mother had predicted, everything had been arranged beforehand. We came over by boat the night before – the *Lady of Mann*, as it happened, though Dad wasn't collecting winnings. It was dark queuing at Heysham Port, and the hearse taking my father over was a hundred yards in front. He always liked being first on. Once boarded, we went to the restaurant for a snack, whilst he stayed in the coffin, in the hearse, down on the car-deck. It was a strange feeling, knowing he was there on the boat, yet not seeing him – as though we weren't on speaking terms any more.

The burial service was the next morning. We'd already had a funeral service in Stoke, so this was just the ashes-to-ashes, dust-to-dust horror, without the friends or sherry to leaven it. After a short service and tuneless singing, we wandered outside. My mother said to me, 'I don't want him put in the ground.' We stared down at a wooden lid in plot no. H24. The vicar threw some earth on top of it. My mother tossed a rose on it. I thought God had been replaced by an evil impostor.

And the vampire? Where does the legendary vampire come into the story? According to local folklore and church tours, the grave next to the wall and to the right of the main gate is a vampire's grave, easy to spot because it's surrounded by chains. It's the resting place of one Mr Matthew Hassall, who seems to have committed suicide in October 1854. As a suicide, his body couldn't be *carried* over consecrated ground. This would normally mean burial in unconsecrated ground, or at a crossroads. In Mr Hassall's case, though, the locals found a cunning way to circumvent the prohibition. They dug his grave next to the cemetery wall, and threw his corpse into it from the unconsecrated field beyond. He must have been popular for people to go to all that trouble.

I bet my father would be rather pleased to know he's sharing his final resting place with a vampire. It would give him something to talk about. If we'd visited Malew Church cemetery pre-Parkinson's, I can just imagine my father relating the folk tale to us, rubbing his hands together with relish. He was one of those fathers who liked to tell you things he knew and you didn't. He liked to 'impart knowledge,' in the form of facts, statistics and, indeed, mild horror stories (when he thought Mum wasn't listening). Knowledge to him was a matter of facts, fragments, snippets, encyclopaedia entries: 'Did you know miners used to take canaries down with them to detect methane?' 'Did you know when you're looking at the Pole Star, you're looking back 500 years into the past?' 'Did you know those first four notes of Beethoven's Fifth are fate knocking at the door?' I thought – and still, on one level, like to believe – that if you strung all my father's 'Did you knows?' together, you'd get the sum total of human knowledge, in a set of green encyclopaedias. As he became ill, though, the fragments got more fragmentary, the snippets more snippety, the encyclopaedia entries dated and repetitive, to the point that we could always pre-empt his 'Did you knows?' with 'Yesses'.

In the case of Malew Church cemetery, he would have whispered to us about the vampire whilst my mother was picking heathers, out of earshot: 'Did you know I share my final resting place with a revenant?' He would have laughed and embellished some of the toothy details. My mother would have overheard and stopped him short: 'Darling! They don't want to hear about that kind of thing.' 'Yes we do.' 'No they don't. It's horrid.'

Oldham

. . . the deep, deep tragedies of infancy, as when the child's hands were unlinked for ever from his mother's neck, or his lips for ever from his sister's kisses, these remain lurking below all, and these lurk to the last.

(Thomas De Quincey, *Suspiria de Profundis*)

My father as a boy of about six

My earliest memory: rushing in from the cold, running upstairs, forgetting that my dad's sister, Auntie Mildred, and her husband are staying in my bedroom, barging in and finding my auntie on the verge of taking off a vast bra. She's not in the least perturbed by my intrusion, and carries on. The bra slips to the floor, and mammoth breasts spill out – down her chest, down her legs, on to the floor, across the floor, till they push me out of the room. Like magic porridge, the breasts grow and grow. Riding on soft flesh, I'm carried downstairs and into the garden. In the street, I wave at passers-by. Some laugh and climb aboard. My father shouts at me to stop this nonsense. But the breasts are unstoppable, and soon they've occupied the whole of south Stoke.

You can say it's a dream – a Freudian field day of a dream – but that's not how I experienced it at the time. For years afterwards, I believed that it had happened, that the mammaries were memories. It's like many of my earliest memories, where realities merge with dreams. No doubt, if I develop dementia when I'm older, this will happen again. But I suppose if the worst I get are hallucinations of ever-expanding breasts, it won't be so bad.

Many memories of my father's family mix the past up with dreams. This is because there were twelve years, between childhood and the late 1990s, when I didn't see this side of the family. Memories of them became distant, jumbled with childhood dreams and myths. My father was too busy having nervous breakdowns, my mother too busy dealing with his breakdowns, to visit Oldham or Llandudno where his sisters lived. Besides which, my father got the heebie-jeebies just from watching

Coronation Street, let alone visiting Greater Manchester. As soon as the dreaded soap's title music started, he'd squeeze his eyes shut and shout: 'You know I can't stand it! You know those terraces make me remember things – things I don't want to remember! You've put it on on purpose, haven't you? Turn it off! Offoffoff!' He was convinced his mother-in-law was a fan of *Coronation Street* just to spite him: 'She has it on whenever I'm visiting. Probably never watches it otherwise.' Given that this was the effect on him of a TV-version of Lancashire, there was no knowing what he might do if confronted with the real thing. So we gradually stopped going.

From the age of twelve onwards, I saw Auntie Mildred only twice more. By the time I realized that there was a history here I wanted to know, it had been turned to ash. Before then, I'd been too busy being a teenager to wonder about – let alone visit – lost aunties. Teenagedom is as much about forgetting as old age, except that it's a *willed* dementia. With beer, drugs and sex, the teenager actively seeks to wipe consciousness clean of aunties and history. You might say it's the besetting sin of our age, the belief in teenagedom at the expense of older genera-tions, aunties, history. You only have to go to nightclubs to realize that even fifty-somethings want to return to the demen-tia of youth. For me, this willed dementia has meant the irretrievable loss of a dozen histories.

Not that Auntie Mildred would necessarily have told the 'truth' if I'd known there were things worth asking about. Exaggerating, fictionalizing, downright fibbing run in the family, as much as knobbly knees. Auntie Mildred's stories, for example, were as grand as her chest. She invented contradic-tory family genealogies, usually in order to 'Welshify' our lineage. She invented celebrity relations: I still don't know for sure if actress Dora Bryan is some kind of cousin; and I could never quite pin down what our connection was with the composer William Walton. And Mildred's particular forte was inventing illnesses from which she and her husband were suffering. As a child, I remember feeling queasy after meals spent hearing case histories of her miscarriages, his missing lung, her elephantiasis, and so on. On these occasions, I can only hope that Mildred *was* exaggerating, that some of the illnesses were fictional.

Unfortunately, the cancer which killed Mildred in May 2001 was all too real. At her funeral service, the vicar kept getting her name wrong. He called her 'Millicent', even whilst eulogizing about her 'ballroom-dancing classes for the elderly'. 'Millicent,' he said, 'was a big lady with a big personality and nimble feet.' He said he'd got to know 'Millicent' or – as he liked to call her – 'Millie' very well over the years. Perhaps he had, but this wasn't Millicent he was cremating. Had he checked the coffin, I wondered?

Not being familiar with what the 'done thing' is in a case of mistaken identity at a funeral, no one in the congregation opened their mouths. No one said, 'Excuse me, are we in the right place?', 'Excuse me, are you in the right place?' or 'Is the corpse in the right place?' Instead, we trooped out of the chapel in orderly fashion, shaking the vicar's hand and agreeing that Millicent's death was a real shame. Even my elder sister, who complains about everything whenever possible, said nothing.

On the way home, I asked her why. She explained that, knowing Auntie Mildred, knowing the family's propensity for embellishment, it had struck her that, well, y'know, there's the slightest possibility that Mildred might actually, for some reason known to herself, have told everyone at the ballroom-dancing classes that her name *was* Millicent. Perhaps she'd created a whole history for herself ('I'm related not only to Dora Bryan and William Walton, but also most famous people from Wales you can mention'). In which case, it was hardly the vicar's fault. Stories, invented identities, casual lies are now easier to believe than a vicar making a thoughtless mistake.

The wake was held at Mildred's flat in Llandudno. I chatted away the afternoon with cousins whom I hadn't seen for years, and wouldn't have recognized on the street. After an hour or two, I noticed a photograph of my brother, sisters and me, in pride of place, next to the TV. I realized that Auntie Mildred had not forgotten about us, however remiss we'd been. There are people who don't see you for years, yet the love is still there, waiting to be rediscovered – people who aren't infected with the dementia of youth. My Auntie Mildred stored up teddy bears against the moment we'd remember her. Honestly, I was about to visit her in hospital the day she died. Honestly.

Mildred had always wanted children, but her own had been born dead. So she spoilt her nephews and nieces instead, with rocking horses, electric trains and sets of Dickens. She even managed to spoil us from the grave. In her flat, amongst hundreds of boxes of junk and teddy bears, there was a set of 100 CDs, still in wrappers. One of my cousins offered it to me: 'Mildred probably bought it thinking of you. She was waiting for a visit to give it you. You're the one who likes this classical stuff.'

And I think of the last conversation I had with Auntie Mildred. It was a Christmas Day phone call, five months before she died. She was asking me what I'd had for Christmas, how university was, whether or not I was courting, etc. Suddenly, she interrupted herself, and asked in her Greater-Mancunian-but-trying-to-be-Welsh sing-song: 'More to the point, what Tchaikovsky symphony do you like best?'

'I don't know. Gosh. The *Pathétique?*'

'Ah, the Sixth. Sad, that one, very B minor. Your Auntie Annie loved that best. We used to argue about it.'

'Which do you like best?'

'The Fourth. I saw it in the Free Trade Hall. Your father liked the Fourth too. Annie was funny that way, with her *Pathétique* and all. You must be like her.'

'Oh,' I yawn, sick of the phone. The last conversation I ever have with my auntie is over.

It's fashionable now to say that 'canonical art' and artists are elitist, that they 'marginalize the working classes', blah blah. Like teenagers, you can try and rub out history, pretend you know better than those writers and composers; you can be what my father called an 'inverted snob' to the snobbishness of the past. But then you have to deal with the fact that many of the 'working classes' of my father's generation hunted out Tchaikovsky, Dickens, Shakespeare and Beethoven. You can say they were 'misled' by a 'false consciousness', but that still implies you know better than them. They didn't want to read Marx and Lenin, or, on the other hand, to listen to George Formby and Vera Lynn – or not all the time, anyway. They had arguments about the relative merits of Tchaikovsky's Fourth or Sixth symphonies, after hearing them played by the Hallé Orchestra under Sir John Barbirolli.

By trying to dismantle the canon, by making everything relative, by deciding that Tchaikovsky and Shakespeare aren't worth the effort, all our generation has done is kick away the autodidact's ladder – that ladder which was so valued by the generation reaching adulthood in the war. Suddenly, they could read Shakespeare, afford Tchaikovsky concerts, even (if they were lucky like my father) go to university and study Shakespeare. But that autodidactic generation is over. Our generation has trampled on such opportunities. And it has done so for the present, the future and even the past, retrospectively speaking, by declaring it wasn't worth it anyway. Forget about the past, says the dementia of youth.

But perhaps I'm being unfair to dementia. My father's dementia wiped out the present far more than it did the past. Perhaps 'retrograde amnesia' is a better metaphor for what I'm talking about. It's amnesiacs, not people with dementia, who live wholly in the present moment, unable to recollect the recent past.

In the blackest moments of his disease, I still assumed that, somewhere in his mind, the past was stored away, ready to be rediscovered – like the CDs in Mildred's flat. Thomas De Quincey says that 'There is no such thing as forgetting possible to the mind.' And I'm sure I wasn't alone in sharing De Quincey's belief. I'm sure it's what most people believe when confronted with so-called 'memory *loss*' in loved ones. To 'lose' something doesn't necessarily mean it's been destroyed. A book can be lost in a library by being put on the wrong shelf. A teddy bear can be lost in a flat simply because it hasn't been collected yet.

Parkinson's is a disease of neurotransmitters, of the chemicals which facilitate communication *between* cells. So I liked to believe – whether or not it was neurologically correct – that the brain cells themselves, and the memories they embodied, were still intact. They were just isolated, unable to communicate with one another. I believed that, at some level, my father remembered his sister Mildred, as she remembered us. He at least didn't have retrograde amnesia.

That was confirmed by something which happened on our return to Stoke, following Auntie Mildred's funeral. There was no way my father could have come with us: he'd only recently emerged from hospital, after weeks of horror, surgery and supposed 'convalescence'. He had nearly died, there was no doubt about that, but had eventually recovered enough to be wheeled to freedom. Then, I had a phone call to tell me that Auntie Mildred had been taken to hospital. Like the figures on Swiss clocks, one sibling comes out, another goes in. Except this time, the latter didn't come out again.

When we returned home after the funeral, my father was shaking, sitting up, falling back, shaking, crossing legs, uncrossing legs, pulling trouser legs up, knocking for help, sitting up, falling back. We thought he hadn't understood our whispered 'code' about the funeral (Mum: 'How was the "wedding" service?' Me: 'It was terrible – the vicar got the bride's name wrong. He thought M. was for Millicent'). But my father was having none of this. As I pushed him from the living room towards tea, I saw a moment when I could have stopped his falling. His feet caught beneath the wheelchair. He rolled slowly forwards. His face hit the floor with a crack. The blood flowed from under him, making butterfly patterns on the floor.

Three of us managed to haul him up, into the wheelchair, and from there back to the living room. His nose was broken, and bruises were spreading across his face. His eyes were clenched shut, his hands shaking, and he was crying. I wondered if I'd seen him cry before. My sister snapped his nose back into place, saying that Accident and Emergency could only make him worse.

'He knew what we were talking about,' said my mother. 'I don't know how, but he picked up it was Mildred's funeral, and he'd missed it.' After years of devastating 'memory loss', a life-and-death operation, weeks of hospitalization – after all this, my father remembered his sister. And he remembered her in the only way he had left – through his Parkinsonian symptoms, through the shaking, fidgeting, falling. The broken nose proves to me that memory is mislaid, not destroyed; that dementia isn't amnesia.

Perhaps that's also the (polite) way to see my father's propensity to lose touch with people when he was *compos mentis*: not forgotten, mislaid. In these terms, he 'mislaid' Mildred for many years, as he did all his relatives from Oldham. Between 1944 and December 1966 – between, that is, my father's sixteenth birthday and second marriage – his three sisters, Annie, Mildred and Edith, didn't hear from him. My Auntie Edith says, 'I didn't lay me eyes on him after one evening when I were nineteen. I gave him a bronze medal I'd won for a dancing contest, as a keepsake – as if I knew I wouldn't see him for years.'

Twenty-two years later, the sisters finally managed to trace their brother. According to Mildred, she and Annie turned up on my parents' wedding day, out of the blue. Edith – the only sibling still alive – says she couldn't go to the wedding because she was ill. A couple of weeks later, my father and his new wife drove up to Oldham to visit her. Edith was excited, of course, as were her children. It had been a protracted build-up: for years, a week hadn't gone by without her telling them about a lost uncle 'who's somewhere being a *teacher*. A *schoolteacher* no less.'

One of Edith's daughters was less than impressed, however, by the prospect of a visit from a schoolteacher: 'It's like an 'ouse inspection. He'll want to see me exercise book. He'll inspect it and find blank pages where the homework should be.' She was worked up further by being told she had to be polite. Best Sunday accent for best Sunday people: 'Everyone says 'is new wife speaks like the queen.'

As well as enjoining politeness, Edith prepared her children for the visitors by listing various subjects which should *not* be mentioned: 1. previous marriages; 2. previous wives; 3. children

from previous marriages 'who are in care, so it's a sensitive subject'; 4. divorces; 5. most other things. Best to stay quiet. Of
these injunctions, all Edith's daughter took in was that the big-
bad-homework-inspector had two children from a previous
marriage – two children who might be good to play with. Aha:
perhaps the afternoon wouldn't be a glorified lesson, after all.

But when my parents did turn up, the two children weren't
there. Edith's daughter looked round them, behind them. But
no children. Sitting in the front room with a cup of tea, she
huffed and puffed and suddenly broke into the conversation
with: 'So where *are* your children, then, eh? Locked up?'
Storming upstairs, she left the room to the silence of rattling
crockery and reddening faces.

My father, I'm sure, would never have made light of the situation. He would never have laughed and reassured his hostess,
'Don't worry, it's just a joke, she's a child, never mind.' He
wasn't one to make light of situations, this man who, later in
life, took *Coronation Street* as a personal affront.

We can laugh about it now, of course. Edith, her daughters,
my mother and I can sit round a different front room and say,
'Wasn't everyone silly, how we've changed since then, don't
worry, it was just a joke, she was a child, never mind.' In retrospect, we can ask, 'Why didn't everyone relax, ditch the
politeness, talk things through, have a laugh? Why this uptight-
ness over a schoolteacher and his wife's southern accent?' But
it's only hindsight that allows these questions. Questions like
'Why did?' and 'Why didn't?' are only conceivable in the past
tense. When the 1960s was in the present tense, I don't think
my father could have relaxed or learnt to laugh at himself. I
think he would have preferred silence and the rattling of crockery to 'talking things through'. Auntie Edith was probably right
to enjoin politeness at any cost.

And the costs were high. In the case of Edith, it prevented her ever saying what she wanted to say to my father. Between 1966 and his death, she never asked him about his adoption out of the family. She never asked him: 'Did you resent it?', never reassured him: 'You didn't miss much, our John. It were terrible in our 'ouse after you'd gone.' 'Now it's too late,' she sighs to me. 'I wish I'd said it back then. I'm sorry I didn't. But it never seemed the right chance. And I felt he didn't want to talk about the past. Unlike you, Jonathan.'

The cliché is that it's the older generation who endlessly recite stories and regrets from the past. That's not my experience, and was certainly not the case with my father. Remembering is an expensive commodity, it takes time, and my father's generation never had time to waste on anything but the here-and-now, the next hunk of bread and jam. Later on, when my father did have spare time for remembering, dementia got in the way.

Even if he hadn't had dementia, though, I can't imagine him talking frankly about the past with us. I can't imagine him laughing and exclaiming: 'Weren't we silly back then? All those years wasted on politeness. Why didn't we say what we wanted?' Herein lies the fundamental difference between, on the one hand, my father and, on the other, my generation: my father would never have laughed with a 'how silly I was, how I've changed since then'. Or, at least, not the father I knew.

The father I knew would never have recanted his politeness. He would never have talked about the past – except in the form of fictionalized fragments – let alone apologize for it. He looked forward to others apologizing, so he could say 'I told you so (even when he hadn't).' But as far as his own past was concerned, what was done was done. Yes, dementia isn't amnesia;

certainly, my father kept the past safe, stored in his memory; but this wasn't so he could revisit it with a regretful sigh.

If there has been a familial *glasnost* since a letter from the Salvation Army, this has nothing to do with my father. Rather, it's because my half-brother, Colin, looked back and decided, 'Perhaps I was wrong in the past. Perhaps Dad wasn't the Stalin I thought. Perhaps I'll contact the Salvation Army.' After years of my father's official, *Pravda*-version of history, after years of my aunties' studied politeness, here was real news. More revelations followed that first thaw. Here was a family undergoing *Perestroika*: Edith looked back in regret at her politeness; my mother looked back in anger at being 'such a mouse'.

History, I think, is made up of regrets and apologies. History wouldn't be possible without people willing to apologize, talk and laugh about past mistakes. But my father was never one of them. This, for me, is what made him the Romantic hero I can never be – his propensity for never saying sorry. He wasn't one to laugh disparagingly about his past selves; he moved unflinchingly from one episode in his life to the next, without looking back. No wonder he liked Edith Piaf and that much-misunderstood song, 'Non, je ne regrette rien'.

People with this 'je ne regrette rien' attitude are always going to seem ambivalent to us latter-day navel-gazers. As Colin knows only too well, it's easy for them to be seen as the Stalins of history, airbrushing out pasts they don't want remembered. Take my father's father's second wife – let's call her Mary G. For all their differences, I think my father's hard attitude towards the past echoes hers. I wrote to her a couple of years ago, asking for information. The letter I received back showed that, for her, the past is a list of facts, nothing else. Mary's comprehensive list of facts spanned four generations. It even included a note that 'John your dad died in November

2001' – as if I needed reminding, as if it were something to learn by rote for Trivial Pursuit. Finally, she added:

Why your dad was adopted:

Mr and Mrs Taylor wanted him so much. Your grandad gave him the chance to have a better education . . .

Your dad went to university.

He wanted to make his life as he pleased.

I think you can get any information at the London Register Office.

I hope you can make something of these notes, I am 91 yrs and not very clever at writing.

With which conclusion – which one can't help thinking a little disingenuous – she signed off. I wrote to Mary G. a second time, asking for more details. She didn't reply. 'Je ne regrette rien': the past for Mary is something kept at the 'London Register Office', not a matter for debate, or apologies. I gained a similar impression during our only meeting, at Mildred's funeral. There she sat, this nonagenarian grande dame, dominating everyone with her age, her stick and her facts: 'You're one of John's sons [not a question]. You're a university lecturer. His side of the family were the clever ones. We are not, are we, Edith [accompanied by a jab of the stick in Edith's direction]? None of us were ever clever,' she concluded with pride.

Mary G. is one of the Stalins of Edith's history. For Edith, any list of facts does nothing to erase the ultimate 'fact' that

Mary, her stepmother, has never said sorry. 'I remember Mary punching Mildred straight in the face,' declares Edith, enjoying the seventy-year-old gossip. 'She used to give Mildred a right pasting, pulling her along the ground by her 'air. That's why I wanted to say to our John, you didn't miss much being adopted. When we were young, Mary were even cruel with the furniture. She never let us sit on the settee. That were reserved for me father and Mary's darling firstborn. We had to sit on 'ard chairs. If we slouched or looked comfortable, we'd get a word or worse. Before yer dad left, there were three of us crammed in a single bed: John, me and Mildred. After he'd gone, things got worse and worse. I s'pose Mary were just a girl like us, suddenly forced to be a mother to new children.'

Mary G. would have been in her early twenties when Mr George Davies, my father's 'real' father, married her. He was struggling as a wireman for the GPO, after being a cotton piecer for some years. (A cotton piecer's job was winding the cotton on to bobbins after the spinning process was finished.) George's first wife, Nellie, had died at the age of forty, in August 1931. She'd worked as a cotton doubler-piecer, married George Davies in 1911, watched him go to war, watched him come back, had five children, lived in poverty and then died. Her youngest – my father – was three-years-and-a-week old. I wonder if it's a coincidence that, many years later, he was to pretend on birth and marriage certificates that the first three years of this life, from August 1928 to August 1931, didn't exist. By doing so, he was airbrushing out of his life his real mother and the tragedy of her premature death.

Nellie's death certificate states as causes of death '1. (a) Generalized Peritonitis (b) Appendicitis, [and] 2. Operation'. The operation referred to would have been an appendectomy. The appendix must have ruptured and the infection spread.

Following this tragedy, Nellie's husband was left with five children: Annie, Nellie, Mildred, Edith, John. Well, at least I think it was five. My father was characteristically vague when I used to ask how many siblings he had. I found it hard to equate the father who was so good at doing my maths homework with the man who couldn't count up brothers and sisters. A conversation driving back from Oldham: 'So how many sisters have you got, Dad?' 'It's . . . hard to say. It depends on how you look at it.' 'What about brothers?' 'Oh, I didn't have any brothers. Maybe one. He was either older or younger. Or did I have two? Again, it depends how you count them. But no. One brother. I think he went to war, or something. Erm . . . Ah, I've got to concentrate on this roundabout. Why don't you count the Christmas trees in the windows?' Let's count Christmas trees rather than siblings – it's obviously easier.

In hindsight, I think my father's ambiguity about brothers was due partly to the dubious status of Mary G.'s firstborn. Was he a 'real' brother or not? Maybe my dad wasn't sure. Mary G.'s son himself died without ever finding out that George Davies wasn't his biological father.

When Mary G. met George Davies, she needed a father for her son, and he needed someone to take the place of a deceased wife. They met at Oldham Market. Shopping for fruit and veg was one of the many 'womanish' jobs George had had to take over since his wife upped and died; and Mary was working on one of the stalls. He came there regularly until 1933, when they reached an agreement. Late one night, Edith, Mildred and John were woken up by their father's announcement that tomorrow was an important day: 'Sunday clothes. Sunday accents. Polish over the holes in yer shoes. Go back to sleep.' Tomorrow morning was the wedding of Mary and George Davies at St Paul's Church, Ashton Road, Oldham.

And the next morning after that was hair-pulling and furniture cruelty. There was no honeymoon. Mary G. installed
herself and her darling firstborn on the settee, and my father
started his long goodbye to the Davies family. Even before the
marriage, the widowed George Davies hadn't been able to cope
alone with his three-year-old. Like fruit shopping only more so,
three-year-olds were a woman's job. So he'd started 'farming' his
son out to a childminder on Heron Street called Mrs Taylor:
'You look after him. I've got enough on me plate, looking fer
work. And I've got to go t' market. Take him, for God's sake.'

In a lucid moment on her deathbed, my father's mother had
foreseen what would happen. She'd begged her eldest daughter,
Annie, to take care of the family in her absence – especially her
youngest, John: 'Don't let John go.' Annie reassured her: 'I
promise I'll take care of him.' And she was burdened with guilt
till her own death in 1984. 'Annie, the poor girl, were only
nineteen,' explains Edith. 'She'd got married, and was living in
a tiny room. Her and her 'usband hardly had a cup of tea to rub
together, let alone anything for a growing boy. So she *had* to let
John go, and felt terrible ever after.' It would seem that my
Auntie Annie wasn't of the 'je ne regrette rien' school of history. She was willing to look back at the past, with an 'I'm sorry'
or 'I wish it had been different'.

As for Mr George Davies, throughout his life nothing
seemed to touch him. I suppose veterans of the First World
War trenches learnt *not* to remember. Newly married, my
mother remembers going to Oldham to meet Mr Davies. It was
the first time my father had seen his 'real' father in decades.
For an hour, they sat facing each other on hard chairs. They
had a cup of tea. Some crockery rattled. They left. That's all
my mother remembers: 'No sorries, no tears like TV reunions.
It was a "hello again", "hear you're a teacher", "bad weather",

"goodbye" kind of nothing. That was the last time they saw each other.'

It was past mending for my father and George Davies. But there was a later scene, another deathbed scene, which shows the latter in a different light. It was in 1969, and the dying George Davies asked his daughter, Annie, to perjure herself once more: 'Tell me I've been a good father, Annie, to you all. Tell me, won't you?' The question suggests that this inflexible, stoical, despotic man was warding off regrets at the end; that the past finally came back to nag him, pull him around by the hair. Warding off his last-minute guilt, though, meant compounding Annie's, because now she felt compelled to lie a second time: 'Yes, sir, you were a good father. I promise.'

'Whatever she said, he must have known 'imself he weren't no Father Christmas,' snorts one of my cousins. 'He never showed any interest in us, his grandchildren. We had to sit on hard chairs and not say a word. No, he weren't no Father Christmas.'

Or, at least, he wasn't to his own family: to Maggie Taylor, he must have seemed very Santa-like. He gave her a son, as if the latter were a teddy bear, a set of CDs. People recall slanging matches over washing lines: 'You're a bastard, George Davies! Imagine, giving away yer own son, bit by bit! How can you live with yerself?' And there were the darker rumours, of a mercenary Father Christmas who hadn't opened his sack for nothing: 'You're a bastard, George Davies! Imagine, *selling* yer own son, bit by bit! How can you live with yerself?' 'How much did you get for him from't Taylors?' 'It's 'er what's to blame, that new wife of 'is.'

This isn't, of course, the version suggested by Mary G. in her letter to me. She claims that George Davies made a conscious decision to give my father away to a better life: 'Mr

and Mrs Taylor wanted him so much. Your grandad gave him
the chance to have a better education. Your dad went to
university.' According to Mary G.'s positive spin, George
Davies managed to please everybody: Mr and Mrs Taylor got
the son they couldn't have, my father got the education he
deserved, and George and Mary got the satisfaction of seeing
my father 'better' himself. Incidentally, it also meant that the
financial burden on their new home was lessened. And, incidentally again, it meant that Mary's firstborn had no male
competition to challenge rampant favouritism.

In fact, one problem with accepting the 'incidentalness' of
these advantages is Mary's darling son. If the reason for giving
away my father was purely altruistic, motivated by the desire
that he have a better life, then why did Mary not give away her
firstborn instead? No, there is a convenience about my father's
disappearance from the family which is more than incidental,
and which does not square with the motives Mary names in retrospect.

Nor do those benign motives square with the few times my
father mentioned Mary G. to me. Far from remembering her
fondly – as a sort of fairy stepmother, conjuring up a better life
for him – he named her at times of desperation and Capgrasian
horror. In disorientating moments of cross-gender misrecognition, he'd mistake me for her – and he'd take a swing, shrieking:
'It's you, isn't it, Mary? Leave us alone, won't you? Please please
go away!'

Whatever Mary's motives, my father drifted away from the
Davieses to the Taylors, from Lee Street to Heron Street, mislaid bit by bit, hour by hour . . . until he was spending not hours
there but whole afternoons . . . until he was spending not afternoons but nights . . . until Annie, Mildred and Edith were
transformed from sisters into weekend visitors.

'We'd go round Sundays,' says my Auntie Edith. 'He had things we didn't, like Mickey Mouse comics. And the meals were right different from what we 'ad – what were luxuries then. They had oranges cut into segments and poached eggs on toast, not too runny and not too hard. He had a bike too. Some Sundays, we'd ride out to Daisy Nook, me on the back of it.

'He didn't come to our 'ouse any more. Mary and me father made it clear they didn't want him there. On t'other side, I thought Mrs Taylor didn't want her new son coming to see us. She were worried he might not come back to 'er. It seemed like he had everything at the Taylors', Mickey Mouse included. But it was also a bit boring there, kinda slow. The clocks used to send me to sleep sometimes. The Taylors seemed old. And there weren't no one else for your dad to play with.

'When John were living with us, there was a beggar on our street who he used to play with. The beggar didn't have any arms from the war. He'd sing "Three Blind Mice", and yer dad'd stand behind him, mimicking him, like. He'd even hide his arms behind his back. When yer dad went to the Taylors', the beggar got bored and moved away. And I reckon yer dad got bored too in his new home. He were lonely. No sisters, no beggars.

'I wish I'd said to 'im, just cos our dad doesn't want anything to do with you, doesn't mean we don't.' I get lost somewhere in the negatives. 'I hope that's not what he thought about us. It must've been terrible for a child that age, being sold to strangers. It must've haunted him forever. But I hope he didn't feel like we'd *all* rejected him. I wish I'd said that to him – like I wish I'd told him that he didn't miss much, adopted away from us. I never told him these things, and then he got ill and it were too late.'

There's a pause, the unsaids hanging in the air.

Suddenly: 'It were a rotten life when your dad had gone. Mary were a terror at home, and school weren't much better. We got to the end of our elementary school – Werneth, it were called. I passed for Hollins High School, but there weren't no money for uniforms. Unlike t'other kids, we had to go to school in our everyday, worn-out clothes. And as fer the school dinners – we had to 'ave the free ones and sit separate from everyone else. Right horrid, it were, knowing you were "charity cases", and knowing that everyone else knew too.

'I left school at fourteen. I worked in a cotton mill called Lancashire Handbag. I went into service for a while. Every Thursday, I had to take me wages home to Mary. I didn't live there then, but it made no odds to Mary. She'd give me half a crown back out of twelve 'n' six. That were nothing, especially when you liked to go out of a night t'dances or pictures.'

Meanwhile, my father grew up in a different environment. Only a mile away, but this was a world where there were uniforms for High School, where my father didn't have to sit separately for school dinners – or, at least, not separately from other children, just from his sisters. The proprietors of this new world, James and Margaret Taylor, were by no means well off – he was an iron moulder – but this provided a stable income by comparison with George Davies. Moreover, the Taylors didn't have other children to support. So they could afford Mickey Mouse, poached eggs and holidays on the Isle of Man.

The Isle of Man was where Margaret Taylor's family came from, and it was where the Taylors would eventually return to, once my father married and moved away. Here at last is a little Manx heritage I can adopt and cling to, as it adopted and clung to my father.

Because of what happened to my father as a child, this is all we can do: adopt an incomplete family history. The basic choice is between two inadequate genealogies – between a family which wasn't my father's except in terms of adoption, and a family which wasn't my father's because it rejected him. Taylor or Davies, Davies or Taylor? Neither of these genealogies quite work, and we end up half-identifying with both, which is the same as wholly recognizing neither. It's significant that I think of neither the Davieses nor the Taylors as 'grandparents'. That traumatic first fracture in my father's past – when his mother died and he was carried off by strangers – leaves its marks on the next generation as well.

Of us all, only my brother Robin remembers using the term 'grandpa' for a relative on my father's side of the family. Only he was born in time to recall Sunday visits to 'old Oldham grandpa' in the early 1970s. And even he didn't know, until recently, exactly whom this memory concerned. He didn't know that this was our adoptive grandfather, Mr Taylor, not Mr Davies, our (so-called) 'real' grandfather: 'To me, he was just "old Oldham grandpa". There was never any explanation. He was just there, in a home with lots of other "olds".' By this time, Margaret Taylor had died, and Mr Taylor had moved back to Oldham, where he was living in a rest home.

'We used to drive him out to the old cotton mills being demolished. We'd sit in the car and watch them being smashed up with those huge iron balls on cranes. Old Oldham grandpa smoked a pipe and didn't say much. Then we'd drive him back. That's all I remember.'

When Nellie Davies died and my father was given away, it seems as if our family's past was shattered into a multiplicity of fragments – fragments of Taylors, Davieses, Marys, aunties, faux-aunties, faux-grandparents. All we have to look back on are second-hand shards such as:

. . . watching Oldham's mills being levelled, with an ancient pipe-smoker . . .

. . . watching a Second World War documentary with my father . . . He was suddenly lucid, and recalled hiding under the kitchen table as V-1s buzzed overhead: 'You only had to worry when the buzzing stopped – like tribal drums in *Tarzan* films. That's when the engines ran out of fuel, and the rockets dropped from the sky' . . .

. . . watching the original *Flash Gordon* . . . and Dad telling me that, during 1930s summers, he'd go to the pictures every afternoon: 'Because of the cliffhangers, you had to go next day to see if the world was going to end. You hoped it would, of course' . . .

. . . watching *Match of the Day*, whilst Dad told us about going to see Oldham Athletic: 'Children were allowed to sneak in for free, half an hour before matches ended' . . .

. . . hearing the song 'A Windmill in Old Amsterdam' on Radio 2, and Dad reminiscing about the sound of clogs on cobbles.

These fragments are all we have. My father never provided us with any sense of totality. He never provided any explanation as to how one isolated memory related to another. He never told Robin who 'old Oldham grandpa' was. He never explained whom he was with during the blitz, when he saw *Flash Gordon*, or when he went to Oldham Athletic (though now I think that might have been because he was alone, lonely). 'Je ne regrette rien': in the same way that Mary G.'s history was disconnected facts, my father's consisted of disconnected fragments.

And, actually, it strikes me that fragments were all he had. How can you possess a sense of totality, of connectedness, when, in the first instance, your past is based on fracture, rather than wholeness? From the beginning, my father's history consisted of separation. The formative event in his life was one of loss, of familial fragmentation. I wonder if his whole 'je ne regrette rien' attitude to the past originates from this. Why look back if, in the first instance, there's nothing solid or whole or singular to look back to?

And perhaps that first fracture, when he was wrenched from the Davies family, explains the many subsequent fractures in his life. Perhaps that formative trauma determined the fractured structure of his subsequent life and, indeed, memory. No doubt adoption has similar effects on others, even if it's more sensitively handled than it was with my father.

Why did the Taylors decide to adopt my father? Margaret Taylor, so the story goes, couldn't have children of her own. So she became a childminder and took a special shine to my father. Certainly, the Taylors loved him as their own child; and (I think) he loved them back as his own parents. To the point that, when he was seventeen, the adoption was formalized and he became John Taylor. To the point that, when he died, he was buried with Mrs Margaret Taylor in plot H24 of Malew Church cemetery, Isle of Man. To the point that I thought that Mrs Taylor was his real mother.

This wasn't merely because my father never explained his family history. It was also because we, as amnesic teenagers, abetted his taciturnity by not being interested. Believe it or not, I never bothered to ask who the Mary was for whom I was occasionally mistaken. Or, at least, I didn't bother after I'd failed to understand the first explanation from my mother – an explanation which was whispered, hurried. She didn't want to disturb him whilst he was sleeping off the paranoia.

Sometimes he laughed in his sleep, sometimes he screamed. And sometimes he recited hour-long mathematical formulae to an unseen class. The formulae would be mingled with names – names like Mary, Margaret, Marilla, Mildred, Heron Street, Lee Street – some of which I recognized, some of which I didn't. Being a mathematical disappointment to my father, I certainly never recognized the formulae. What was he calculating? Maybe he was trying to solve the past in an equation, as Mary encompassed it in a list of facts. He never got to the end of the equation, though. His somno-arithmetic was usually interrupted by a violent awakening, a yelp in the dark. And as Parkinson's gripped him, the equations became less and less distinct. Years passed, and the names, pasts and mathematics finally disappeared into a generalized Parkinsonian mumbling.

All Over

'*I* did that,' my father said once, pointing at a TV documentary about the Korean War – as if he were personally responsible for it. 'I was in that.'

'No, you weren't. Don't be silly . . . Were you?'

'I was. I went to Korea. The war. Yes. I . . . went to . . . During National Serv . . . Kore . . . a . . . And . . .'

'Are you serious?'

'Can I have that . . . square, please?'

'Dad! Look at me. You said you were in Korea. Are you sure?'

He yawns and starts rolling up his trouser legs – and I know I've lost him to vagueness. A rare smile lingers on his face, though, and this infuriates me.

'Dad!' I shake him a bit, as if the information might fall out of him. 'For goodness sake. You can't say something like that and stop. Dad! You said you went to Korea?!'

'Stop it,' he says angrily. 'Switch the channel over. The programme's boring.'

And that's the end of our non-conversation.

Most likely, it was Parkinsonian nonsense, inspired by the television. He was echoing the documentary, the TV using him

like a ventriloquist's dummy. It often did this. A trailer for
Crufts would interrupt a request for salt: 'Would you pass me
the . . . erm . . . Irish setter . . . I mean . . .' An advert for tomato
soup would infiltrate a bout of paranoia: 'He's out to get me, I
tell you! He's trying to . . . He's trying to . . . to . . . Campbell's
soup me. Stop the soup!' Somehow, Parkinson's eroded his
resistance to the suggestive power of television. It undermined
his ability to differentiate between his own thoughts and the
voices blaring at him from across the room.

With the Machiavellianism of carers, I latched on to television's ability to ventriloquize him, and tried to do the same.
When anger and confrontational bossiness failed, I resorted to
various modes of ventriloquism. For example, there was the
simple 'Bugs Bunny' technique. Here, one confused the 'enemy'
(i.e. my father) by suddenly swapping positions during an argument – just as Bugs often befuddles Porky Pig: 'Dad, you've got
to sit down for lunch. The soup'll get cold.' 'No. The soup's a
trap. I won't sit down.' 'Yes you will.' 'No I won't.' 'Yes you will.'
'No I won't.' 'No you won't.' 'Erm . . . Yes I will.' 'No you won't.'
'Yes I will.' 'Okay, Dad, have it your way. If you insist, you can
sit down for lunch.'

That was the Bugs Bunny technique. If that failed, there
was the more complex 'Jedi' technique. In *Star Wars*, one of
the Jedi mind tricks practised by Alec Guinness consists of
telepathically dictating what stormtroopers will say next. In
Care Wars, the Jedi technique was deployed at moments of
optimum confusion: 'Dad, you've got to sit down for lunch.
The soup'll get cold.' 'No. The soup's a trap. I won't sit down.'
'How can the soup be a trap?' He's so furious he starts repeating what I'm saying: 'How? How? How can the soup be a trap?'
'It can't be, can it?' 'It can't be, can it?' 'No, it can't, so you
may as well sit down.' 'No, it can't, so *you* may as well sit

down.' 'I *will* sit down then.' 'I *will* sit down then.' 'Good.'
'Good.'

If the Jedi technique was reliant on the echolalic structure of
Parkinsonism, then the 'Schwarzenegger' technique depended
on my father's forgetfulness. In the film *Total Recall*, false memories are implanted into Schwarzenegger's brain; I tried to do
the same with my father: 'Dad, you've got to sit down for lunch.
The soup'll get cold.' 'No. The soup's a trap. I won't sit down.'
'Oh okay.' Long pause, waiting for him to forget his first
response: 'Dad, can you sit down for lunch?' 'I won't.' Another
long pause, followed by lies: 'Oh, Dad, I'm sorry I made you get
up during lunch for no reason. I was wrong, you were right –
there was nobody at the door. You can sit down again now like
you wanted to.' Self-righteously: 'I will.'

All three of these techniques failed when it came to Korea.
The Bugs Bunny technique failed: 'Dad, will you tell me about
your National Service?' 'No.' 'Yes.' 'No.' 'No.' 'Erm . . . Yes.'
'No.' 'Yes.' 'Go on, tell me about it, then.' 'What?' 'Your
National Service.' 'No.' The Jedi technique got me nowhere:
'Dad, you said you went to Korea?' 'You said you went to Korea.'
'Well, did you . . .?' 'Well, did you . . .?' '. . . go to Korea?' '. . . go
to Korea?' 'Yes?' 'Yes?' And finally the Schwarzenegger technique failed too: 'Dad, you said you'd tell me about your
National Service.' 'No.' Long pause. 'Ah, it's funny what you
were just saying about your National Service.' 'Ha ha.' Another
long pause. 'Go on then.' 'Go on with what?' 'You were going to
tell me about your National Service.' 'What National Service?'

Years later, I trace his National Service records at the RAF.
Unsurprisingly, I find no evidence of a posting in Korea. The
only information the records contain is that he enlisted on the
10th of October 1949, a year after leaving Manchester
University; that he was initially an 'Airman class 2', and was

later promoted to the rank of sergeant; that he took a course for educational assistants; and that he was discharged from whole-time service on the 23rd of September 1951. The documents are disconcerting. They're certainly about my father, insofar as they concern a John Taylor who was born on 5 August 1928, and whose 'parents' live on Heron Street, Oldham. But this is a John Taylor who has dark brown hair, not black, and whose complexion is 'freckled', which it certainly wasn't. Like his passports, birth and marriage certificates, here are papers which reproduce yet another John Taylor clone, slightly different from the one I knew.

I think it's unlikely that any of these John Taylor clones went to Korea. The television was probably playing games with him. Or perhaps he was playing games with me. I'm still not sure. Though there's no mention of Korea on the RAF records, I'm told this doesn't necessarily rule it out. So, all we have is the huge balance of probabilities against his being in Korea on the one side, and a couple of throwaway comments on the other. Add such circumstantial evidence that his National Service did overlap with the war, and that he used to watch M*A*S*H avidly, you still don't have much of a case. It's just that neither do you have a definite, unarguable 'no'.

Another myth about my father's National Service was provided by Auntie Mildred, Myth-Maker-General of the family. She claimed that it was during this time that my father met his first wife. Supposedly, he came down with pneumonia and was sent to military hospital. His first wife-to-be was working on the ward, and nursed him back to health and marriage.

Above and beyond the romance of the story, I catch at the mention of pneumonia. I think of the chest infections in his last year, and the one which carried him off. Over his lifetime, there are strange patterns of illnesses: the repetition of nervous breakdowns, of pneumonias, the bouts of depression, the pre-disposition for forgetting people re-enacted in his dementia. Most probably, I'm trying to impose a retrospective structure on what was an episodic and fragmentary life. But I can't help feeling there are recurrences, patterns, destinies hidden in his mind, body and history. Whether or not they actually mean anything is a different matter.

If one of the recurrences in his life was pneumonia, it's quite possible my father did meet his first wife while sick in the RAF. The date of their marriage was 18 March 1950, six months after his National Service commenced. So, for once, it's conceivable that a 'Mildredian' myth is based on fact.

It isn't, though, how my mother heard about their first meeting. Shortly after showing me a certain letter from the Salvation Army, she explained: 'I think he met his first wife when he was at Manchester University. She was working, he was skiving lectures. He saw her and was instantly besotted. He followed her round for months, waiting on street corners, badgering her after work. Finally, she gave in, and they got married.

'I never saw a photo of her. He'd got rid of most photos. But I guess she was glamorous, sophisticated – especially to a boy who'd grown up in Oldham. She was from a different class. She was independent, a headstrong woman, a woman of the world.' My mother grins. 'She was also fourteen years older than he was, which is a coincidence.'

'Why?'

'Because his second wife – me! – I was exactly fourteen years younger. There's a peculiar pattern for you, if you want patterns.' She pauses. 'I suppose I represented her mirror image. I was not glamorous or independent, and certainly not sophisticated. I was a mouse from the sticks.'

I don't have to agree with my mother's modesty to see that she represented the opposite of Barbara Muriel Jane Taylor née Matthews. With one, my father was controlled, with the other, the controller. My mother was timid, young, stable, settled, dependent and, above all, didn't like moving home. For Barbara Muriel Jane Taylor née Matthews, on the other hand, the grass was always greener, home was always somewhere else; and my father spent ten years chasing her from one town to the next. Every so often, he'd come back from work of an evening to find the flat cleared out, his family gone – and he'd have to search for them, move houses, move jobs . . . until he'd come back from work of an evening to find the flat cleared out, his family gone –and he'd have to search for them, move houses, move jobs . . . until it happened again . . . and again. By contrast, with Marilla Margaret Taylor née Kelly, he moved only once, during thirty-four years of marriage. From 1971 till his death, he stayed put in Stoke-on-Trent. And however much my father hated being 'Stuck-on-Trent', never moving from a place he detested was preferable to moving every few months between places he didn't know.

'Stuck-on-Trent' was also one of the few cities he hadn't moved to with his first wife. So it was free of associations – unlike Coventry, for example, where I lived for a while, and where he'd look from wall to wall with terror-struck eyes: 'Let me go. I want to go home. This is Coven . . . isn't it? You've brought me here on purpose, haven't you?' He'd grab the wrist of a passing housemate and bemuse him with paranoia: 'Help me. Get me away from here. It's a conspiracy. I mustn't be here.' I'd laugh and make 'cuckoo' sounds to explain away my father's behaviour; only now can I understand the desperation inspired by Coventry. I mean, Coventry inspires desperation in many of us, but his was of a peculiar kind – as was the desperation inspired by Sheffield, Wolverhampton, Wellington, Birmingham, Nottingham, Sussex, parts of London, and so forth. You have to wonder if the 'Reduplicative Paramnesia' of the 1990s – whereby he felt disorientated everywhere, even found it hard to recognize his own home – had its roots much earlier, in his first marriage. The horror of always moving, never finding a settled home, determined his future illness.

Before that illness, Stuck-on-Trent was at least a safe distance from past events. Stoke allowed him to forget his first marriage, to disappear it to an extent I can scarce believe. Stalin blacking out enemies from old photos was hardly as thorough. He never mentioned the name Barbara Muriel Jane Taylor née Matthews in more than thirty years. The fifteen years between 1950 and 1965 might never have existed. While other traumas resurfaced in his dementia, he never seemed to return to the disaster of his first marriage. 'It was wiped out,' says my mother. 'Perhaps he couldn't remember because of the ECT. Whatever the reason, 1950 to 65 was absolutely, utterly gone for him.'

Except for once, when my father pushed me away with a twisted face, calling me Colin . . . Oh, and another time, when he got cross at the name 'Jane Taylor'. 'Jane Taylor' was how Barbara Muriel Jane Taylor, née Matthews was known to friends and family. And 'Jane Taylor' was also the name of one of my mother's friends. Though the two Jane Taylors were entirely unrelated, the mention of the latter once caused him to drop a milk bottle: 'Where's my wife?' 'She's gone out for a bit to visit Jane Taylor.' Smash. 'Dad! What did you do that for? Just my luck – Mum pops out for a second to see Jane Taylor and . . .' Thud. 'For Christ's sake, Dad! Now you've fallen in it too. Wait till Mum gets home from Jane Tay . . .' Smash thud bang.

So my father's first wife and marriage weren't quite 'absolutely, utterly gone', even if they only resurfaced in half-noticed names and broken milk bottles. Of course, I didn't understand these things till later, after the Salvation Army letter. Since then, I've also come to see how more general aspects of his illness and, indeed, his relationship with my mother relate back to that first marriage. Take, for instance, my father's over-protectiveness towards my mother. He wasn't happy with my mother having friends of her own; he wouldn't let her have her own car, in case she drove away and didn't come back; and he was unhappy when she returned to teaching after years at home. Parkinson's let these jealousies run rampant: by the 1990s, he couldn't cope with my mother being out of sight. 'Where's Mum?' 'In the kitchen.' Pause. 'Help help help! Darling darling darling!' 'Dad, she's in the kitchen.' 'She's not. You're hiding her.' My mother comes in: 'What's the matter, darling?' 'I wanted to see you, darling, to know where you are.' 'I'm in the kitchen.' 'What're you doing in there, for God's sake?' 'Cooking.' My mother goes back out. 'Where's Mum?' 'In the kitchen.'

Surveillance, supervision, paranoia. I thought he was being old-fashioned, a 'stick-in-the-mud' (to use his own phrase back at him). I was right and up-to-date, he was wrong and old and silly: 'Things are different nowadays, Dad. You've got left behind in 1930s Oldham, when wives weren't independent people.'

Undoubtedly, with my mother, he was the head of the household, the paterfamilias. He earned the money, paid the bills, had the final word on what my mother would or would not wear. When his control began to slip, he clung on to it ever more desperately, with his 'Help help helps' and his paranoiac furies. But this urge to stay in control must have been a hang-

over from his first marriage, where he'd disastrously lost any
control. He wanted my mother to remain dependent because
his first wife had been so fiercely independent, unpredictable.
Rather than being a stick-in-the-mud by design, I can see now
that my father's 'old-fashioned' opinions were born of his first,
new-fashioned marriage. In patterns of behaviour like this, I
now discern the ghost of his first marriage stalking him, its horrors looming larger and larger as he became iller and iller.

There are many examples of such ghosts. His need to know
where my mother was all the time was determined by his first
wife's disappearing acts. His jealousy of me, I think, came from
the same source.

As his Parkinson's developed, he became increasingly jealous
of my relationship with my mother, to the point that . . . Well,
I don't need to spell it out, do I? He'd shout at us: 'It's you and
him. You've always been in it together. You're my wife, not his.
I know what's going on behind my back. You're . . .' – and I'd
interrupt him, stop him finishing the sentence, stop my cheeks
going red: 'Stop it, Dad. It's not nice.' 'Yes, stop it, darling. Be
quiet and watch the television and drink your pop and have
your pills.' This multi-tasking was beyond him, though, and
he'd spit the pills back at us: 'You're in it together, I tell you!'

As ever, his paranoia was *partly* right, in that my mother and
I did gang up on him. For years, my mother and I chatted over
meals together, whilst my father sat in the corner, losing his
teeth in his food. For years, we shared complaints about his
toilet problems, whilst he drooled at the television. For years,
we laughed conspiratorially at his paranoiac terror of Hem
Heath Colliery. Obviously, I regret some of this ganging up. But
it was a way of surviving, a way of differentiating ourselves from
paranoia, dementia, surreality. It was a way of asserting: we're
not ill, he is, we're not going mad, he is, we're not going to lose

our minds to paranoia, however much he barrages us with it. I
won't say sorry for our conspiratorialness to anyone who hasn't
themselves cared for a sick relative. Care is by nature a form of
conspiracy – a conspiracy in which the carers gang up together,
because they think they know what the patient needs better
than him- or herself. No wonder so many of the chronically ill
suffer from paranoia.

Now I find, though, that our conspiratorialness and my
father's paranoia have a pre-history, BP (Before Parkinson's). In
grotesque, Parkinsonian form, we were rehearsing over again
my father's failed relationship with his first son, Colin. This is
one of the things I've realized since meeting Colin in 1999.
'Like a conspiracy,' he says, 'I teamed up with my mother
against Dad. He'd try and discipline me, I'd go to her, and she'd
say he was wrong. She let me have whatever I wanted. He was
the "baddie", she the "goodie". He must've felt terribly frustrated.' It all sounds strangely familiar.

Meeting my half-brother Colin has provided a wider context in
which I can understand some of my father's behavioural patterns,
paranoias, jealousies – as well as some of my own. Quite whether
it's provided anything comparable for Colin is another matter.
Whilst I find patterns, connections and answers in my father's
past, Colin has found asymmetries, disjunctions, and questions on
bursting into my father's future. 'I don't know how to reconcile
the dad you had with the one I remember,' he says. 'They're two
different people. The one I remember was, well, *mean*.'

'That doesn't sound like a different person,' I laugh. 'Dad was
notoriously stingy.'

'Not mean with money – though there was that too – but I
mean *mean*, emotionally mean. He seemed to find it hard to
give us affection. I was frightened of him. Probably he felt he
had to be harsher to make up for my mother, who was a "soft

touch". I don't understand it, how he was such a different person to you.'

While he's saying this, I wonder if there are more continuities here than I'd like to admit. Like Colin, I used to be scared of my father, of being chased upstairs by his smacks. And I did see my mother as the 'soft touch', who was more easily persuaded that I needed a day off school, a new electric train, a Sherbert Dib Dab. After my father had refused my request, I'd trot off to her, and she'd usually say yes. I caused various rows between them in this way, with my father accusing my mother of undermining his discipline.

Okay, I never thought of Dad as 'emotionally mean'. I continued hugging, holding his hand and kissing him into old age. I sometimes wonder, though, if this would have been the case had he been well, had he not been 'gentleized' by illness. As Parkinson's took hold, it became easier than before to express affection 'at' him. Touch became necessary, in that holding his hand stopped it shaking; putting an arm round his shoulders stopped him falling forwards; gripping his arm stopped him 'doing a runner'. These forms of contact were necessitated by illness. I was glad of this; at least I could be physically close to him, if not mentally. But I do wonder what our relationship would have been like if he hadn't been ill. Would I have understood more Colin's complaint that Dad was 'emotionally mean'? It's possible, I suppose. There were times when he shook off my hands and shouted: 'Stop touching me. You're one of those queers, you are.'

For all their differences, I can't help but find connections and patterns between my experience and Colin's. Colin can't help but find discontinuities, chaos. Colin's memory seems to have been structured in terms of discontinuity and disjunction from childhood, made up as it is of alienation from his father, constant house-moving, constant school-moving, 'care' . . . and finally the most terrible discontinuity of all – thirty years of not seeing Dad, only to find a 'different person' at the end.

He found that different person in 1999. Following the Salvation Army letter, my sister set up a meeting between my father and Colin in the Lake District. We were primed for horrors on both sides. Bishops Solicitors had warned us about 'gold-digging relatives', though they were working in ignorance of my parents' bank balance. More seriously, there was the issue of my father's state of mind: here was a conspiracy his paranoia could really get its teeth into. I had recurrent visions of him in the town square, shouting at passers-by: 'Look! A conspiracy! I was right all along! They're all in on it, kidnapping me to meet *him*!' Conversely, it was also a possibility that Colin might be the one to shout at my father: 'You bastard. Look what you did to me. I wanted to meet up so I could tell you how I feel, once and for all.'

In the event, nothing like that happened. Karen brought Colin to see my father, and asked him: 'Do you know who this is, Dad?' Dad didn't say much, and nor did Colin. But they seemed to recognize each other. Even my father didn't have much difficulty recognizing a face so very like his own.

I first met Colin in Stoke, a couple of months later. He brought his wife and family with him. His children seemed to have no problem with gaining new aunties, uncles and a grandpa out of the blue. I, on the other hand, was terrified. So I spent the afternoon upstairs, being buried alive under a heap of teddy bears by Colin's youngest. Being buried alive seemed easier than conversing with a brother who was also a stranger. My father said nothing too, shaking in his chair and staring into space. 'What can it be like,' my mother wondered afterwards, 'to trace your father after thirty years, and find a shell – to find him unable to answer the questions you've stored up? You remember your father when he was young. When you find him again he's old and hardly there. It's not like those reunions on TV.'

All afternoon, I wondered if my father knew who was visiting. But when the visit was over, and everyone was leaving, he sprang out of his chair, and kissed his new-found granddaughter. At the door, he and Colin faced each other. It was my father who leant forwards and rubbed his son's arm, in a kind of semi-hug. Colin turned and left, no doubt bewildered how semi-hugs equate with long-ago memories of emotional meanness.

I've met Colin on various occasions since. I no longer feel the need to hide from him amongst cuddly toys. Instead of hiding, one snowy weekend in March 2004, Maria and I visited his home in Scotland. We helped his youngest hang her dolls. We talked over Colin's memories of meanness, and mine of semi-hugs. We had a drive into the country, towards the Cairngorms. Colin hadn't decided where we were going beforehand, so we ended up driving round in indecision for a couple of hours, and heading home. Inevitably, I was reminded of my father's reputation for indecision – and dozens of similar car journeys to nowhere when we were young: 'Where are we going, Dad?' 'Don't know yet, let's drive round and decide.' Two hours later, we're eating sandwiches in a lay-by on the A34. 'Where are we going, Dad?' 'Home. I think.'

Twenty years later, the car journey with Colin ends with sledging. Finally, he takes Maria and me to see his bookshop, lost in a corner of the town. I buy armfuls of stock, thinking how our father had often talked about giving up teaching and opening a bookshop – a dream realized a generation late.

'It's been a lovely weekend,' I say, books spilling on to the floor, 'and lovely visiting you. I was wondering if . . . I know it's difficult . . . but I wonder if it'd be possible to arrange a visit to your sister, Emma, as well?'

There's silence.

'I understand,' he says. 'I should have told her about tracing Dad from the start. I never got round to telling her, and now I think it's too late.'

He goes on to justify his indecision – something my father would never have done: 'I don't know whether it'd achieve anything, especially now Dad's dead. She doesn't know you exist. Ever since she was a teenager, she's had mental problems. She's paranoid, probably schizophrenic.

'If you asked about Dad, mentioned his name, you wouldn't get anything coherent out of her. You'd get a torrent of irrational abuse. That wouldn't answer any questions, or solve any mysteries, would it? There's only hatred left. Hatred has replaced all the memories. And hatred for him is what you'd find if you went to meet her. Apart from, maybe, hatred for you too. She'd probably not let you in the house.'

Here – in a vision of a middle-aged woman answering her door in gnashing fury – is where the continuities and patterns end. Here, my attempt to point up continuities between my father's life with us and his first family fails. I can understand Colin's deeply contradictory emotions towards our father. But I cannot understand unalloyed hatred for him. I can only dismiss it as a symptom of Emma's illness. It is an isolated anomaly which has no analogies in the distant past of Oldham, or the nearer past of Stoke-on-Trent. For no one else was my father an object of detestation. There are no continuities, no repeated patterns, no doubles in Emma's hatred.

The tragedy, of course, is that my father loved her, as he did

Colin. My father lost contact with Colin for thirty years and Emma for good; but evidence turns up – at the bottom of drawers, in the corner of attics – that he did try to trace them, at least till the mid-1970s. One letter, which I find folded into the tiniest possible space, is dated May 1974, and informs my father that the 'Taylors' have moved from Hepworth Road, London. The landlady doesn't have a forwarding address. Almost hidden on the back of the letter, my father has scrawled the address of the Salvation Army Information Services, London – a prophetic gesture, given later events. The letter is my father's tragedy in miniature: in a few words, here is his separation from his first family, their rejection of him, their constant moving, his failed – maybe half-hearted – attempts to find them again.

I wonder what his feelings were in the thirty years when he didn't see them. I wonder what his feelings were when his son reappeared. I wonder what his feelings were when his daughter didn't. This inscrutable, stoical man who was my father – he never talked to anyone about these feelings. And by the time of his reunion with Colin, he was incapable of talking about them.

If I'll never know the story from my father, at least Colin has provided me with his version of events:

January 2005

Dear Jonathan

As I'm sure I told you, my memories of Dad are few. I don't know why this is. Partly it's because we did not spend much time with him; and partly because I made him the villain.

I remember nothing before when I was about four. About that time, my mother [Jane Taylor] contracted TB. My sister and I were put into foster care. My mother later said this was because Dad was teaching full-time. I suppose that it was also the norm then that fathers did not take sole care of

children. I do know that I was unhappy with these foster
parents (this was near Ludlow; we'd been living in
Wellington, Shropshire). I could not understand why I had
to be separated from my parents. I think this was the
beginning of my resentment of Dad. I remember the foster
parents forcing me to eat things I didn't like.

I remember returning to our new house in Wellington
before my mother came home. This was during the summer
holiday. I remember that we watched and counted different
types of cars at bedtime [we used to do this too, Colin]. We
subsequently moved near the railway, and I have a few
memories of Dad taking me to the station to see the steam
engines coming through [again, we did this with Dad as
well]. We moved house a lot. I know that Dad did not sell
the previous house in Wellington because we lived in it
later. It was usually my mother's decision to move, because
she thought the 'grass would be greener' elsewhere, although
I know that Dad used to make money by renting out
property. I think my mum had expensive tastes which he
had to cater for.

My mum went on convalescence to Dawlish, and took us
with her. This was our first of many experiences of staying in
guest houses and holiday lets. I remember Dad coming to
visit a bit and us children being clingy to our mum – to the
point of insisting that we sleep in her bed.

Our first visit to the Isle of Man was also during this time
(when I was between about four and six). It was quite an
adventure in those days. Even at that age, I used to chase
round the ferry, mess about in the ropes, and it's a wonder I
wasn't lost overboard. My memories of that holiday are
good: going on the Manx railway, eating fish and chips in
Peel, visiting Laxey wheel, the wildlife park, the boating

pool, etc. My memories of the Taylors in Castletown are few, except that there was a nice cosiness about their house, and always the sweet smell of tobacco.

I suspect things started to go wrong soon after this holiday. The next house we moved to was in Wolverhampton. Perhaps we moved so my mum could be nearer her parents, who lived there. Or perhaps my refusal to go to school may have forced us to move – because of truancy officers. I think that I was a bigger problem than my sister when I was fiveish. I had particular problems with school dinners, and also separation anxiety. My mother certainly could not cope with the schooling situation, particularly after my sister's nervous breakdown when I was about eight. Possibly Dad was worried about this, and I do remember him forcing me (unwillingly) to school.

A few times Dad took time off work, so he could make sure I went to school. As soon as he'd left me in the yard, I'd bunk off anyway, over the wall. When I went to a new school, I'd last a few days, then come home one evening and cry to my mother about this or that event. I'd say I couldn't go back. My mother would say, oh well, never mind, let's go somewhere else then. And we'd move to a different place and different school.

My memory of Dad at this time (mid- to late 1950s) is of someone who did not *seem* sympathetic or caring about my 'school-phobia'. Certainly, from when I was six, I remember there being lots of rows between my parents, some about my school problems, and feeling totally on my mother's side. I do not remember violence. I can only recall one occasion when he smacked me, and that led to another separation.

We stayed intermittently at my grandmother's in Wolverhampton. We went there sometimes when we ran away from Dad. The house was a posh, middle-class house, my grandfather being a retired director of education. I don't think my grandmother had worked, and she was quite the Victorian, middle-class lady (she was born about 1880). I know from a letter I found that she had emotionally manipulated my mother; and she had expected to be looked after in old age by her daughter. When my mother got married, it must have been a disappointment. Long before this, though, my mother had already moved away from home. She did war-work in her early twenties – she talked proudly about working in aircraft factories and the Land Army, and dodging bombs in Birmingham.

That first separation between mother and daughter was completed by my mother's marriage. To my grandparents, Dad was a bit 'beneath' them, coming from working-class Oldham and all that. Of course, he was also a bit of a socialist, so that did not impress my grandparents either. When relations soured between my parents, my mother used to be quite snobbish about him and his background. She used to joke about how she had to buy Dad platform tickets, so he could get out of the rail station when he visited her from Manchester.

Where did we go next? Spent a short time in Wellington again (I was sevenish). Moved to Birmingham and lived with Dad some of the time. For a while, it was a bit like the early years, going trainspotting and so on. It was around this time that my sister Emma became ill. I may have said to you that at first they thought it was polio, or paralysis, and then some extreme nervous condition. She was in and out of hospitals in different places for years, having different treatments for different things. In a hospital in Camberwell, she had Electro-Convulsive Therapy (ECT). We also took her to a hospital on the Isle of Man, whilst we stayed in a hotel in Douglas. I do not know how Emma's hospital treatment on the Isle of Man was paid for; I suspect Dad had a stressful time financially during my early childhood.

Dad also had a nervous breakdown around this time. One day he got in a temper and smashed things up in one room, although he was not violent to us. I think he spent a few weeks in a hospital, or rest home . . .

This, the first of our father's two nervous breakdowns, was in 1960. He told my mother that he'd been driven beyond desperation by coming back from work in the evening, finding his family cleared out, searching the country for them, finding them again, getting a new house, new job, settling down for a while, then coming back from work in the evening to find his family cleared out, and so on, again and again.

He was put in the Queen Elizabeth Hospital, Birmingham, and was transferred to Roffey Park Hospital in Sussex. I read this in his GP notes. When I tried to find out more about Roffey Park Hospital, no one had heard of it. Its records, buildings and staff were lost. It's as if the whole NHS had had ECT, wiping away any memory of the place.

Finally, the elderly mother-in-law of someone in Sussex Primary Care Trust said she remembered Roffey Park: 'It was one of them looney bins.'

'But we have no way of finding out what treatment your father received,' says the bureaucrat who relays this information to me: 'There were no records kept.'

'My mother thinks he had Electric Shock Treatment?'

'What did he suffer from?'

'A breakdown.'

'It's possible. At Roffey Park, they did prescribe ECT for

severe depression. Still do, of course, in many places. But, as far as your father goes, we can't know either way. At all. Whatsoever.' The bureaucrat is obviously trained to be cagey, detecting court action in every enquiry – even ones about forty-five-year-old cases, in hospitals which no longer exist. 'Obviously, don't quote me on any of this.'

Not quoting the NHS bureaucrat is as far as I get on this subject. No one can tell me for sure if my father had ECT, and my father disappears down Roffey Park Hospital corridors into myth . . . a myth involving muscle relaxants, straps, 220 volts, seizure, the disruption of communication in the brain, the destruction of neurons, the erasure of short-term memory, and the random destruction of other memories. It's no doubt one reason ECT sometimes 'works' – it gets rid of painful memories, and you simply forget what you were depressed about.

It seems odd to me (though I'm no psychiatrist) that the same health service which spent the last fifteen years of my father's life trying to retard a memory-loss disease would actively encourage memory-loss when he was younger. Nor can I help thinking that 220 volts to the head might have had something to do with my father's illness, a couple of decades later.

After Roffey Park and (maybe) ECT, my father and his first wife lived apart for a while. Solicitors began to get involved, as Dad tried to keep track of his family and his children's schooling. There are letters from 1961 and early 1962, requesting that Dad not visit his wife 'because of the disturbing rows'. Colin writes of this period:

We then spent about two years moving from pillar to post!
We'd get to a new place, and mum would say something
like, 'It'll be better here', 'Emma will get help here', or 'I

used to work here.' So much moving around: Bournemouth, back to Birmingham, Great Yarmouth, back to Birmingham . . .

We next settled for a few months when I was nearly eleven. We saw Dad infrequently during these years, and when I was eleven he was in London. There was some attempt at a reconciliation and we moved down to live with him (in Hither Green near Lewisham). It seemed to be OK for a while. My mother started work (Civil Service). I remember being anxious if she was late back. I did not feel secure with Dad. It's a difficult realization, but it may be that we, my sister and I, were more than a small part of the reason things never worked. We weren't close with Dad, and we didn't hide it. I remember one occasion when I dismantled his radiogram! I always felt he was mean with money, although I had no idea of his circumstances.

I was not happy with the school I was in. My mum moved me to a Roman Catholic school while we still lived with Dad, about six miles by train. A couple of months later, we moved nearer the school without Dad. We were on our own again – permanently, it transpired. This was early 1964. A few months later, we were on our way once more, to Coventry. I guess this was because the school truant officers were after us again!

We moved to Coventry because of the secondary schooling system. Neither Emma nor I had taken an eleven-plus, and my mum wouldn't contemplate us going to a secondary modern. So we had to go somewhere with comprehensive schooling. Not that we stayed in comprehensives long, whether in Coventry or elsewhere.

In fact, late one evening, we moved again, this time to Sheffield. We had no particular place set up, and we ended up in a bit of a doss house after a night or two in a hotel. We often knocked on the doors of Catholic charities for money, sometimes because the maintenance from Dad had run out. Come 1965, we moved back to London – again, the same scenario, on to a train (an overnight one this time), into a hotel, find a boarding house.

We spent nine months going from place to place in 1965. We had not been to school at all. We spent our days while Mum was at work going to museums, parks, zoos, etc.

Matters came to a head in May 1966 when the divorce proceedings were going through. Quite unexpectedly, for us, we were put into care, in a children's home. I was particularly upset by what happened and, to make matters worse, what was meant to be a temporary measure as far as the court was concerned was made into an indefinite measure by the council responsible. Two social workers told me I'd 'never, never go home again'. I hated it. There is more I could say about this episode, but the reason I subsequently 'renounced' Dad was that I blamed this trauma on him. I thought, rightly or wrongly, that he was responsible for us being put into care.

We eventually came out of care because the case was transferred to other social workers, and brought back to court. I was almost fifteen, and Emma sixteen, so we could not be made to go to school. Back we went to Mum, who at least was in regular employment. We stayed in South London and I left home to go to university in 1971. I had written to Dad in 1968 to say that I was reverting to my mother's name and saying that I blamed him for what had happened.

'I was very blunt,' says Colin, 'I said what I felt – that I blamed him for everything. I never got a reply.'

'It's strange Dad never mentioned such a letter,' says my mother, 'and I've never come across it. Gosh, it's hard to imagine how it must have been, getting something like that through the post. I wonder: was I there when he read it? Did I think it was a gas bill? Did he read it over breakfast and not even flicker? Did he excuse himself from the table, or carry on with his toast? Poor Dad, receiving a letter like that. Poor Colin, having to write it.'

The letter is the missing climax of my father's disastrous first marriage. It was the last contact between father and son from the late 1960s until the late 1990s.

Colin ends his letter of 2005 to me by wondering . . .

. . . Jonathan, perhaps you can put a bit more of this whole puzzle together. Why did you have such a different experience of Dad? Had he changed and learnt from the past? Was your mother the strong, stable woman who saved him? Was my mother more of a problem than I realized at the time? I also think that many of these family patterns have been repeated: for example, Dad being separated from his Oldham family and then cutting them off, as I later did.

Love and best wishes, Colin.

So even Colin, for whom life has been a matter of discontinuities and contradictions, can retrieve some patterns from the wreckage of my father's life. And I agree with him when the patterns he finds are ones of repetition, doubleness: '. . . for example, Dad being separated from his family and then cutting them off, as I later did.' Looking back over my father's life, it seems that things come in twos, like some cloning experiment gone wrong:

. . . two families – Davieses and Taylors – one real, one adoptive . . .

. . . a pairing which is in turn echoed by the two families of his own . . .

. . . two wives, echoing the two wives of his real father, and echoed by the two wives of his son, Colin . . .

. . . two sets of disapproving parents-in-law . . .

. . . a forgotten father – George Davies – just as he was forgotten by Colin . . .

. . . two Salvation Army enquiries . . .

. . . two nervous breakdowns . . .

. . . two paranoiacs – my father and Emma – and two doses of ECT . . .

. . . two school-phobic sons – Colin and I – who excited his jealousy by being too close to their mothers . . .

. . . and then the weirder pairings, including two threatening young men with long hair – Mr Gil-Martin and myself . . .

My father's life was so full of these repeated patterns and doubles, I wonder if Capgras syndrome just mixed them up a bit. The pattern of doubles was already there, structuring his life and mind; all Capgras had to do was collapse a few of the pairings into each other – until I became a Jonathan-Gil-Martin or Colin-Jonathan or Jonathan-Mary fusion, and my mother became a potential second-first-wife. Capgras: it's the end-point of finding patterns and establishing connections: everything collapses into everything else.

Headmaster

Injelititis or Palsied Paralysis . . . is the disease of . . . organizational paralysis. The first sign of danger is represented by the appearance in the organization's hierarchy of an individual who combines in himself a high concentration of incompetence and jealousy . . . The two elements fuse, producing a new substance that we have termed 'injelitance' . . .

The next or secondary stage in the progress of the disease is reached when the infected individual gains complete or partial control of the central organization . . . The injelitant individual is easily recognizable at this stage from the persistence with which he struggles to eject all those abler than himself . . .

The next or tertiary stage in the onset of this disease is reached when there is no spark of intelligence left in the whole organization from top to bottom. This is [a] . . . state of coma.

(C. Northcote Parkinson, *Parkinson's Law*)

Institutions can get Parkinson's disease too. We've all seen it, whether in a hospital, a school or a university (mentioning no names). This is where Parkinson's disease meets Parkinson's Law.

My father graduating from Manchester University

The book *Parkinson's Law* (1957) contains a chapter on organizations and institutions, and how they become infected with a disease called 'Injelititis, or Palsied Paralysis'. The book's author, C. Northcote Parkinson, must have known what he was doing. He must have known that, with a name like Parkinson, you can't write about a paralytic disease without bringing to mind the great James Parkinson's 'An Essay on the Shaking Palsy' – without bringing to mind Parkinson's disease. He was consciously lending a name already associated with a paralytic disease affecting individuals, to a paralytic disease affecting institutions.

For a long while, I assumed that Injelititis, or Institutional Parkinson's, was what had destroyed Willfield High School. Willfield was the huge comprehensive in Bentilee, Stoke-on-Trent, of which my father was headmaster. Some time in the late 1970s, I thought, Willfield had become infected with Institutional Parkinson's. Eventually, Injelititis had paralysed the whole school. By the time of my father's retirement, the school was in the tertiary stage of the disease, and had to be shut down three years later.

There's a neat, micro-macrocosmic symmetry to the idea that what was already happening in my father's brain was mirrored in his workplace – that a disease which operates on a microscopic level was magnified a billion times, and played out in a huge institution. In Willfield High, the disease was played out with teachers in place of brain cells, bureaucrats instead of neuro-transmitters, school inspectors instead of Lewy bodies.

It was the deputy head, Mr Gil-Martin, who was the initial carrier of the disease – the very deputy for whom my father would misrecognize me, come the 1990s. Back in the 1970s, it was he who was the 'injelitant individual', mixing together 'a high concentration of incompetence and jealousy'. It was he who infected Willfield, gaining 'control of the central administration', spreading Injelititis downwards into the school, and upwards into the Local Education Authority. Mr Gil-Martin schemed against, and ultimately succeeded in getting rid of my father, because injelitant individuals struggle to 'eject all those abler' than themselves from organizations.

I'm not saying this is really what happened. It's what I wanted to believe, in order for my father to be the 'abler' man ousted by the disease. I was only ten years old when he retired from his job, when undiagnosed Parkinson's started grinding him through its mill. The shaking, the slowness, the forgetfulness developed during my early teens. It didn't need a diagnosis for me to see that he wasn't what he had been. But what he had been was only half-remembered. Whilst my older siblings can recall his years at Willfield vividly, I was too young. So I constructed a mythical past to look back to, a past in which he was what he had been.

Yet another myth to add to the family album – a heroic myth, a myth in which Dad was a genius who knew a dozen languages, had ingested a dozen encyclopaedias, had been an inspirational teacher of any subject you could mention (barring PE), had gone on to manage a huge school . . . but was ultimately defeated by low-down Stoke cunning. Here was a Potteries Passion, with my father as the suffering Christ, the Local Authority as the council of elders, Bentilee's councillor as a foul-mouthed Pilate, and Mr Gil-Martin as the (injelitant) Judas Iscariot of Willfield High.

Such myth making was inevitable given the taboo on Willfield. We weren't allowed to talk about Willfield, ask about Willfield, mention Willfield. Back in 1983, when he was 'being retired' from the school, he never spoke about it. One day, he just stopped going to work after breakfast; he just stopped coming home in the evening with *The Dandy* (ostensibly for me).

He had a nervous breakdown, and all I remember is my mother wearing her hair in curlers more often. All my brother recalls is being asked by my mother to 'Keep an eye on Dad,' whilst she was out at the Co-op, 'especially if he goes for a shave.' All my mother recalls are a couple of horrid phone calls during which a local councillor swore at her, and a kangaroo court at the Local Education Authority. My father asked her if she'd go along with him. At the meeting, he asked meekly if he could go part-time till he was better. The members shook their heads and the councillor swore.

Other than that, we remember nothing from 1983 because there is nothing to remember. As normal, my father didn't confide in anyone. He had his nervous breakdown alone, locked in his office and his nightmares. Afterwards, the subject was unmentionable, and words like 'Willfield' or 'Bentilee' were worse than 'fuck', 'shit', or even 'Coronation Street'. He expunged these words from consciousness, and we were expected to as well. This was collective amnesia – as though we'd all had ECT, and our memories of my dad's workplace were destroyed. 'Electro-Convulsive Therapy: Memory Loss for All the Family.'

'When Dad left Willfield,' says my mother, 'he went round the house, removing all the files, books and photos from the school. He took all the paintings off the walls. The school's art teacher had given him some lovely stuff, but he got rid of it.' Two years after my father's death, I poke round the attic, and come across a dustbin liner, shoved into a far spider's web, next to a forgotten Teasmade. I pull the cobwebbed bin liner apart, and find two paintings which beautify Stoke-on-Trent pot-banks. There's also a photograph of my father on his graduation day, and a mirror of dust. The photo's old frame comes apart in my hands. Lurking behind the lost picture of my father is a doubly-lost picture of his adoptive parents, a photo ghostly in its fadedness. There are questions here my father will never answer: why hide a picture of your graduation? Why doubly hide a picture of your adoptive parents? Why hide them with stuff from Willfield, a part of your life they surely had nothing to do with? For my father, the past seemed to be something you lumped together in a dustbin liner, and shoved amongst cobwebs in a corner of the attic.

James and Margaret Taylor, my father's adoptive parents

For some years, the Willfield past was forgotten amongst the cobwebs. The taboo on subjects pertaining to Willfield was enforced throughout my teens. In the later 1980s, during a prize-giving evening at my high school, my father walked out when he recognized in the speaker an old enemy from the local authority. As early as this in his illness, he thought it was some kind of trap: 'What's going on?' he muttered half a dozen times. 'Why have I been brought here? Why's *he* here?' 'I'm getting a prize.' 'From *him*?' 'Well, from the school.' 'Why are you getting a prize from him? What have *you* done for him, eh? Eh? I'm getting out of here.'

Rather than relaxing over time, the taboo was more strictly enforced. In the mid-1990s, one of the night-nurses exclaimed brightly to him: 'I know who you are! You're the Mr Taylor who used to be 'ead of Willfield 'igh! You taught me son, Billy!'

He screwed up his eyes and answered through grinding teeth: 'No. I'm not. I never taught a Billy. You've got the wrong man.'

'Come on, don't be all modest-like. I knows a name when I sees one.'

'No no no. There're no Mr Taylors or Willfields here.'

'But . . .'

'I'm not. Not.' Not Mr Taylor of Willfield 'igh had had enough: 'Get this mad woman away from me! Shut down the school! Send the pupils home! Help me . . . I'm not head of this school. No one is . . . There's nothing here.' Nothing to see here, nothing to remember, move along please. 'Shut the school!'

By the 1990s, the mere mention of Willfield triggered delusional behaviour, and cries of 'Shut the school!' These delusions ranged from fairly benign instructions ('Come on, it's the end of break, line the children up, won't you?'), to paranoia ('What're you saying in the staffroom about me?'), to Capgras syndrome ('You're Gil-Martin, aren't you? You sod – what have you done with my son?'). As Mr Gil-Martin, I had the front door slammed in my face ('That . . . bloody bastard isn't coming back on school premises!'), meals thrown at me ('I'm not eating school dinners you've poisoned!'), and slaps aimed haphazardly in my direction ('I'll get you for what you said to those inspectors!').

In turn, I entered into the part of villainous double like a method actor. As Mr Gil-Martin, I slammed doors on his 'helps', swore back at him, force-fed him the remains of ruined dinners and retaliated with slaps of my own: 'Okay, you're at school and that's corporal punishment for you! I'll get you sacked over again if you don't fucking behave!' My father would put his hands over his eyes, and clench his eyes shut, blocking out the remembering that I embodied. Maybe, if he'd got the chance, he'd have sealed me up in a dustbin liner and hidden me amongst attic spiders.

If my father tried desperately to forget work, his work returned the favour. Willfield High was closed in 1986. Thereafter, it was wiped from Stoke's memory. The earth, where once had stood a haunted house called Willfield, was sown with salt. Following my father's death, I tried to find out what had happened at the school. But there were no records at the local newspaper; no one had heard of either school or father at Stoke Local Education Authority; there were no minutes of LEA kangaroo courts; the school logbook had been relocated and lost; ex-staff were retired, dead or unwilling to return calls. As with Roffey Park Hospital, Willfield High School might never have existed. My father's headship might never have happened.

It did happen, though, and some of the details were hidden, not lost.

The hidden story starts in the late 1940s, when my father was studying French and English at Manchester University. He asked a careers advisor what jobs he could do after his degree. The man snorted: 'Jobs? You mean job singular. You should know your plurals from your singulars, if you've done arts subjects. Go into teaching. You won't get much money, but that's all there is for arts types, sonnyboy.'

My father used to tell this story quite often, to warn me against financially unremunerative arts subjects. 'You won't make any money that way, boy,' he'd say, repeating the advice he'd been given. 'I've spent my life reading books, getting degrees, learning languages. Look what good it's done me. Grey hairs, shaky hands and a poor pension. Music and culture are all well and good, but they don't pay bills. Do medicine or business instead. There's nothing at the end of arts subjects except becoming a teacher. Watch out, boy, or you'll end up like me.'

My father said this as a threat – he threatened me with himself. He used himself as an example of something *not* to aspire to. And I felt doomed by the threat, doomed to be my father, doomed to do arts subjects, doomed to become a teacher – perhaps doomed ultimately to sit in a chair, tremoring slightly, telling my son to avoid arts subjects in case he ends up ill like me. No one can tell me if the feeling of doom about illness is justified (the feeling of doom about teaching certainly was). There are lots of conflicting reports, some that say 'Parkinson's is by no means hereditary', some that say, 'People whose parents have Parkinson's are twenty times more likely to develop it themselves.' This is my genetic terror: in 1997, the National Human Genome Research Institute announced that they'd discovered a gene that might cause the disease. Sometimes the gene malfunctions, causing a build-up of Lewy bodies. Whether the malfunction is itself hereditary or genetically determined remains uncertain. My feeling of doom isn't yet genetic science.

My father's pronouncements of doom, by contrast, did have the inevitability of science. When he said 'Don't do arts subjects, boy, or you'll go into teaching and end up like me,' the implication was that these things formed an inevitable continuum. Studying arts subjects meant being a teacher, which ultimately meant developing Parkinson's. Arts subjects = Teaching = Parkinson's.

I think that's probably how he felt about his life. Things would have been different had he done medicine instead of French and English. Things would have been different had he not seen a careers advisor in 1948. Things would have been different had the advisor not told him that he had no alternative than to become a teacher, get married, have a nervous breakdown, marry a second time, become a headmaster at a terrible school in Stoke, have a second nervous breakdown, and then retire into Parkinson's.

Back at the beginning of this story, my father took an Education Assistant's course whilst in the RAF, and taught the troops French. After the RAF, he went straight into high school teaching. Formal qualifications weren't demanded in the 1950s; any teaching qualifications he had were taken on the job.

From one of these later education degrees, I found a lever-arch file full of quotations he'd copied down. One quotation which kept recurring was by George Bernard Shaw: 'The only time my education was interrupted was when I was in school.' My father probably felt Shaw summed up his own ambivalent attitude towards education and school. For my father, education in an abstract sense was inevitable – without it, you were barely breathing. The institution of school was equally inescapable; but this didn't mean it was the same thing as education, that it was anything more than sound and fury signifying nothing. My father and I agreed on this, though I never realized it at the time. The only inkling I had that he hated school as much as me was his peculiar relish for 'I don't like Mondays' by the Boomtown Rats and 'The Wall' by Pink Floyd – songs he quoted as often as G. B. Shaw.

No doubt his first son, Colin, would also have agreed with the Boomtown Rats. But what he and his mother did not agree with was my father's belief in the inescapability of school. Colin found school rather easy to escape. My father must have had a difficult time in his early career, trying to hold down teaching jobs, while his own children weren't attending school. There he was, disciplining truants at his schools, whilst his own family was pursued by truancy officers, up and down the country. No wonder he had a breakdown in 1960.

By 1963, he'd managed to stabilize the work side of his life. Between April 1963 and 1965, he was head of Modern Languages at Christopher Wren Comprehensive in Shepherd's

Bush, West London. From there, he moved on to a deputy headship at Charles Chute School, Basingstoke. On this school's 'Friends Reunited' webpage, I came across some reminiscences about him: 'Which teacher was it who used to rev up his Hillman Imp on the school drive, as if it were a F1 race car?' 'Was it Mr Taylor, the deputy with the clapped-out Hillman Imp?' 'Just to confirm that, yes, it was Mr Taylor with the Hillman Imp. I think he was revving it up so as not to stall on the speed-humps whilst keeping under the 5mph limit.' I showed the website to my mother, and she was indignant: 'He achieved so many things there, and the only thing these "Friends Reunited" remember is the Hillman Imp!' 'At least they remember him at all,' I said.

If he was remembered afterwards only for the Hillman Imp, at the time other achievements were recognized, and he received a glowing letter of recommendation from the school ('a quiet man of real, natural dignity'). This went a long way towards securing the headmastership at Willfield High School in Bentilee, Stoke-on-Trent. It was 1970, and he was forty-two – then an exceptionally young age for a headmaster, especially when you consider he'd started off in the slums of Oldham. Given his meteoric rise through the profession, the testimonials from senior colleagues, the fact that he managed to achieve what he did despite Oldham slums, a failed marriage, a breakdown, a divorce – given all these things, I now find some truth in the heroic mythology I constructed round him when I was young.

What went wrong at Willfield? In 2004, twenty-one years after my father retired, I wander past an old man digging in his front garden. He's smiling and humming Bach to his azaleas. I recognize him as Mr Turner, former art teacher at Willfield, and I ask him about Willfield and my father's headship. Leaning against his spade, Mr Turner tells me he has uniformly good memories of working with my father.

'If there are only good memories, why do you think they got rid of him?'

'I only ever knew rumours. Your dad and me sometimes drove home in the same car. Towards the end, he seemed distressed, looking out at the road. He didn't want to talk about what was going wrong, and I didn't feel it right to ask him. One morning, he called a staff meeting. He announced he was leaving. Everyone was surprised. Well, almost everyone. There was a faction in the school who ganged up with a local councillor, and who hunted your dad out. I'd like to think there were good reasons for savagery like that.

'Before your dad announced his resignation, I remember wandering past the staffroom and overhearing a huge row. One of the voices was the local councillor. He was swearing that your dad was a born "something" bureaucrat, not a headmaster. The councillor said your dad was in the wrong "something" job in the wrong "something" place.'

Many people seemed to have felt that my father was in the wrong place at Willfield: he seemed doubly displaced, historically and geographically, in 1980s Stoke.

This is the version of the story, for example, provided by my old headmaster, who was retired from another school in south Stoke. I wrote to him, and asked him if he knew anything about what happened at Willfield. He wrote back:

11 July 2004

Dear Jonathan

Your father was an extremely academic person, intellectually astute and with a wide range of knowledge. It was felt that a comprehensive school in Bentilee – one of the most poverty-stricken areas in the city – was not the best place for him to display his undoubted gifts. With some severe disciplinary problems in the school, I'm told your father tended to leave these to the two deputies. They controlled things well, but after a time they were both promoted or retired and their successors didn't have the same authority.

This was when your father felt that the situation was weighing heavily upon him, leading eventually to his retirement. It was a very difficult school, which of course eventually had to close. In the final stages of his time there, I think your father found it hard to communicate both with the pupils and with the staff and so became somewhat remote from them.

'That sounds like Dad,' my mother says when I tell her this. 'And I suppose all of them're right when they say the school was the wrong place for him. After teaching in London, he found Willfield frustrating by comparison. It was so deprived. And I don't just mean in terms of money. He said he couldn't understand the lack of aspirations above coal-mining. No one was interested in his Shakespeare, Cicero or Beethoven. He came from a family where they'd grown up in even worse surroundings. But he'd wanted to get out. His whole family had tried to educate themselves out of poverty. He couldn't understand why people here didn't have the same attitude.

'It was representative that, when the Bentilee councillor was swearing down the phone, Dad couldn't cope with it. It was a different language to him. He didn't understand the attitude to education, or the councillor's pride in being working-class "Stoke". For Dad, being working class wasn't something to be proud of. It's like when they were shutting Hem Heath Colliery down the road. There were people on television saying they wanted their children to get jobs in the mine. Dad watched in disbelief. His family had spent their lives trying to get away from mines and mills.'

Ultimately, my father hadn't got away. He'd come full circle, starting off in Oldham slums, and ending up teaching in a similar area of Stoke. After forty years, though, he no longer recognized the class from which he'd originated. The working-class terraces of Stoke seemed like an alien environment.

For my mother, it's the shadow of Stoke-on-Trent which looms largest. In her versions of Willfield mythology, it's Stoke which is the arch-villain. My mother's myths are a kind of Zolaesque naturalism, where the tragedy was pre-determined by 'Stuck-on-Trent', and the massive social and economic forces therein.

Zolaesque naturalism is particularly suitable for the city which spawned one of England's greatest naturalist writers, Arnold Bennett, and novels like *Anna of the Five Towns*. 'I hadn't heard of Arnold Bennett before we got here,' says my mother. 'When we moved in, in 1971, the first person who spoke to us was a neighbour. Her head popped over the hedge, and she asked us where we'd come from. When we told her, she shook her head and came out with that saying everyone quotes round here: "No one ever comes to Stoke, no one ever leaves Stoke, apart from Arnold Bennett, and even 'e 'ad to write about it."'

Certainly, my father always felt trapped in Stoke-on-Trent. He wasn't happy, the school was not his kind of place, his indecision got worse and worse, and he gave up looking for other jobs. But none of this explains what happened in 1983 to induce a crisis, to trigger his nervous breakdown and resignation. For a long while, I thought any explanation of 1983 would escape me and the stories I had. With the school records lost, the local authority's minutes destroyed, ex-staff members silent, the Bentilee councillor long-since dead, the school closed, it seemed impossible to reclaim anything tangible from this traumatic moment.

Then, in 2004, finding his address in the phone book, I wrote a letter to the one man who would know what had happened. I wrote a short letter to my double, my bodysnatcher, my doppelgänger, my other self: Mr Gil-Martin. And, eventually, I received a phone call back from him. Suddenly, here I was, speaking to the wicked bodysnatcher himself, my double. His voice was that of a quiet, uncertain old man: 'Hello? Is anyone there? Am I speaking to a Jonathan Taylor?'

The hairs on the back of my neck prickle up.

'I'm Gil-Martin. I got a message that you want to speak to me.'

'I do. It's a little hard to explain.' But I try, and end with: 'So I'm calling you up because I thought you might shed some light on Willfield, and why he mistook me for you.'

There's a pause.

'Strange,' he says, in the nostalgic tone of an old man looking back. 'Of course I remember your father. We had a . . . difficult professional relationship. He was aloof from the community and staff. I felt he was an old-fashioned autocrat – the kind of headmaster that was out of date.

'Maybe your father saw me as a young firebrand, trying to shake things up. By the end, our relationship had degenerated to the point of stand-up rows.'

At the end of our phone call, Mr Gil-Martin agrees to write a letter for me about Willfield. Then he adds:

'I would be devastated if I felt that I was a cause of your father's illness. Devastated.'

I feel like a traitorous journalist when I reassure him: 'You weren't, of course you weren't. Parkinson's is a neurological condition, not a mental disorder. No one knows what causes it.'

His letter arrives a few days later:

15 March 2005

Dear Jonathan

There is some dark humour in your circumstance as a teenager being perceived as 'Gil-Martin'. I can understand your frustration at not being recognized by the father you loved – how you must have wanted to be rid of this person who was troubling to your dad. Clearly, I had become an obsession for your father that had its origins in a professional relationship that was strained from our first meeting.

I was at Willfield High School between 1976 and 1986. You might appreciate there are memories of my time there that I do not wish to revive. Willfield is a long way away to me. I will confine my recollections to those of your father, the head teacher – Mr Taylor.

Mr Taylor was out-voted by the Chairman of the Stoke-on-Trent Education Committee and the LEA's Senior Advisor at my interview for the post of Second Deputy Head. I had responsibilities for Upper School, pastoral care, examinations and community links. My enthusiasm for developing close links with the community was soon to cause friction. I realized Mr Taylor did not want me to talk to parents. He also did not seem to be at ease with our students. He had wanted a 'disciplinarian' as his deputy.

Mr Taylor seemed most secure in his room.

There were those staff who sought his favour, but I don't think he had a close friend in the school. He was John to no one. He was always referred to as Mr Taylor. I found it

difficult to understand how a person could handle such a
role as head teacher without a relationship that was truly
professional – a critical friend.

I do not think he enjoyed Bentilee, at that time the
largest council estate in Europe. The school reflected its
community insofar as there were a few young people
behaving in ways that reflected the irrelevance of schooling
for them. What I found difficult was the reluctance to
challenge the stereotypes of a large housing-estate school.
Without leadership from the top, many influential staff were
cynical and negative in their approach to the curriculum
and the young people.

Willfield was not attracting students. Our rolls were
falling dramatically. External exam results were well below
the average even for Stoke-on-Trent. Expectations were low,
as was the proportion of young people moving on to further
education. Teachers were being redeployed or retired.
Though the ethos and performance of any school is
determined by the overall enthusiasm, commitment and
expertise of the whole staff team, its leadership will always
be critical.

On the other hand, there were havens of peace and
excellence, like Bob Turner's art room – a place that
confounded the grind and was uplifting.

It is possible for an experienced and talented teacher to
secure a headship in the wrong school and community.
Indeed, the one time I caught a glimpse of Mr Taylor happy
in his work was when he decided to timetable himself to
teach Latin to the first year 'A' class.

Jonathan, I am sure your father had his own clear
rationale for his feelings towards me. I did challenge his
leadership on the final day of a school inspection. It was

chaired by an advisor whom I had earlier made a private appointment to see. I wanted his advice as to whom a deputy can talk to about the situation in their school when the head teacher is perceived to be the problem rather than the solution. This advisor felt unable to offer even such advice as 'find another job', but rather said I was unprofessional to raise my concerns when the head was not present. So, when the state of the school was being heavily criticized (today it would have been placed in 'special measures') by the inspection panel, showing either deterioration or at best no change since their visit three years previous, I suggested that all the issues had been tabled at senior staff meetings. I said we had been unable to initiate remedies because of the head teacher's inability to take risks, have a vision and trust his senior colleagues.

You can imagine that Mr Taylor's reaction was not enthusiastic. I know this meeting was followed by a period of absence by your father. This became ill health and the appointment of an acting head teacher.

So, what was a challenging ten years for me at Willfield had its moments of mutual stress and frustration for Mr Taylor and myself. I hold no regrets. However, many a time I wished that Mr Taylor would see that I was different, yes, but nevertheless an asset – an under-used resource. I am sure I could have done much more for his school with professional encouragement.

Jonathan, I am sorry your father was not able to enjoy the kind of retirement he deserved. Your expectations of a father have been blighted by a cruel illness.

I have never challenged anyone in my career except in terms of professional understanding and educational practice. I stand by what I stood for when I worked with Mr

Taylor, though I admit my tactics may well have been impetuous and ill timed. From what you have read, it may seem strange when I tell you that I am not comfortable with conflict. I got no satisfaction from those occasions that are remembered as difficult. My overwhelming feeling remains that Mr Taylor and Willfield were not right for each other and I personified that dysfunction, that misdirected energy.

Kindest regards,
Mr Gil-Martin

So we all have our myths for my father's teaching past. Whilst mine are Parkinson's Law and Potteries Passions, and my mother's are naturalist novels, Mr Gil-Martin's story is one of heroic resistance to my father's pedagogical despotism. It seems everyone tries to understand my father's time at Willfield through different narratives, in lieu of what my father never provided, what we want but can't have: his own version of events.

No doubt there's truth and falsehood in all these stories. What they have in common is that they're retrospective impositions on the past, reshapings of it, contortions of it. When the past was actually happening, I saw nothing but my mother in curlers; my mother understood nothing but her husband's suicidal distress; Mr Gil-Martin saw nothing but his own professional frustration.

When the past was the present, none of our different stories were really happening. They only happened in retrospect, when we imposed them on our fragmentary and chaotic experiences of my father's breakdown. We used these different stories to order the past into coherent shapes and to give it meaning. At the time, there was no shape.

Parkinson's disease is like that: when it's happening, minute to minute, day to day, it's such a flux of changing, flickering, on-off symptoms that it seems mere bodily chaos. What's happening is happening, and neither me nor my father is conscious of the illness as a story, with beginning, middle . . . and end. Similarly, my mother complains that she was never warned from the start what Parkinson's meant in the long term – what story was ahead of her. She only found out what story she'd been in retrospectively.

'All is in retrospect,' says Katherine Mansfield: only in retrospect can we trace the story of my father's gradual decline. Only in retrospect, after his death, can we look back on it and shape it into something meaningful. Only in retrospect do we become conscious of a long-term, linear narrative, moving from the disease's origins to its end. The stories which make up consciousness come after the *real* story's over, when the world has already yawned and moved on.

PART FOUR

Hospitals

A phone call, after midnight, 19 November 2001, Karen's voice: 'Daddy . . . is . . . dead.'

I can still hear the spaces between those words.

'Oh.'

'Can you ring Mum? She's in a state.'

'Of course. Karen, I love you, you know.' No answer, a pause and a click.

How did we reach that click?

Three years after his death, I found a way of tracing the story of his Parkinson's from beginning to end. It was when I obtained copies of his medical notes. In my father's GP and hospital records, I found a half-familiar story running parallel to what I'd witnessed. Where I remember disease-ridden spots of time, my father's medical notes read like a joined-up narrative. Where my memories are isolated nows in the present tense, my father's doctors use past, present and future tenses to narrate a long-term case history of chronic depression, graduated symptoms, progressive illness.

Not that the narrative in my father's medical notes is a simple one of wellness to illness to death. At least it wasn't on

first reading. Since the most recent medical notes were on top
of the pile, the oldest at the bottom, they took me backwards in
time – from death to illness to wellness. They read like one of
my father's cine-camera shows: to make us laugh, he'd play
everything backwards, and we'd slide up slides, dismantle sandcastles, un-bury the cat.

In these old medical notes, my father is un-buried too, and
his life put into reverse. It's a miracle: death to illness to wellness, just through reading . . .

> I am Lazarus, come from the dead,
> Come back to tell you all, I shall tell you all.

At 11.40 pm on 18 November 2001, my father was being transferred from a trolley to a bed in the hospital's assessment ward.
He breathed in deeply, let out a long sigh . . . and then stopped.

My mother couldn't speak for a long time. The staff were
milling round, chatting. She tried to say something to one of
them. He wasn't listening. The moments went by. She looked
at my father. He still wasn't breathing. Desperate, she tugged
one of the nurse's sleeves. No one did anything. A doctor came
to prod my father and pronounce him dead. The doctor's clip-
board said in big letters: 'DO NOT RESUSCITATE.'

On the certificate, the causes of death were given as: 'I. (a)
Left Lobe Pneumonia, and II. Renal Failure'. My father had
caught his first cold of the winter, it had settled on his chest
and killed him.

I had a cold on my last visit.

But let's not think about causation.

Instead, let's go backwards to the morning of 18 November
2001. That day, my father was visited at home by two doctors –
one in the morning, one in the evening. The morning doctor

noted that 'John Taylor has been vomiting all night and is chesty.' The doctor suggested a follow-up appointment. That took place at six in the evening, when another doctor diagnosed a 'chest infection', and recommended my father be admitted to hospital. Once in the assessment ward of the hospital, he was transferred from a trolley to a bed and . . .

Backwards, backwards in time, not forwards . . .

In one of her letters, my mother recalls the days before he died:

2 November, 2004

Dear Jonathan

This time three years ago were Dad's last days.

In the end, everything seemed to come full circle –

One Sunday afternoon, we sat together on the settee just as we always used to do and watched a video. Dad chose *Sweet Charity* without any hesitation from several titles I suggested. It was always a favourite of ours. It was the first film we went to see after Robin was born.

In those last days, we were very close. He was loving again. He caught hold of my arm one afternoon and 'proposed'. At least, what he actually said was: 'I want us to be married.' It is a special memory.

I asked him where he would like to go if I took him out. He wanted to go shopping. When you came home for the weekend, we managed to get to Stafford. He enjoyed a big cream cake in the café and wanted to buy some Christmas cards with robins on. This was his last outing.

He seemed to be so well that last week. It was a busy week, the dentist came, the physiotherapist came – she wasn't too hopeful about his mobility. I booked a holiday for the following July on an Isle of Man farm, with a cottage adapted for the disabled and little fluffy animals to play with. Unlike you or me, he always liked animals. I ordered a special car seat. I spent some time trying to make the garden 'low maintenance' (!) to have more time to spend with him.

On Friday morning when Doreen from Social Services got him up, he stood up twice, and looked intently out of the window. What was he looking for? Doreen said, 'We'll get you walking for Christmas!' He was so well on Friday. Saturday night he was very sick – and Sunday – I miss him so much.

Love, Mum x

I try so hard to remember the last time I saw him after our trip to Stafford, after he'd bought the Christmas cards with robins on. I try so hard to remember him, as I said goodbye and left for the train station. He'd have been sitting in his chair in the living room. He'd have been arranging the 'squares' in front of him into a Gothic monument of some kind. I'd have kissed him. He might have taken my hand, and gestured towards a 'square' he needed adding to his Cushion Cathedral. I'd have disengaged my hand, said goodbye, and left. I just hope that, before I left, I gave him the 'square' he needed to complete his cathedral.

I went back to Loughborough that week for a job interview. Two days before my father died, my mother announced to him that his second son had finally got a permanent job (as a lecturer). She said his Parkinson's mask cracked for a moment. He seemed pleased, despite no longer being able to say 'I told you so' about 'that lazy hippy-son who'll be sponging off us for life'. Although he was almost right: I'd sponged off him for his whole life bar two days . . .

But let's go further backwards in time. Photos from the six months between his operation in March 2001 and his death the following November shock me now. At the time, he was what he was and I didn't notice. Believe it or not, I had no idea in the summer of 2001 that he could ever die. It's only looking at photos now that I see how fragile, bent, saggy he'd become. In one photo taken in my parents' garden, it's the morning after his birthday party in August. There he is, at the centre of us. He's leaning forwards, bleached by illness, his skin loose, his face masked, his tremoring hand holding mine so it's not blurred by the camera – and so he doesn't fall forwards like he did after Mildred's funeral.

From left: my sister-in-law Anna, Karen, Dad, Helen, Maria, me, my mother

The brutal process of gentleization, cardiganization is complete, rounded off by surgery, Intensive Care Units and Intensive Neglect Units. I hardly recognize in the man in the photo the same father who used to run upstairs smacking me. Nor do I recognize in him the father who believed that his son had been bodysnatched. Capgras was a long time ago.

'He lost the hallucinations, anger and paranoia in those last few months,' says my mother. 'That negativity about everything was gone. He started enjoying things again. We went to the shops, and he looked at dinosaur books with you. We went to the Lake District. He loved his food, and meals would last forever' – it's true, breakfast, lunch and tea started joining up – 'It was lovely watching him eat huge pies in Cumbria after he'd lost so much weight in hospital.' He liked his pies so much, he continued the chewing motion long after they were finished. He chewed even in his sleep. Maybe those Parkinsonian nightmares had vanished with the paranoia, replaced at the last by dreams of huge Cumbrian pies.

But before that final, dependent, pie-loving period, there was Saturday, 17 March 2001.

For the seventh time in three years, my father had developed a distended abdomen which was hard to the touch. He wasn't eating. His skin was grey. All the colour was ejected from his body as sick. He wasn't moving his bowels when lifted on to the commode. He wasn't moving anything except what Parkinson's was moving for him. He'd screwed up his eyes to block out the world – as if the pain were outside himself. For the seventh time, he was sent to hospital with a 'sigmoid volvulus'.

One of the unmentioned or unmentionable symptoms of Parkinson's is bowel problems. I suppose people (my father included) find it easier to talk about shaky hands than chronic constipation. The lower section of my father's large intestine – the sigmoid colon, above the rectum – had become elongated,

maybe due to Parkinson's or years of Parkinson's medication.
Consequently, it was prone to twisting. This caused him to
become dangerously blocked, constipated. Constipated to the
power 10,000.

I wasn't there the seventh time he was admitted for this
uber-constipation. I found him the next evening in a distant
ward of the hospital. He lay on the bed, bloated and contorted;
he'd bitten through his lower lip, inside to outside, with one of
his few remaining teeth. The way his head was tipped back, his
face screwed up, the muscles in his neck strained, he looked like
the agony of a Salvador Dalí painting.

I sat with him for a little while, holding his hand. Then I left
for Loughborough where I was teaching next day. Early the following evening, I got a phone call from my mother telling me
to come home. Now.

That day, the consultant surgeon, a Mrs S., had tried the
usual procedure twice. The 'usual procedure' involved shoving
a colonoscope (or 'flatus tube') up my father's bottom, and using
it to deflate, decompress, and untwist the bowel. No anaesthetic, no sedative – just up, wrestle, untwist, out. To use the
phraseology of the consultant, they usually 'popped in a flatus
tube' and 'that did the trick'. This time it failed. The twist had
become too tight, and it was causing ischaemia – i.e., it was cutting off blood to one segment of the colon.

Surgery for his sigmoid volvulus had been threatened before,
but only as a last resort. As Mrs S. had explained: 'Surgery for
Parkinsonians is fraught. We must avoid it if possible. Not only
is there the seriousness of the operation itself, but then there's
the difficulty of getting these patients going after general
anaesthetic. It ruins their mobility, they get bedridden, they
become prone to chest infections.' Parkinsonians are suscepti-
ble to chest infections because of the difficulty they have in

swallowing and clearing their throats. Sufferers have difficulty initiating muscle movements, including internal muscles like those in the throat, so they find it hard to cough up stuff that settles on their chests.

Mrs S. continued: 'If the operation itself didn't "do away" with your father, a chest infection might. Surgery is our last option, something to reserve for the distant future.' In March 2001, the future arrived.

During the hour-long journey home . . . during the search for a parking space . . . during the walk to the ward . . . whilst waiting with my mother . . . whilst not reading *Hello* magazine . . . whilst visiting the hospital shop to buy some sweets ('Refreshers' to be exact) . . . during the gradual appearance of the rest of the family . . . during all this, any one of the white coats rushing past the room could have been the one to tell my mother he was dead.

None of the white coats stopped, though. And eventually we were led to another waiting room, down a corridor labelled 'Intensive Care Unit (ICU)' – a corridor I'd never noticed before. Mrs S. turned up in a plastic hat, rubbing her hands together: 'Excellent,' she said. 'Everything went excellently. Surprised even myself. An excellently smooth laparotomy one can be proud of.'

What she didn't say was that, by the time they opened my father up, the colon was so twisted it had become gangrenous. It was starting to infect everything round it. Without the operation my father would only have had a few hours to live. Under general anaesthetic, they slit him open, drained his insides and removed the infected section. They replaced it with an artificial anus in his abdomen; this was fitted with a plastic mouth on to which colostomy bags could be screwed. Sewing-up over, they packed him off to intensive care.

'You'll be able to see him in a while, when everything's set up in ICU. He'll be under general for a while. Then it's sedative time.'

We waited. I went to the shop to buy another packet of Refreshers. I got lost on the way back, unable to find the right corridor. I ate a yellow Refresher, approached from a different direction, and found the corridor again. By the time I got back, my mother and sister were in with my father. We were only allowed in two at a time. I waited till my mother and sister returned in tears. To avoid their tears, I decided it was my turn. Clutching my Refreshers, I stepped up to the door and was buzzed into the Intensive Care Unit.

Everything was suddenly white (everything except a man with a black foot in the corner). There were mumblings and bleeps and rustling clipboards. There was no daylight, nothing to tell what o'clock it was in the 'real' world. Or perhaps this enclosed, timeless place *was* the real world, and it was the other one which was a fake, a sham.

I saw my father and some machines. I ate a pink Refresher.

Two in the morning in the outside world – none o'clock in ICU – and we left for home, Refreshers finished.

Over the next month, I became addicted to Refreshers. I hadn't eaten them since I was a child, but now couldn't leave them alone. I'd buy them from the hospital shop every time I had to leave the ward – when they were turning him over, x-raying his chest, or other visitors had come to see him. When I was allowed back on the ward, I'd smuggle the sweets in, past security. Settling next to Dad's bed, I'd fish them out of my pocket when the nurses weren't looking. I tried eating one every time a particular machine beeped.

I could never work out if different colour Refreshers had different flavours. I discussed the issue at length with my siblings.

Robin remarked that only orange Smarties taste different to other Smarties, so perhaps it's the same with Refreshers. Helen tried two or three Refreshers at once to see if that decided the matter; she came to the conclusion that no, it was the tingly sensation that was their distinguishing characteristic. Karen, on the contrary, felt that they *did* all taste different, but couldn't describe what the different flavours were. My father didn't comment.

Inevitably, he developed a severe chest infection in the days following the operation. The doctors performed a tracheotomy and connected him to a mechanical ventilator. They cut a hole in his throat and screwed in a concertina-like tube. This was attached to a longer tube, which in turn was attached to the ventilator. Watching the blood seeping out round the bottom of the tube in his throat, I politely withdrew, strolled to the nearest Gents – and threw up the Refreshers, with rainbow sick.

Every half hour, a nurse would temporarily disconnect the tube from the ventilator, take a long straw from another machine, and pass it down the concertina-like opening. The straw would go down and down – through the tracheotomy, down my father's windpipe, into his lungs. It would then hoover up the mucus from his lungs and trachea which he couldn't clear himself. Don't look now, I'd think.

A dentist came to wrench out the tooth which had bitten through his mouth, and which was still chewing at the hole. The dentist didn't dare give him much local anaesthetic, in case it reacted with the previous doses. There was a crunching noise and some blood. Don't look now, I thought again. I concentrated instead on the sweet wrapper I was clutching: 'Refreshers: Fruit Flavour Fizzy Sweets, Ingredients: Sugar, Malic Acid, Sodium Bicarbonate, Release Agent, Calcium

Stearate, Stearic Acid, Hydrogenated Vegetable Fat, Flavourings, Gelatin, Colours (E104, E124, E122, E132).' I wondered if these numbers might eventually give you sigmoid volvulus.

I accidentally glanced at my father's face, and saw it was screwed up in pain. Since the operation, this was the first time I'd seen him register anything from the outside world. Perhaps, though, he'd screwed up his face many times before, and I'd been looking in the other direction, sucking a Refresher.

Suddenly, standing there in front of a father having his tooth pulled, three yards to the left of a man with a black foot, I was horror-struck by the thought that the body is a booby trap . . . a trap like Stuck-on-Trent but worse: you can at least drive out of Stoke. There's no A50 or M6 out of the body. No doubt this sudden horror wasn't really sudden, but had built up over years. I'd been witness to thirteen years of Parkinson's disease, which is nothing if not the brutal assertion of the body *über alles*. Dyskinesia, tremors, rigidity, tics, drooling – these are symptoms of the body winning out over mind. Body 5, Mind 0. The mind can no longer even pretend to be in control of what's going on.

When he was younger, my father had memorized most of Shakespeare, could name symphonies within a couple of bars, had mastered half a dozen languages. But by those last three years, he found it hard to control his muscles long enough to enunciate one English sentence. He couldn't tell the doctors or nurses in the hospital how he felt, what he wanted. He couldn't tell the surgeon if he wanted the laparotomy, couldn't tell the ICU staff if he wanted the tracheotomy, couldn't tell any of us if the agonies of surgery, pneumonia and tooth-pulling were worth it. The doctors and (to a lesser extent) his family made the decisions for him. That might be me, I thought, trapped in agonies and unable to say, 'Stop, enough.'

My father couldn't, didn't say anything. He didn't open his eyes. Hours, days, eventually two weeks of Refreshers went by. My brother and I read him stories from the Reverend Awdry's train books, which he'd once read to us. My sisters arranged a teddy-bear entourage round him. My mother held his hand and told him she'd take him for big, Cumbrian pies when he got better. Visitors came, cried a bit, went. The man with the black foot died and vanished. My father stayed plugged in.

Time performed strange contortions, as if it were dyskinetic. Moments crawled between machinic bleeps, whilst hours jumped from none o'clock in the morning to none o'clock in the evening. Now and then the bleeps seemed further apart from each other. I'd become anxious that I'd heard his last trump. But finally the next one came along. Then, five hours had passed, and it was none o'clock again, time to leave.

The house would be cold and Dennis the Cat supperless when we got home. A Chinese takeaway and Hitchcock film later, I'd go to bed and find myself back in the ICU of my dreams, reading endless stories about derailed trains: 'Ooh! Look! There's been an accident!'

Sometimes, these dreams were interrupted by other, waking dreams, in which I had to return to Loughborough and work. The only reality left was ICU, but I was a part-time tutor at a university, and had to return now and then to my job.

Ten days after my father's admission, I remember dreaming to work through Loughborough town, wondering how many people I was passing had fathers in intensive care wards. This was the real secret life: not that at weekends you had leather-clad orgies in your front room, but that, at weekends, in the evening, any days you could get away, you went down a corridor to a place no one knew existed, to read train books to someone living through a machine. People who didn't have this secret life seemed unreal. I looked hard at passing faces, wondering if you could detect traces of ICU in them, wondering who was a fellow human being. It's a shame, I think, that there aren't telltale signs of ICU in people's faces. Then we'd know not to bump into their trolleys in supermarkets, not to take their seats on buses, not to hoot at them when they distractedly cut us up.

Unfortunately, that kind of ICU recognition is impossible. But there is another, different kind of recognition which can and does happen, in rare moments – a kind that happened to me and my father, in a moment which is more important to me than anything else in this book.

It happened when my father had left ICU, and had been moved to a Victorian prison-house of a building called the 'Infirmary'. Over the two weeks in ICU, his body had finally made the decision to live (whether his mind liked it or not). His eyes – shut for days – had opened. The vertiginous terror of that reawakening was obvious, as he stared ahead, hardly blinking. After a while, his unblinking eyes started following things around – things like doctors, nurses, straws.

He was moved to his own room in the Infirmary, where he continued to stare with darting eyes, on the look-out for new torture devices. He started to squeeze my mother's hand. He got a bit cross when the nurses tried to hoover his chest. He swiped at one of them when they turned him over. One day, he yawned at a Thomas the Tank story. The nurses hoisted him out of bed into a chair, which gave him a different angle for staring.

More days and weeks went by.

I went to Liverpool for three nights to visit a friend. Then I came back to Stoke and the ward for a quick, half-hour visit. It was a Sunday afternoon, 22 April. The ward was quiet. None of my family was there. My father's only company was his favourite teddy, Cord the Dog. They were both sitting in a chair, propped up by cushions, a 'comfort' blanket over their knees. My father looked round when I came in, no doubt expecting incoming pain of some sort.

In Liverpool, I'd bought my father two tapes from a second-hand shop – a shop where old men sit round discussing the relative merits of Barbirolli's versus Bernstein's Mahler in broad Scouse. The two cassettes were compilations of opera and ballet excerpts. I'd bought them for Dad to listen to on his radio, now he seemed bored with train books. He needed something to fill his ears with other than bleeps and nurses' gossip. Tchaikovsky, Smetana, Verdi, and someone I'd never heard of called Franz Schmidt seemed a good bet.

In the hospital, I sat with my father a while, forgetting Tchaikovsky and Verdi. As I was about to go, I felt them in my coat pocket. I handed them to him. 'They're from Liverpool, Dad. I bought them for you.' His eyes looked down at the cassettes on his lap, and then up at me, and then down at them again. I held his hand, and I felt him squeeze it a bit.

'Are they good, Dad?'

His eyes looked up at me once more. He tried to croak something through the tracheotomy. He nodded. He stared at me with watery eyes. I croaked, nodded and cried too.

The croaks seemed to say: 'Yes, boy, I like the tapes.' That's all. But after life-and-death surgery . . . after weeks of intensive care and pneumonia . . . after years of bodysnatching delusions, dementia, paranoia . . . nothing, no croaks before or since seemed so important.

I don't care if I'm being sentimental. My memory has not been kind to me – I was only ten years old when he had his nervous breakdown, only fifteen when his disease was diagnosed, only eighteen when he started misidentifying me. All those happy memories of Toros, Lumps, Jellyfish, Sledging are so distant. I can't find 'the Cave' where we used to eat picnics again, can hardly even visualize it. Getting at these things is like trying to find the other side of a twisted forest.

I do, though, have this one precious moment. It was quickly over. I squeezed his hand, kissed him, put Cord the Dog on his lap and left – though not before putting one of the tapes on for him. From the doorway, I looked back. He was staring straight ahead, listening with Cord to the 'Intermezzo' from Franz Schmidt's opera, *Notre Dame*. I thought it was the most beautiful music in the world.

It'd make a nice end, wouldn't it – the moment of recognition, with Franz Schmidt's 'Intermezzo' as a closing theme tune? It must already be obvious, though, that the story didn't end there. The moment in the hospital was not a finale but an intermezzo. A few minutes after I'd left him, one of the nurses popped her head round the door and said to my mother: 'Why, he don't want heavy stuff like that in his condition. He wants fun things like Britney Spears.' So she brought in her own tape of Britney, ejected the 'heavy stuff' halfway through, and subjected my father to an hour of girlie pop.

Post-Britney, there were more horrors to come. My mother arrived at the prison-house one morning to find my father's right leg cut because the prison-house staff had forgotten to cover up the bed rails. In response, his eyes had gone backwards, and were screwed shut again. A few days later, my mother turned up to find my father sprawled unnoticed on the floor. His eyes were shut, his tracheotomy rasping.

My mother tackled the ward sister: 'I found my husband on the floor this morning.'

'How dare you?'

'How dare I what?'

'How dare you speak to me like that in my ward?'

'Speak like what?'

'I'll not have you talking like that in my ward, to me or any of my staff.'

My mother speaks quickly before another 'How dare you?' can get in the way: 'My husband had fallen and no one had noticed so perhaps if you left the door of his room open so the nurses on duty could check on him now and then . . .'

'How dare you insinuate that my staff aren't doing their jobs?'

Realizing she wasn't going to get further than the 'How dare yous?' my mother decided to get my father and Cord the Dog out of the prison-house as soon as possible. Cord was at particular risk, since many of my father's teddies had already vanished, lost forever somewhere in the institution. Cord needed rescuing before the same happened to him.

But institutions don't yield up their inmates lightly. Once you've been ingested by an infirmary, asylum, care home, there's no easy way out. 'If you're going to get him out,' whispered a young doctor who looked like Michael J. Fox, 'watch out for the nurses. They're suspicious of your family because none of you have Stoke accents.'

April tick-tocked by, every day interchangeable with every other. Visit Dad, talk at him about nothing, read the notice-board whilst they turn him, talk to Dr Michael J. Fox, think about Refreshers, talk to Cord the Dog. From day to day, week to week, visiting days slid into one another. Time stood still. And so did my Dad. He wasn't getting better. Only days when he hurt himself, when the nurses forgot his tablets or when he fell afforded variations. Otherwise, a continuum of sameness.

Early on in the Infirmary, the chest infection had cleared, the eyes were open, and he was drinking and eating a bit of what we gave him. For the Infirmary, progress had been made, stability reached and that was enough. No Further, Saith The Institution: He Is Alive, He Canst Sit In A Chair And He Canst Sip Ribena. None Shalt Pass Beyond Ribena – Let Alone Get As Far As The Rusty Gates Of This, Our Auspicious Hospital.

The institution clung to its paralytic inertia. Setting up impossible challenges, it decreed: 'Thy Father Canst Leave When He Is Able To Sippeth Ribena Through A Straw.' 'Look, he can do it.' 'Thy Father Canst Leave When He Is Able To Cheweth Solids.' 'Look, we've got him chewing cow biscuits.' 'Thy Father Canst Leave When He Canst Walketh On Water.'

Finally, at the end of April, the discharge forms were signed by Dr Michael J. Fox. But that wasn't enough for the institution, which now bore down on my father with all its might.

An occupational therapist was sent round to my mother's house to deem it 'unsuitable' for my father's needs. The occupational therapist phoned up Social Services, who withdrew their help until further notice. Social Services phoned up the ward to tell the ward sister that there was no 'care package' in place. The occupational therapist phoned my mother to tell her that the discharge would have to be postponed: 'You won't be able to cope at home without a care package in place,' she said.

'But it's you who's taken the "care package" away,' said my mother.

'We advised it be taken away because your house is at present unsuitable for the patient's needs. And because it's been taken away, you now won't be able to cope.'

My mother arranged a meeting with the ward sister, who shouted 'How dare you?' at her. 'He can't cope outside. He fell out of his chair the other day.'

'But that was your fault for not . . .'

'How dare you?'

'He said he wanted to be at home. He'll be better there.'

'How dare you suggest that home is better for him than my ward? Your husband isn't to leave.' None Shall Pass.

On 30 April 2001, six weeks after admission, my mother lifted her husband into his wheelchair, covered his legs with his comfort blanket, sat Cord the Dog next to him, and wheeled him out . . . Wheeled him past the ward sister, out of the ward, through the corridors, through the doors, and out of the prison-house.

The institution was spiteful in its defeat. For ten days, my mother had to look after him alone, because the occupational therapist had rung up Social Services and the district nurses to double-check that any help she might get was cancelled.

None of this was recorded for posterity, of course. In my father's medical records, the only thing noted about his fraught discharge is that: 'His family were keen that he leave, so Social Services were contacted, and he was discharged home with a full care package in place. Everything was in order, and Mr Taylor had recovered fully.' According to its own official records, the institution bestowed a blessing and saith: 'Go forth.' I suppose one can't expect a palsied institution to rehearse anything but its own side of the story, its own greatness. One of the chief 'symptoms' of institutional Palsied

Paralysis, says C. Northcote Parkinson, is untrammelled 'self-satisfaction'.

Nor is there a hint of anything but self-satisfaction in the story told by the institution six months before, in Autumn 2000. This was the time of my father's fifth, fourth and third stays in hospital with sigmoid volvulus. It was also the time of our most protracted tussle with the hospital.

During the first of these three stays, my father was treated as normal by Mrs S. However, the flatus tube didn't work as well as before and, a few weeks later, he was admitted again. This time, Mrs S. was away, and he was discharged before the sigmoid volvulus had been properly treated. Shortly afterwards, he was admitted for a third time. He was taken to far-away Ward 101, and the palsied institution forgot his existence. Over a few days which seemed like weeks, his skin went greyer and greyer, his abdomen harder and harder.

Amongst the pile of medical notes, I found a letter from the 8th of December 2000, in which Mrs. S wrote about this episode to my father's GP:

> Mr Taylor was admitted as an emergency on 26 October. He was put in Ward 101. I was on annual leave, and he was looked after very well in my absence by my experienced colleague, Mr M.
>
> Mr Taylor was referred back to me by Mr M. at the end of October when I returned from leave. There had been quite a lot of family angst during my absence. All of the staff reported that the family had telephoned and been rude to various nurses. This was unacceptable. Whilst I can accept that major anxiety was causing the problem, Mr M. and I had quite a stiff hour's meeting with the family trying to put things right.

During the meeting which 'put things right', my mother found out that there had been no negligence at the hospital; that everything had been done in my father's best interests; and that her husband was going to die: 'Whether he dies today or in a couple of years' time, you've got to get used to it. And what standard of life does he have at the moment? All he's got left are his symptoms. It's all very well for *you* to cling onto him. But is it in *his* best interests to go on?'

And no doubt, from a hospital perspective, Mr M. had a point. Certainly, in institutions which regularly forgot his pills, abandoned him on the toilet floor for hours, let him almost die of dehydration, left him naked on the bed for all to see, brought his lunch, left it at the end of his bed, and collected it half an hour later – certainly, in institutions like this, my father didn't have much of a standard of life, and the question of 'his best interests' might seem more pressing than it really was.

A year later, with a bit of paper on which was written 'DO NOT RESUSCITATE,' the hospital decided this question once and for all.

But we're not meant to be talking about November 2001. We're meant to be retreating from it, making him well again.

Between 1993 and 1997, there are various letters to-ing and fro-ing between neurologists, neuropsychiatrists, Parkinson's nurses and the GP. Most of these to-ing and fro-ing letters are about the to-ing and fro-ing of my father's medication: increase this, decrease that, try this, take away that, move the L-Dopa doses around the day, round and round the garden like a teddy bear. Risperidone makes him see goblins, so take that away. Try Selegeline for concentration. Take away Selegeline, because it makes him go to the police to report his own kidnapping. Oxybutynin interferes with the Sinemet, so take that away. Reinstate Oxybutynin because it helps his bladder problems. Increase the Sinemet for mobility. Decrease the Sinemet because he reported a fraud called Jonathan to Barclay's bank.

The medication never stabilized. It was never right. He was never right, drifting between pills, specialists and limbos between appointments: 'We made arrangements to see him again in six months' time.' 'Mr Taylor's appointment will be in a few months, give or take.'

Time and my father drifted. I can see it in the medical records. Every six-month appointment with the neuropsychiatrist reads like the last – as if my father is starting Parkinson's all over again. Most of the letters begin with the words: 'This man has severe Parkinson's disease,' as if it's breaking news. Years late, a letter from a nurse in 1999 solemnly announces that 'The patient now seems to be developing dementia alongside his Parkinson's.' There seems to be a constant return to Go in Parkinson's Monopoly.

By the time of an appointment in November 1997, the neuropsychiatrist was despairing a little. So he referred my father to a neurologist, who in turn referred him for a CT ('computerized axial tomography') scan. The patient lies with his or her head in a cylinder, and the computer builds up a three-dimensional picture of the brain. Unsurprisingly, my father's scan showed that his cortex had shrunk considerably. This happens to all of us: by the age of seventy, our brains are five per cent lighter, by ninety, twenty per cent. Parkinson's and Alzheimer's, though, accelerate this neuronal holocaust; the latter disease can reduce some parts of the brain by half, sending millions of precious memories up in smoke.

By going backwards – now to 1994 – we're watching the cells

grow back, the cortical atrophy reverse, the brain expand once more. From 1994, there's a detailed case study of my father's condition from the neuropsychiatrist:

> Thank you for referring this sixty-six-year-old, married former teacher who attended the clinic today along with his wife.
>
> His main problems include the following:
>
> (i)   Impairment in concentration. He forgets what he is talking about.
>
> (ii)   Memory impairment. He forgets what he has been told and feels that his family have moved things about in the house without his consent.
>
> (iii) During the day and night, he is extremely restless.
>
> (iv) He says he is always worrying about something. He was particularly upset and concerned about failing to recognize his son. This is quite a complicated problem. Initially, it seemed that he didn't recognize his face. Then it seemed that he did recognize him, but felt that he was not his son but a 'fraud' who was playing a trick on him. This sounds like so-called 'Cut Grass Syndrome'.

Reading this, I no longer recognize my father's misrecognition syndrome: 'Cut Grass Syndrome'? Sounds much more benign than 'Capgras syndrome' – more like hay fever than delusional misidentification. No doubt it was just a typo.

The case study continues, littered with other typos and bizarre errors:

> Mr Taylor's family history was that he was adopted. He knows his natural father died in his eighties, but is unsure when his natural mother died. He was fostered out and had a disrupted

childhood, though he is unclear about any specific episodes of
abuse. He has four sisters and two brothers who are alive.

I have no idea how some of this information squares with what
I know: two brothers? Four sisters who are alive? Abuse before
or after fostering? He didn't know when his natural mother
died? I can only wonder if my father knew less about himself
than we do. Or perhaps he was being his normal obfuscatory
self, even with a neuropsychiatrist. The letter continues:

> Mr Taylor's premorbid personality was that he has always been
> a quiet, withdrawn man. He has never been temper prone. He
> has always been interested in studying, reading and collecting
> degrees.
>
> At interview, he was restless with marked choreiform [flick-
> ing] movements of his neck, arms and trunk. He showed
> marked features of Parkinson's, with cogwheel rigidity,
> bradykinesia [slowness of voluntary movement] and akathisia
> [involuntary restlessness], associated with involuntary move-
> ments of the head, neck and limbs. His gait was a little
> shuffling. Speech was slightly dysarthric.
>
> His thought was coherent but he was easily distracted. He
> said he has experienced various Lilliputian hallucinations. He
> did not appear overtly depressed, but did get upset when talk-
> ing about beliefs that his son was being impersonated by
> someone else. He is paranoid. Turning to his cognitive func-
> tion, he knew the day and month, but not the date or years.
>
> This man has Parkinson's disease. Recently, he has also had
> some cognitive impairment. His memory is not as good as it
> was. It is possible that he may be developing early stages of a
> cortical dementia, and a Lewybody disease woud be the most
> likely given his Parkinson's.

Four years after I first read Arnold Bennett's novel, *Clayhanger* – and cried because I recognized some of my father's symptoms in Clayhanger Sr's mental illness – four years late, diagnosis catches up. The diagnosis of 'cortical dementia' explains what's already been happening. It's not a starting point, but an end, a summing up, a last judgement. When the disease is incurable, there's nowhere to go after diagnosis: 'You have Lewy body dementia.' 'Oh.' 'There's nothing we can do.' 'Oh.' From 1994 and diagnosis onwards, it's drift, drift into nowhere.

Retreating back from nowhere, we get to 1992. He had an operation on his prostate, after years of 'nocturia'. Nocturia was the doctor's rather poetic term for my father's five-toilet-visits-a-night, night-wanderings, night-fallings and night-rows with my mother. Every night this nocturia, interspersed with hours of shakes, nightmares about giant bees, and waking paranoia about the chip-chip-chip of coalminers far below – it went on for months, years. Until my mother thought there was no sleep left in the world. Until my father decided there was nothing for it but surgery – surgery so that his wife could sleep. A doctor passing an endoscope up his urethra and burning away the enlarged prostate gland: this was one of the last big gifts he gave his wife.

Like many of the birthday presents he bought for me, though, this gift didn't work properly. The bladder weakness was only marginally better. There's a letter from March 1993 from a follow-up appointment with the surgeon: 'As is usual in these cases, prostatic surgery did not give a particularly impressive result. From his history it does not sound to me as though he has a "plumbing" problem. I think Mr Taylor understands that the nature of the abnormality lies in the nerve control of the bladder, and this control has been impaired by his

Parkinson's disease.' So Parkinson's thwarted even this, the last present my father tried to give my mother.

Let's move away from failed operations. Let's retreat back from 1992.

Surely we're getting somewhere now? Surely we're moving from doctors' letters about sigmoid volvulus, to letters about a Platonic wellness? Dad, are we there yet?

As early (or late) as 1993, the outline of my father starts appearing in the doctors' letters and diagnoses, half-hidden by symptoms. In the later 90s, doctors saw only Parkinson's, the ultimate expression being Mr M.'s 'all he's got left are his symptoms'. Doctors' letters from 1994 on are merely descriptions of my father's illness. Letters from late 1993 back, however, contain the petrified outline of my father as a person.

In November 1993, one doctor notices that 'On examination Mr Taylor was a very pleasant gentleman' – as if pleasantness is a diagnosable condition. The letter continues: 'The patient lives with his wife in a house.' As opposed to what, you may wonder. The point, though, is that my father *as a person* is discernible in the letter. Here is a man, says the doctor, who lives in a house with his wife, and who is pleasant. In a few, throwaway phrases, here is the outline of a *whole* person – not just bits and pieces of tremoring hands, distended abdomens, choreiform movements, Lewy bodies. Illness takes the patient apart. Travelling back to wellness puts Humpty Dumpty together again.

Take me by the hand, my collection of GP letters, and guide me back through the symptoms, guide me back to a complete Humpty Dumpty . . .

Back in September 1991, my mother is 'complaining that her husband does very little during the day'. There were a

thousand rows round this time about my father spending afternoons in bed: 'Don't go to bed again.' 'Why not?' 'You won't
sleep again at night.' 'Yes I will.' 'No you won't, you'll keep me
awake.' 'There's nothing to do. I get all stiff and shaky. So I
might as well go to bed.' 'You shouldn't give into "it" like that.
Why can't you fight it?' 'Blah blah blah. What I've got is incurable, so there's no giving in or not to it. It's just a fact. I'm going
to get worse and worse and worse, whether you like it or not.
Draw those curtains and let me go to sleep.'

   You weren't a 'fighter', Dad, when it came to Parkinson's.
And this was in character. You were never an optimist; you
were cynical about other people's optimism. A psychiatrist
comments in a letter of September 1989 that: 'Mr Taylor
describes himself as an anxious and apprehensive type of person
who generally looks on the black side of things.' Your pessimism
constantly upset people. Why couldn't you resist your illness
like the people we saw on TV?

   We're bombarded with heroic, 'inspirational' stories about
illness on chat shows: a woman with cancer who cycles round
Europe for charity; a brittle-boned girl who does a sponsored
run for other brittle-boned girls. Besides these self-help heroes,
there are few other images of illness available. You don't see
many people on television declaring of their disease: 'There's no
giving in or not to it. I'm going to get worse and worse and
worse whether you like it or not.' No, television illness is all
about heroic resistance, raising charity for other sufferers, the
cared-for becoming carers. But not all cared-fors can be carers.
There have to be people at the bottom of the heap.

   And you could look at it another way. You could say that,
despite the barrage of 'positive' media images of illness, my
father's heroism consisted of being ill in his own way. His
heroism consisted in not being a hero as the TV understands

the term. His resistance was resistance to resistance. There's an unrecognized courage in not fighting, in saying: 'It's an incurable, degenerative disease, so I'm going to shrug my shoulders and go to bed.' It takes a lot of strength to answer back to the world: 'Sod you. I'm not going to play that TV game show for the sick. I'm not going to pretend everything's all right, cos it bloody well isn't. I'm not going to do what's expected of me – never have, and I'm not going to start now.' So bed it was.

No doubt the 'giving up and going to bed' side of his personality was part of his unending depression. Back in 1990, there's a doctor's letter which bewails my father's 'chronic depression, which underlies everything'. Seven years after his nervous breakdown, the depression is still there. In the early 1990s, it merged into paranoia and dementia; the mental illness of the 1990s formed a continuum with the depression and anxiety of the 80s. There are letters from the 1980s which could just as easily be from the 1990s, and vice versa. In January 1990, for instance, there's a letter about a hospital stay which reads: 'We admitted Mr Taylor in an attempt to rationalize his treatment and understand why he gets easily upset. He said he forgets things and thinks people are talking about him. He is depressed and worried about everything. In fact he said he had lost about a stone in weight worrying about his admission to the hospital.' He is discharged with no change, except a new pill which does nothing.

Letters to and fro about pill modifications, pill timings, depression and car crises. In May 1989: 'Mr Taylor is still much the same as he always was. He has resolved his car accident crisis now, but he says he is perpetually waiting for the next crisis to arise.' In January 1989: 'Mr Taylor said that he was in a car accident because of his own fault, last November. The police informed him that they would prosecute him. This has caused him considerable anxiety.'

1988 is the Year of Diagnosis. Oddly enough my father's anxiety is less for a while: 'I reviewed Mr Taylor in clinic today. He seems to be satisfied with the diagnosis of Parkinson's, since it has removed any worry from his mind as to his condition. He still finds it difficult to shave, dress and write, but the Sinemet has helped a bit. However, I am not sure he is aware of the prognosis of Parkinson's disease in the long term.' 'I wish they'd sat us down and told us what the word Parkinson's meant,' says my mother now. 'I wish they'd told us what to expect of the future. Instead, they said it was an old person's illness, what a shame Dad had got it so young, there was nothing to be done. Diagnosis was the end of the matter. They'd found out what was wrong with him, hurrah, the end.'

That end was June 1988.

And now, going backwards again, we enter the prehistoric World Before Parkinson's.

In March 1988, a consultant psychiatrist writes: 'Mr Taylor seems to have become more hesitant with a shuffling gait and complains of a shaking of his left arm, so I have referred him to a neurologist about this.' The psychiatrist wonders if there's been an underlying neurological problem all along.

The thought must have provided some relief, after the bleak mid-80s – years in which psychiatry despairs in letter after letter: 'Mr Taylor remains much the same as ever', 'Mr Taylor doesn't seem to be getting anywhere', 'On or off the Amitriptyline [anti-depressants], the depression and nightmares about school continue to be bad'. My father attends a day clinic for chronic depressives, and eventually gives it up, like everything else. In September 1986, the psychiatrist comments: 'This fifty-eight-year-old gentleman doesn't seem to be benefiting from the day clinic, or anything else. He remains introspective and indecisive. He is dependent on his wife. He feels that he cannot cope when she leaves the house, and is afraid when she visits her parents.'

Back to September 1983, and the psychiatrist reports that: 'Mr Taylor has calmed down since he first attended the clinic. He still finds it difficult to make decisions. He feels guilty that the children have less money now he's retired. In his opinion, he was forced into retirement and therefore feels humiliated. He is reluctant to meet anyone whom he knows professionally – so much so that he avoids going to shopping centres on days he is liable to meet them. He is planning now to sell his present house and move somewhere away from Stoke-on-Trent.' Of course, he never did.

In August 1983, my father is debating whether to look for a different 'part-time teaching job outside the state system, or whether to accept a job at a lower level within the state system'. In May 1983, the doctor advises him to look for a different job, outside teaching. Between March and May, there is the trauma of the retirement from Willfield, and his breakdown. The beginning of this is marked in the medical records by a letter from his GP:

This man apparently has been advised to retire from work on account of his medical condition. As far as I can understand anything from him in this state, he has been headmaster of a school for the last few years. Recently, the standard of his work has been criticized by superiors. He says he finds it difficult making decisions about things. He is tense and anxious and of late has been depressed and feels very inadequate. He has four children. He gives a history that in 1960 he was admitted to hospital for a mental con-

dition. I really don't know what to make of his story at all.
Perhaps you can help?

In the years preceding the doctor's plea for help, the medical
letters peter out, the records are lost, the trail of breadcrumbs
out of the forest vanishes . . . Though not before a strange
moment of déjà vu – or, given the reverse chronology, *avant-
déjà* vu. In February 1983, there's a letter saying that my father
has received 'a barium enema, after his piles were ligated.
During the procedure, his sigmoid colon started spasming.'
Sigmoid colon – where have I heard that before? In hindsight,
this throwaway comment on a 1983 letter reads like a prophecy
of doom. Perhaps as far back as 1983, sigmoid volvulus was
lying in wait. Perhaps many illnesses are like Parkinson's, lying
dormant in the body for decades before they surface.

Writing backwards in time assumes a linear process, from
death to sickness to wellness. And certainly Parkinson's is a
degenerative condition, where things get worse over time,
better if you reverse time. But if Parkinson's is genetic, there's
no escaping from it, however far you go back. Even if it's not,
there's no escaping from the complex patterns of symptoms
from which my father suffered: 1983's sigmoid spasms, for example, come back in the late 1990s with terrible force.

When it comes to illness, whether you go forwards or backwards, linearity breaks down. Chronology turns into swirls,
cycles, fractals, where every moment is connected to every
other: 1983's depression mirrors 1960's; November 2001's chest
infection joins up with 1950's pneumonia; the dementia of the
1990s forms a continuum with the depressions of the 80s . . .
which in turn forms a continuum with the 1950s.

So there's no getting out of the woods with breadcrumbs;
there's no simple retreat from illness to wellness by going back

in time. How stupid of me, I think: of course one can't use medical records to trace the way back to total wellness. Of course there are no medical records marking a moment of perfect wellness. Of course there are no GP letters saying: 'Dear Dr J., just to say that we have diagnosed your patient as one hundred per cent well at this moment, hurrah. Yours, Dr Quack.'

No. When it comes to medical records, in place of wellness, there's just an empty space.

Aftercare

When did you last see your father? . . . I keep trying to find the last moment when he was still unmistakably there, in the fullness of his being, him.

(Blake Morrison, *And When Did You Last See Your Father?*)

My father on holiday in Esjberg, Denmark, 1998

I can't answer that question, Blake. I don't know when I last saw my father 'unmistakably there, in the fullness of his being, him', because I'm not sure who my father was.

I tried to locate the last time he was 'unmistakably there, in the fullness of his being, him' in his medical notes. But that moment was missing. And if I were to ask other people when they last saw my father 'unmistakably there, in the fullness of his being, him', I would receive different answers from everyone. My father was all sorts of fathers, husbands, brothers, symptoms, heroes, villains and paradoxes to different people at different times.

Or perhaps I should put this another way. Perhaps I do know who *my* father was – or at least the person I like to think he was. He was the gentle man in the Infirmary whose tracheotomy croaked, 'Yes, boy, I like the tapes.' That moment was my father.

But that means my father was a man gentleized and reshaped by surgery, care, neglect, Parkinson's, dementia. It means that the disease wasn't extraneous to his character but was part of it. Normally, we see such things as extrinsic to identity. Illness is something from beyond the self which infects and tyrannizes it. But the man in the Infirmary was *both* the end point of a brutal disease *and* the person I recognized as my father. Unlike my older siblings, I don't have many memories of the pre-Parkinson's father, of the pre-diagnosis, pre-nervous-breakdown father. For me, Lumps, Toros, Sledging, all seem such a long time ago, in a galaxy far, far away. The memory of my father's shaky hand is much closer.

So it's inevitable that *my* father is a Parkinson's father.

Parkinson's is part of what and who he was.

The others see things differently, of course. 'Their' fathers aren't like 'my' father. Karen and Robin remember as much wellness as Parkinson's. For them, Parkinson's is an afterword, something they watched transform him.

You see, we all have our different fathers, different John Taylors. That's what struck me, looking round familiar faces at his funeral:

For my mother, he is the charming man with the mac on his arm whom she met at King's Cross, August 1965. He's also the man who proposed to her a second time in November 2001.

For my Auntie Edith, he is the Prodigal Brother. His disappearance in death merely echoes his many disappearing acts (literal and mental) during his lifetime.

For my elder brother, he is the genius with the green encyclopaedias who could speak a dozen languages. He represents a model of manhood, fatherhood and snooker playing to be emulated. He is decidedly *not* the man we saw last in the funeral parlour, laid out and made up, with the ever-faithful Cord the Dog beside him. It was the one time I saw my brother sob: 'That man wasn't Dad. That was a stranger.'

For my elder sister . . . well . . . Dad was everything. I don't want to put words into her mouth. She was his favourite and he hers. There's nothing I can say to put things right.

For my younger sister, he is doubleness personified. On the one hand, he is an old man defined by illness – sometimes enraged, sometimes paranoiac, sometimes kind. On the other hand, there is his distant, pre-Parkinson's self, half-myth, half-memory. The pre-Parkinson's self was the Perfect Gentleman as well as the Greatest Genius in the World. According to myth, he swallowed a dozen green encyclopaedias and digested all human knowledge.

For Colin, he was once the criminal, now the mystery. That is, my father's life is a detective novel in reverse. And Colin is left wondering: if Dad wasn't the guilty criminal, who was? How was the father who semi-hugged him in Stoke the same as the Freudian nightmare remembered from childhood? How does the man whose second family wept at his funeral equate with the man who'd once been the damnèd villain?

For Emma – who, of course, wasn't at the funeral – detection is far more straightforward. With her, my father becomes the uncomplicated criminal, the Moriarty, the Ripper, the Macavity of fathers. Which is a tragedy, because this Macavity adored his daughters.

But I'm not in a position to say that Emma is wrong, I'm right. I can't claim outright that 'her' father is the wrong one, 'my' father the bona fide John Taylor. They're just the contradictory John Taylors who 'belonged' to each of us. Neither takes us closer to understanding our father himself. All we have, 'belonging' to Emma, Colin, Robin, Karen, Helen and myself, are multiple fathers orbiting a black hole in the centre.

Quite what this means for the afterlife is beyond me. I don't want to meet a black hole in heaven. However atheistic or agnostic we think we are, most of us cling to some rosy notion of the hereafter. The notion usually involves meeting our deceased loved ones, Shakespeare, Tchaikovsky and Cord the Dog in a cloudy, Michelangelic painting. We're talking bargain basement Dante here, who also met old chums in the afterworld. What this view of eternity assumes is that you meet up with people as they *really* were, when they were at their best (or most characteristic) in life. Not many people think, ah, my grandma had Alzheimer's when she died – so that's how she'll be in heaven. Oh no. Alzheimer's is seen as alien to Grandma's real identity. When we meet her in the world beyond, she'll be back to 'normal', back to her ideal self.

The problem for me is that this dream of a heavenly reunion is rather ambivalent. I can't find in it the reassurance it provides for lots of people, because I'm not sure I'd really know my father if we met. The idea of meeting my father in heaven has something disturbing in it. Who would he be? The defeated man in the Infirmary who liked Franz Schmidt? The man who thought I was being bodysnatched? The pre-Parkinson's father who took us sledging? And who would I be? The young boy on the sledge who knew nothing about past or future, the twenty-something my father misrecognized, the thirty-something he never knew? How could we find a moment when he would really know me and me him?

The possibility of mutual recognition in an afterlife shatters into a million questions. Perhaps I could be one age, he another – I could be the age I was in the Infirmary, he a younger, healthier father. But then, would he know me? Would he like the person I became in his future? Would he like the tape of opera extracts?

And, anyway, whatever age I chose for him, for his 'ideal' moment of selfhood – whether it's in the Infirmary or sledging in the park – there remains the question of other people, for whom his ideal self would be something different. Would we all meet a different 'father in heaven'? And, for that matter, would Emma laugh at *her* father in hell?

Michelangelic heavens and Dantesque hells disappear in a puff of questions. In their place, I'm left in limbo, a mental Stuck-on-Trent full of unanswered questions and phantom fathers. I suppose that sums up this book. Where once my father was, in his place stands this book, which like him is full of unanswered questions and phantom John Taylors.

Of course it's a pathetically inadequate substitute for the 'real' phantoms. I loved him and he's gone. That's all that really matters.

I was a part-time carer for him, and that raison d'être has been taken away. Welcome to limbo, Stuck-on-Trent: may you enjoy, no, sorry, *fill* your time here. Where once you spent time looking after him, now you spend it filling this book. The book is an afterword to what really mattered.

In fact, everything since my father's death seems like an afterword. No doubt that's what it's like for many people after someone dies – especially a parent. Walking away from my father's grave in the Isle of Man, it's almost as if we, the survivors, are the ones who have become the zombie-undead. It's we who are condemned to walk the earth for eternity, banished from *paradiso*. For the victim, death is sublimely absolute. For those left behind, it feels like real life is over, and everything afterwards is half-living. This limbo is mourning, I suppose. But it goes on for a hell of a long time.

In his great poem of mourning, *In Memoriam*, Alfred Lord Tennyson proposes one way of ending such a limbo: a wedding. The only way to counterbalance an overwhelming event like a funeral is to stage an event which is (almost) as momentous. Weddings are a way, Tennyson suggests, of coming back from half-life, of returning zombies to full health. It's a nice thought: 'It is thy marriage day,' he writes, and 'nor have I felt so much of bliss . . ./Since that dark day a day like this.' If it's good enough for Alfred Lord Tennyson, it's good enough for me.

In Spring 2004, I showed a draft of some of the chapters of this book to my girlfriend, Maria. I gave her the chapter 'WHSmith's, St Pancras' last. After she'd read the final line, she cried and croaked: 'Is this real?' And I said, 'I s'pose so.'

The next day, we rang her parents to tell them. She spoke to them first. Then I said I'd talk to her father. Our first extended phone conversation in eight years went something like this:

'You asken them to marry you?' ('Them' is one of the pronouns Maria's father uses when talking about his daughter. It's as if she's been so much trouble, she seems like two, three, four daughters rolled into one.)

Stammering, I'm turned into Hugh Grant by his guttural, Grecian masculinity: 'I . . . I . . . did. I hope that's okay by you.' No answer, because I've tried not to make it a question – I don't want to ask his permission. The silence makes me nervous, though, and I give in: 'That is all right, isn't it?'

'I letten them make their own mistakes. They do whatever they like. I telling them – I arrange nothing. I arrange no matches for them. It is their lives.' This isn't strictly true, of course, given his and his wife's misfired attempts to introduce Maria to possible matches of the large-moustached-second-cousin variety. But I'm happy to let Maria's father get away with his fiction of the liberal, tolerant parent. And I'm happy to be one of Maria's 'mistakes'.

'When will eet happen? It should be verree soon, I think, because I am bored.'

'Oh,' I say, glad to know that the wedding will alleviate his ennui.

'Yes. I am bored of dees countree. We are soonen both retired, and there is nothing here to do in dees flat. Nothing in England. Just television and parks. And sometimes, de horses. Just same walk'n round the same parks all the time. Eet is verree boring. Parks, parks, parks. Dat ees all there ees here.'

'Oh,' I say, sorry to hear that West London is letting him down.

'Anna and me, we want to go. We going to go'n to Cyprus to live there. We have verree big house there, and rabbeesh flat here. Boring here, good there. No bladdy parks in Cyprus. We go.'

'Oh,' I say, thinking: going, going, but never gone.

'So dees wedding, it must be verree soon. And then Anna and me, we go'n to Cyprus, away from parks.' A pause. 'I paying for some things at de wedding, yes?'

'That's kind. Thank you ever so much. We'll let you know when we've made some arrangements.'

'I said to them that I pay for some things. But not too much.' He chuckles. 'I need to win'n on gee-gees first.' Then abruptly he's had enough: 'Goodbye.' Click.

The bizarre conversation is finished . . . and suddenly I feel good about it all.

I feel buoyant.

I feel Maria's father has come close to recognizing me as his son-in-law, close to saying: 'Congratulations. I am verree happy.' As close as his anger and William Hill permit. As close as one can ever expect, in infirmaries, on phones, in parks, any-where.

GLOSSARY

Akathisia extreme, involuntary restlessness

Anomia *see* Anomic Aphasia

Anomic Aphasia a condition in which the sufferer finds it difficult to recognize and name objects

Bradykinesia slowness of voluntary movement

Capgras syndrome a delusion in which the sufferer believes that a significant other has been replaced by an impostor

Dementia with Lewy bodies (DLB) a common form of dementia associated with Parkinson's disease, and which exhibits some of the same symptoms

Dopamine a chemical used by the brain as a neurotransmitter. Parkinson's disease is associated with a shortage of dopamine.

Dyskinesia loss of control over voluntary movements

Echolalia the repetition of other people's words

Echopraxia the repetition of other people's actions

Festination a kind of hurrying which gets nowhere

Fregoli syndrome the mirror-image of Capgras Syndrome, in which a stranger is mistaken for a significant other

L-Dopa, Levodopa (Sinemet) the medication for Parkinson's sufferers, which artificially boosts levels of dopamine in the brain

Palilalia the incessant repetition of words

Palipraxia the incessant repetition of physical actions

Paramnesia *see* Reduplicative Paramnesia

Parkinson's disease (also known as 'Shaking Palsy') a disease caused primarily by dopamine deficiency in the brain. Symptoms include tremors, shaking, rigidity

Prosopagnosia a neurological impairment whereby sufferers are unable to recognize familiar faces

Reduplicative Paramnesia a syndrome in which the sufferer believes that a familiar place has been duplicated

Thanks

My thanks to: Arts Council England for the initial grant which made the research and writing of this book possible; the Parkinson's Disease Society for their continuing support; members of the Department of English and Drama, Loughborough University, for their invaluable help, and particularly John Schad, Simon King, Marion Shaw, Clare Hanson, Andrew Dix, Jodie Clark, Mystie Hood, Gareth Watts, Robin Webber-Jones, James Holden, Laura Smith; Blake Morrison and Michelene Wandor for their kind advice and suggestions; Robert Turner, Ken Lowe and 'Mr Gil-Martin' for their help with the chapter called 'Headmaster'; and Andrea Roberts and Michael Roberts who supplied information on the folklore of Malew Parish. Thanks to everyone at Granta, including Ian Jack, Helen Gordon and Sajidah Ahmad, for their kindness, time and support.

Thanks to the many people who helped me with drafts and re-drafts, especially the best friend anyone could wish for, Helen Lingwood. Other friends whom I should thank include Jenny, Lucie, Gordon and Gordon's mother. My best wishes to Doreen from Social Services.

Thanks and love to 'Colin' for his letter and invaluable help, and to Auntie Edith and Linda – the chapter 'Oldham' wouldn't exist without the former's memories and the latter's research. I also want to send my thanks to Raymond and Gill, Susan, Auntie Jo and Uncle Edgar, Christopher, Roberta and Steven, Steffi and, of course, Reni.

Thanks to Margaret H., Ted H., Charles (Jonny) H. and, of course, Cath Q., for their hospitality and help.

Robin, Karen, Helen and Anna have made my life and this book what it is. Karen deserves a special mention for her help in the chapter 'Hospitals'; she is the unwritten heroine of this tale.

I want to send my love to my parents-in-law, Dimitrios and Anna. Maria's family have been welcoming, generous and warm since our engagement.

I also want to send my love to my grandparents, Albert and Margaret Kelly, both of whom died while I was writing the book.

More than anyone, I would like to thank my mother, Marilla Taylor, for her support, understanding, help and love. Without her, the book couldn't have been written. If the book is for anyone living, it is for her.

I would like to thank my wife, Maria Taylor née Orthodoxou, whose constant artistic advice shaped and structured the book. Like my mother, she is at the very least the book's co-writer.

And, finally, I'd like to thank my father. In wellness and illness, you were my hero, my ideal self.

ACKNOWLEDGEMENTS

The article in 'Help Help Help', in which my father features as 'Case 1,' is: N. M. J. Edelstyn, F. Oyebode and K. Barrett, 'Delusional Misidentification: A Neuropsychological Case Study in Dementia Associated with Parkinson's Disease,' *Neurocase*, 4 (1998), pp. 181–8.

The Katherine Mansfield quotation in 'Under the Clock, King's Cross Station' is from a letter of 28 December 1921 to Sydney and Violet Schiff; see *Adam International Review*, 300 (1965), pp. 88–118, 113. Mansfield writes: 'There is a moment which is the perfect moment. But so often, until it has passed by we don't see it. We only see what we have missed. All is in retrospect.'

The 'Parkinsonian Urban Myth' in 'Public Toilets in Venice' can be found in Oliver Sacks, *Awakenings* (London: Pan Macmillan, 1991), p. 10 n. 14. On Chaos Theory and Parkinsonism, see the wonderful chapter in *Awakenings*, pp. 351–65.

In 'Bottom of the Bookcase', the poetic description of the finale of Mahler's Sixth Symphony is purportedly what Gustav Mahler said himself, as quoted in Alma Mahler, *Gustav Mahler: Memories and Letters*, trans. Basil Creighton, ed. Donald Mitchell and Knud Martner (London: Sphere Books, 1990), p. 70.

The short essay by J. B. Priestley which I talk about in

'Isle of Man' is in his collection, *Delight* (London: Heinemann, 1951), pp. 46–7. On the Isle of Man during the Second World War, see Connery Chappell, *Island of Barbed Wire* (London: Corgi, 1984).

On 'Injelititis, or Palsied Paralysis', see the chapter in C. Northcote Parkinson, *Parkinson's Law, or the Pursuit of Progress* (Harmondsworth: Penguin, 2002), pp. 98–110.

In 'Hospitals', the quotation 'I am Lazarus, come from the dead' is from T. S. Eliot, 'The Love Song of J. Alfred Prufrock'. See, for example, T. S. Eliot, *The Waste Land and Other Poems* (London: Faber and Faber, 1999), p. 6. The quotation 'Ooh! Look! There's been an accident!' on page 240 comes from Rev W. Awdry, *Small Railway Engines* (London: Kaye and Ward, 1972), p. 54.